The **Rough Guide** to

Seoul

written and researched by

Martin Zatko

JUN 11

Contents

Traditional Seoul
colour section
following p.80

Seoul food
colour section
following p.144

Seoul University
Gwanaksan Park

Colour maps
following p.216

◄◄ Seoul skyline at dusk ◄ Shoppers in Myeongdong

Introduction to
Seoul

An intoxicating mix of high-rise buildings, neon-saturated streets and pounding commerce, Seoul is one of the world's great 24-hour cities, and a true feast for the senses. Within the space of a single day, you could be gazing out over Seoul from a mountaintop, setting your tastebuds on fire with spicy Korean food, taking in an absorbing cocktail of aromas at an open-air market, then bouncing the night away at a karaoke-style singing room. The city's open-all-hours culture gives it an almost unmatched vitality, and the temptation to throw yourself in at the deep end is impossible to resist. It's also a joy to see the city's other side – palaces, temples, royal tombs and ancestral shrines are evidence of Seoul's five centuries as a dynastic capital. With its hyper-efficient transport system, a negligible rate of crime and an astonishing wealth of locally produced modern art, it's little wonder that so many who visit Seoul come away hugely impressed.

Seventy-five percent of visitors to Korea get no further than its fascinating capital. By some counts, this is the world's third most populous city: including the wider urban area, it is home to over 25 million people. That Seoul exists at all constitutes a minor miracle, since the Korean War saw it laid to waste in the early 1950s. The city sits just 30km from the border with North Korea, one day's march should the DMZ separating the countries ever be breached, and until the mid-1970s, Seoulites were poorer than their counterparts in the North Korean capital of Pyongyang. The city's transformation since then has been nothing short of incredible – just a few generations down the line, it's one of the most modern and richest cities in the world, a major financial centre whose skyline is continually being enriched with gleaming skyscrapers.

But for all its non-stop consumption, Seoul is also a place of considerable tradition and history. Six wonderful **palaces** in the centre of the city proclaim its status as a seat of regal power from as far back as 1392 – this was the year that Seoul became capital of the **Joseon dynasty**, whose line of over two dozen kings ruled over all Korea until the country's annexation in 1910. Elsewhere, the tiled roofs of wooden *hanok* houses gently rise towards the ash-coloured granite crags north of Seoul, and the ancient

▲ Jongno Tower

songs and dances of farmhands and court performers are clashed out in a whirligig of sound and colour along Insadonggil, a particularly traditional and tourist-friendly road in the palace district.

It's impossible to talk about Seoul without mentioning the **food**. Received western knowledge of Korea's wonderful cuisine tends to be hugely ill-informed, generally starting with dog meat and ending with *gimchi*; these days very few Koreans eat dog (though a few curious foreigners manage

◀ Gyeongbokgung

5

to hunt it down), and *gimchi* is a mere (if ubiquitous) side-dish. Those who know where to go can **barbecue marinated beef** at tables inset with charcoal briquettes, stuff themselves with the dozens of side-dishes available at a **royal banquet** and take their pick from a bewildering array of super-fresh **seafood**. In addition, Korea boasts Asia's best selection of indigenous alcoholic drinks – many visitors find themselves pining for one more bottle of **makkeolli**, a milky rice-wine, after they've left the country.

Seoulites themselves are a real highlight of any visit to the city: fiercely proud, and with a character almost as spicy as their food, they're markedly keen to welcome foreigners who come to live or holiday in their city. Within hours of arriving, you'll probably find yourself racing up a mountainside – new friends in tow – lunching over a delicious barbecued *galbi*, throwing back *dongdongju* until dawn, or singing the night away at a *noraebang*. Few travellers leave without tales of the kindness of Korean strangers, and almost all wonder why the country isn't a more popular stop on the international travel circuit. Tourist numbers are, however, rising – the secret is well and truly out.

What to see

Although Seoul sprawls for kilometre after kilometre in every direction, most visitors to the city go no further than the compact city centre. The **palace district** is the hub of proceedings: there are no fewer than six gorgeous palaces to stroll around, with **Gyeongbok-gung** and **Changdeokgung** particularly popular with tourists. The others are

◀ Bukchondong

▶ Shoppers in Apgujeong

all delightful in their own way, and those visiting **Changgyeonggung** can head by footbridge to **Jongmyo**, an ancient ancestral shrine venerated by the kings of the Joseon dynasty. In between Gyeongbokgung and Changdeokgung are two of Seoul's most notable districts, each possessing a distinctive appeal: **Samcheong-dong** is a young, zesty area filled with trendy cafés, restaurants, clothing boutiques and art galleries, while neighbouring **Bukchondong** is one of the only places in Seoul where the city's traditional wooden buildings are still standing.

Just south of the palace district is **Insadong**, a charming area that, despite its central location, exudes a markedly traditional atmosphere. You can spend a whole day here, taking your pick from dozens of wonderful galleries, tearooms and restaurants, and winding your way through the mazy side-streets – getting lost is rarely so much fun. A short walk to the west of Insadong is **Jogyesa**, a large temple that provides the best proof of Korea's Buddhist heritage, while just to the south is **Cheonggyecheon**, a recently developed creek whose pedestrian-only banks are arguably Seoul's best walking territory.

Unravelling Korean place names

Many foreign visitors to Seoul find themselves struggling with the lengthy transliterated Korean place names, but armed with a few facts – and perhaps a smidgeon of practice – you'll be able to distinguish your Insadonggils from your Samcheongdongs, and perhaps even Changgyeonggung from Changdeokgung. The key lies in the **suffixes** to these long words: **gung**, for example, means "palace", and once removed you're left with the slightly less bewildering two-syllable name of the complex in question – Gyeongbok Palace, and so on. The **dong** suffix means "district", while **gil** means "road" – all of a sudden, it's possible to break Samcheongdonggil down, and identify it as a thoroughfare in the Samcheong district. Others that may be of use are **gang** and **cheon**, respectively used for waterways large (the Hangang, for example) and small (Cheonggyecheon); **mun**, which means "gate" (Dongdaemun); and **dae**, which usually signifies a university (Hongdae).

South of Cheonggyecheon, the urban character takes an immediate 180-degree turn: this is the capital's prime **business district**, and as such is home to innumerable skyscrapers and other trappings of commerce. Hidden amongst the tower blocks are scores of buildings dating back to the Japanese occupation period, these elegant **colonial structures** now incongruous in their modern surroundings. This is also the main shopping area, and includes Korea's two largest markets, **Dongdaemun** and **Namdaemun**. Both of these are colossal affairs, with a mixture of mall-style buildings and open-air sections. The **market food**, utterly alien to the average traveller, is by far the best reason to visit, though there are also dozens of quality **museums** in this area, and the mini-mountain of **Namsan** provides wonderful views of the capital.

As you travel further out from the business and palace districts, the buildings become smaller in both size and number, thanks to the rugged – even mountainous – topography of the area. In fact, northern Seoul is home to a tremendously popular national park: **Bukhansan**, whose tree-lined trails are steep but surprisingly easy to navigate. Nestled amongst the western foothills is **Buamdong**, Seoul's most relaxing district where the plethora of galleries and restaurants make it a laid-back alternative to Insadong. Heading east instead will bring you to **Daehangno**, a student-filled zone that can hardly be described as relaxed – its hectic street life and cheap restaurants are two reasons why it has long been the base of choice for visiting backpackers.

Seoul is bisected by the **Hangang**, and though most of the big sights lie on its northern side the river itself offers all sorts of enjoyment. Its car-free banks are great for **cycling**, while you can also take a ferry tour, or even a trip by **river taxi**. The river slides gently past two of Seoul's most popular nightlife areas, studenty **Hongdae** and cosmopolitan **Itaewon**. Hongdae has marginally more vitality and Itaewon more variety – it's best to visit both, though your liver may disagree.

Relatively few visitors choose to venture south of the Hangang, but there are certainly reasons to do so. The district of **Apgujeong** is particularly fascinating: this is the place where the city's rich and beautiful come to party, dine and shop. It's worth the splurge to get a glimpse of certain facets of high society, most notably clothing from Seoul's new wave of fashion designers, who are making waves across Asia and beyond. In addition, this is the best place in which to sample **neo-Korean cuisine**, a new take on traditional styles.

Seoul has a pleasing range of sights on its periphery, and most fall easily within day-trip range. Foreign travellers leap at the chance to visit the **DMZ**, the chilling 4km-wide buffer zone separating North and South Korea. In fact, on some tours it's technically possible to walk across the border, under the watchful eyes of rifle-toting soldiers, a surprisingly simple way to generate some travel kudos. Two major cities are easily accessible from Seoul, and actually on the city's subway system. **Incheon** to the west has a thriving Chinatown and serves as a travel base for trips to dozens of **islands** in the **West Sea**, while **Suwon** to the south is home to a stunning fortress. There's an even better fortress in **Gongju**, a small city further south again; this was once the capital of the **Baekje kingdom**, whose astonishingly beautiful jewellery is visible in a fantastic museum.

When to go

Seoul's year is split into **four distinct seasons**. Spring generally lasts from April to June, and is one of the best times of the year to visit: flowers are in bloom, and a fluffy cloak of cherry blossom washes a brief wave of pinkish white over the city. Locals head for the hills by day, and riverside barbecues by night, and the change in weather is also celebrated in a number of interesting festivals.

▶ Cheonggyecheon

▼ W Seoul Walkerhill hotel

The **summer** can be unbearably muggy, and you may find yourself leaping from one air-conditioned sanctuary to the next. You'll wonder how Koreans can persist with their uniformly fiery food at this time, but be grateful for the ubiquitous water fountains. It's best to avoid the **monsoon** season: more than half of the country's annual rain falls from early July to late August. In a neat reversal of history, Japan and China protect Korea from most of the area's typhoons, but one or two manage to squeeze through the gap each year.

The best time of the year to visit is **autumn** (Sept to Nov), when temperatures are mild, rainfall is generally low and the mountains that encircle the city erupt in a magnificent array of reds, yellows and oranges. Locals flock to national parks to picnic surrounded by these fiery leaf tones, and there are plenty of festivals livening things up. T-shirt weather can continue long into October, though you're likely to need some extra layers by the end.

Seoul's **winter** is long and cold, though visiting at this time is far from impossible, even on the many occasions on which the capital finds itself under a thick blanket of snow. There's almost no change to public transport, underfloor *ondol* heating systems are cranked up, and the lack of rain creates photogenic contrasts between powdery snow, crisp blue skies, off-black pine trees and the earthy yellow of dead grass.

Average temperatures and rainfall

	Jan	Feb	Mar	Apr	May	Jun	Jul	Aug	Sep	Oct	Nov	Dec
Seoul												
Max/min (°C)	0/-9	3/-7	8/-2	17/5	22/11	27/16	29/21	31/22	26/15	19/7	11/0	3/-7
Rainfall (mm)	31	20	38	76	81	130	376	267	119	41	46	25

18

things not to miss

It's not possible to see everything that Seoul has to offer on a short trip – and we don't suggest you try. What follows is a selective taste of the city's highlights: fascinating markets, spectacular palaces and a few ways just to indulge yourself. They're arranged in five colour-coded categories, which you can browse through to find the very best things to see and experience. All highlights have a page reference to take you straight into the Guide, where you can find out more.

01 Gyeongbokgung Page **43** • The most popular of Seoul's six palaces, with decades of renovation work bringing it ever closer in appearance to its dynastic heyday.

02 Retail therapy in Apgujeong Page **96** ● The lanes of "Korea's Beverly Hills" are lined with exclusive clothing boutiques, as well as cafés and bars in which to mull over your credit card balance.

03 Huwon Page **52** ● Relax by the pond just as kings once did at this secluded "Secret Garden", which nestles at the back of Changdeokgung, a UNESCO World Heritage-listed palace.

04 Colonial architecture Page **60** ● Seoul spent decades under brutal Japanese annexation, but the buildings constructed in this period are now some of the most beautiful and elegant in the city.

05 Bukchon Hanok Village Page **50** ● In this central but highly traditional district, you can sleep in a traditional wooden *hanok* house heated from underneath by gentle flames.

06 **Art galleries** Page **131** •
The districts of Insadong and
Samcheongdong are crammed with a truly
astonishing number of galleries, which
show why Korean art is gaining an
ever-growing global reputation.

07 **A royal feast** Page **114** • Seoul
gives visitors the rare opportunity
to eat like a king: feast like the Joseon
monarchs, with your table creaking under the
weight of up to forty individual dishes.

08 **Paju Book City** Page **153** • Get off the tourist trail with a trip to Paju Book City, a
superb collection of modern architecture.

09 Ganghwado
Page **157** •

Thousands of years old, the Neolithic dolmens on this island are the area's earliest signs of human habitation.

10 Namsangol Page **70** • This recreated Joseon-era village is a delightful place for a wander, especially in the evening, when it's gently illuminated by paper lanterns.

11 Dongdaemun Market Page **68** • A 24-hour market in a city that never sleeps, Dongdaemun is a Seoul institution, with sights and smells redolent of decades gone by. The atmosphere is best savoured around midnight, with a mung-bean pancake and a few bowls of *makkeolli*.

12 **Samneung Park** Page **94** • The burial place of three Joseon-dynasty royals, and one of Seoul's most pleasant parks to boot.

13 **The DMZ** Page **149** • Take a step inside the world's most heavily-armed border area, and its frostiest remnant of the Cold War – the 4km-wide Demilitarized Zone separating North and South Korea.

14 **Insadong tearooms** Page **122** • The traditional Insadong district remains home to well over a dozen classy tearooms – a rare opportunity to try Korea's fantastic range of domestic infusions.

15 **Jjimjilbang** Page **145** • Take a scrub the Korean way at these sauna-like facilities, which are also Seoul's cheapest places to sleep.

16 Café culture Page 120 • Cafés

have reached saturation point in this city of coffee addicts, and fierce competition has resulted in a glut of distinctive establishments.

17 Noryangjin fish market

Page 87 • There's a mind-boggling variety of ultra-fresh seafood available at this highly atmospheric fish market, which brings together the best produce from Korea's East, West and South seas.

18 Namsan Page 69 • Take a short ride up on Namsan's cable car to see Seoul make

its evening shift from off-grey to searing neon.

Basics

Basics

Getting there

There is no way to arrive in Seoul by land, since such opportunities are choked off by the spiky frontier with North Korea, and most visitors fly in. It may come as something of a surprise to learn that Seoul is not Korea's main international transport hub: that honour goes to Incheon, a city just to the west, yet essentially part of the same gigantic urban conurbation. Incheon is home to the country's main international airport; often referred to as "Seoul Incheon" on departure boards, this offshore beast handles a large and ever-increasing number of international flights. Incheon also has a couple of international port terminals, handling ferries to various cities on China's eastern seaboard.

Korean Air and Asiana are the two big Korean **airlines**, operating direct flights from a number of destinations around the world. **Fares** increase for travel in the summer months, at Christmas time, and during the major Korean holidays of Seollal and Chuseok (see p.37). A **departure tax** applies when leaving Korea, but will almost certainly be factored in to your ticket price.

Those arriving by ferry will be rewarded with a pretty introduction to the country, since the Korean coastline around Incheon melts into countless islands, though the port area is typically industrial.

Flights from the UK and Ireland

Both Korean Air and Asiana have **direct** connections from London Heathrow to Incheon – Korean Air has a daily service, while Asiana has five per week. The journey takes eleven hours, with fares costing around £550; this can rise to over £700 during summer and at Christmas, when it's common for all flights to be fully booked weeks in advance. You can save a bundle of money by taking an indirect flight, with prices often dipping below £400 during low season; good options include Finnair via Helsinki, Qatar Airways via Doha, Aeroflot via Moscow and Emirates via Dubai. It's also worth checking deals with KLM and Air France, whose routes are as close to direct as possible.

There are no direct flights to Korea **from Ireland** so flying indirectly will be your only option.

Flights from the US and Canada

If you are coming from the **US** you have a number of options available to you: there are direct flights to Incheon from New York, Dallas, Las Vegas, Los Angeles, San Francisco, Detroit, Seattle, Chicago, Atlanta, Washington and Honolulu; carriers include Delta, Northwest and United, as well as Asiana and Korean Air. Sample low season fares are $1400 from New York (a journey of around fourteen hours), $1200 from Chicago (fourteen hours) and $1150 from Los Angeles (thirteen hours). In all cases you may save up to a couple of hundred dollars by transferring – San Francisco and Seattle are popular hubs. Fares on many routes can almost double during summer and Christmas time.

Korean Air has direct flights to Incheon from two **Canadian** cities, Vancouver and Toronto, but these can be very expensive when demand is high (over Can$3000). Again, you're likely to save money by taking an indirect flight, in which case Can$1700 would be a typical low-season fare from both cities.

Flights from Australia, New Zealand and South Africa

From **Australia**, there are direct connections to Korea from Sydney (ten hours), twice per day; Brisbane (nine hours), five times per week; and Melbourne (eleven hours) three times per week. There are sometimes direct flights from Cairns during the Korean winter.

Six steps to a better kind of travel

At Rough Guides we are passionately committed to travel. We feel strongly that only through travelling do we truly come to understand the world we live in and the people we share it with – plus tourism has brought a great deal of **benefit** to developing economies around the world over the last few decades. But the extraordinary growth in tourism has also damaged some places irreparably, and of course **climate change** is exacerbated by most forms of transport, especially flying. This means that now more than ever it's important to **travel thoughtfully** and **responsibly**, with respect for the cultures you're visiting – not only to derive the most benefit from your trip but also to preserve the best bits of the planet for everyone to enjoy. At Rough Guides we feel there are six main areas in which you can make a difference:

- Consider what you're contributing to the **local economy**, and how much the services you use do the same, whether it's through employing local workers and guides or sourcing locally grown produce and local services.
- Consider the **environment** on holiday as well as at home. Water is scarce in many developing destinations, and the biodiversity of local flora and fauna can be adversely affected by tourism. Try to patronize businesses that take account of this.
- Travel with a purpose, not just to tick off experiences. Consider **spending longer** in a place, and getting to know it and its people.
- Give thought to how often you **fly**. Try to avoid short hops by air and more harmful night flights.
- Consider **alternatives to flying**, travelling instead by bus, train, boat and even by bike or on foot where possible.
- Make your trips **"climate neutral"** via a reputable carbon-offset scheme. All Rough Guide flights are offset, and every year we donate money to a variety of charities devoted to combating the effects of climate change.

The number of Koreans going to Australia mean that bargain flights are few and far between, but Qantas usually prices its direct services competitively – return fares start at around Aus$1500, while the Korean carriers may ask for almost double that. It's worth checking around for transit flights that connect in a Southeast Asian hub; prices can often drop close to Aus$1000. Likewise, if travelling from **New Zealand** – keep your fingers crossed for a NZ$1400 fare, but assume you'll pay around NZ$1900. There are also direct flights from Auckland (twelve hours), and a few from Christchurch.

At the time of writing, there were no direct flights from **South Africa**.

Flights from Japan and China

There are flights to Seoul from more than a dozen cities in both **China** and **Japan**, but perhaps most notable for western travellers is the handy, and extremely regular, connection between Seoul's Gimpo airport and Tokyo Haneda, both of which are closer to the centre of their respective capitals than the larger hubs, Incheon and Narita. Likewise, some flights from Osaka and Shanghai land at Gimpo.

Airlines, agents and operators

Airlines

Air Canada ⓦ www.aircanada.com.
Air China ⓦ www.air-china.co.uk, ⓦ www.airchina.com.cn.
All Nippon Airways (ANA) ⓦ www.anaskyweb.com.
American Airlines ⓦ www.aa.com.
Asiana Airlines ⓦ www.flyasiana.com.
British Airways ⓦ www.ba.com.
Cathay Pacific ⓦ www.cathaypacific.com.
Delta ⓦ www.delta.com.

Emirates ⓦ www.emirates.com.
JAL (Japan Air Lines) ⓦ www.ar.jal.com.
KLM (Royal Dutch Airlines) ⓦ www.klm.com.
Korean Air ⓦ www.koreanair.com.
Lufthansa ⓦ www.lufthansa.com.
Qantas Airways ⓦ www.qantas.com.
Qatar Airways ⓦ www.qatarairways.com.
Singapore Airlines ⓦ www.singaporeair.com.
United Airlines ⓦ www.united.com.
US Airways ⓦ www.usair.com.

Agents and operators

ebookers ⓦ www.ebookers.com. Low fares on an extensive selection of scheduled flights and package deals.
North South Travel ⓦ www.northsouthtravel .co.uk. Friendly, competitive travel agency, offering discounted fares worldwide. Profits are used to support projects in the developing world, especially the promotion of sustainable tourism.
STA Travel ⓦ www.statravel.com. Worldwide specialists in independent travel; also student IDs, travel insurance, car rental, rail passes, and more. Good discounts for students and under-26s.
Trailfinders ⓦ www.trailfinders.com. One of the best-informed and most efficient agents for independent travellers.

Local tour operators

Aju Tours ⓦ www.ajutours.co.kr. Has a few interesting additions to the regular Seoul tours and DMZ trips, including birdwatching, oriental health or a tour of shamanistic sites.
Grace Travel ⓦ www.triptokorea.com. A user-friendly website – click on "Customized Tours", select your time window, then choose from a range of interesting options.
Rye Tour ⓦ www.ryetour.com. In addition to a few Korea-only itineraries, they also offer week-long tours which combine Seoul and Busan with Beijing, Shanghai or Tokyo.

TIK Tour Service ⓦ www.tiktourservice.com. Offers affordable tours including skiing holidays, temple tours and trips around Jeju Island.

Getting to Seoul by train and ferry

Despite the fact that South Korea is part of the Eurasian landmass, and technically connected to the rest of it by rail, the DMZ and North Korean red tape means that the country is currently **inaccessible by land**. This may well change – two old lines across the DMZ have been renovated and 2007 saw trains rumble across the border as part of a peace ceremony. However, overnight trains from Beijing remain a distant prospect. Until then, surface-based access from the continent takes the form of **ferries** from Japan, China or Russia via a ride on the Trans-Siberian Railway (see box below). Note that if you're heading to or from China or Japan, you can make use of a **combined rail and ferry ticket** that gives substantial discounts on what you'd pay separately – see ⓦ www.korail.com for details.

Ferries from China

There are several ferry routes from **China**'s eastern coast to Incheon's international terminals. The most popular connections include sailings from Dalian, Dandong and Qingdao, while Tianjin's port in Tanggu is the most convenient for those wanting to head to or from Beijing; unfortunately there is no service from Shanghai. All sailings are overnight, with several levels of accommodation available – the cheapest will buy you a bunk-style bed (usually surprisingly

The Trans-Siberian railway

Although you can't actually reach Seoul by train, if you're coming from or via Europe you may wish to consider one of the world's best overland trips – a **train-ride across Russia and China**. There are three main routes from Moscow, the main one a week-long, 9288km journey ending in Vladivostok on the East Sea. The Trans-Manchurian and Trans-Mongolian are slightly shorter rides ending in Beijing. The most popular cities to stop at – other than the termini of Moscow, Vladivostok and Beijing – are Irkutsk, next to beautiful Lake Baikal in Russian Siberia, and Ulaan Baatar, the idiosyncratic capital of Mongolia. Prices vary massively depending upon where you start and stop, and whether you go through a tour agency or not; for more information go to ⓦ www.seat61.com.

Ferry connections from China

Chinese port	Departure days and time	Journey time
Dalian	Tues & Fri at 3.30pm	18 hours
Dandong	Tues, Thurs & Sun at 3pm	16 hours
Lianyungang	Mon at 11pm, Thurs at 1pm	24 hours
Qingdao	Mon, Wed & Fri at 4pm	15 hours
Qinhuangdao	Wed & Sun at 1pm	23 hours
Shidao	Tues, Thurs & Sun at 6pm	14 hours
Tanggu (Tianjin)	Thurs & Sun at 11am	24 hours
Weihai	Tues, Thurs & Sun at 6pm	14 hours
Yantai	Mon, Wed & Fri at 5pm	14 hours
Yingkou	Mon & Thurs at 11am	24 hours

comfortable, replete with a curtain to separate you from the outside world), while private rooms range from 8-berthers to deluxe suites. Prices start at around W110,000 one-way, and though few sailings sell out it'll be wise to book in advance during the summer.

Ferries from Japan

Services from **Japan** depart from Fukuoka and Shimonoseki to Busan, a city in the southeast of Korea; the port is reasonably close to Busan's train station, less than three hours from Seoul by high-speed train. There are, in fact, two different services to and from Fukuoka – one a regular ferry, departing every day except Sunday (6 hours; ¥9000), and a faster jetfoil with at least five services per day (3 hours; ¥13,000). Note that the outward ferry journey from Korea takes far longer than the inbound one, as this is a night sailing and the vessel is required to stay at each port for a few hours. Daily ferries from Shimonoseki (14 hours; ¥8500) leave from a port near the train station, but as times, dates and prices for all sailings have been inconsistent for years, it's best to check with a Japanese tourist office for up-to-date information.

Arrival

Getting into Seoul is simple, however you're arriving. The airports are a little removed from the city centre, but the presence of tourist booths and English-language signage will facilitate matters. Seoul's train stations are all very central, and each is connected to at least one subway line. The main bus stations also have direct connections to the subway, but unfortunately they're all rather awkwardly located to the south and east of the centre.

By air

Most people take the bus from Incheon Airport to Seoul, but following the completion of a **train line** to Seoul train station, via Gimpo airport (the terminus for most domestic flights, and a few short-haul international services), Incheon Airport is now connected to the Seoul underground network. Taking the **AREX** (airport express) train from the airport, you can get off at Gimpo Airport or Gongdeok for line 5, Digital Media City or Gongdeok for line 6 or

Hongik University for line 2, though most will head straight to the terminal at Seoul Station, on lines 1 and 4. Poor planning means that passenger numbers are a fraction of those envisioned (as low as five percent of the forecast, according to some estimates): rather than extend the high-speed rail line from Seoul station, the AREX is little more than a jumped-up subway train, overtaken by pretty much all of the cars and buses on the adjoining highway. As such, you may find it more efficient to take the **bus** from Incheon Airport, which will also take about an hour to Seoul, depending on your destination. There are no fewer than fifteen routes heading to the capital (W8000–12,000), each stopping off at numerous locations, while more expensive limousine buses head straight to many of the top hotels (around W15,000); ask at an airport tourist booth for details of which bus to take. Alternatively you can take a **taxi**, which will take around thirty minutes to get to central Seoul and cost W60,000–90,000 depending upon your destination; the black "deluxe" taxis are more costly.

www.roughguides.com

Getting around

With Seoul's hectic streets making car hire almost tantamount to suicide, and bicycle riding even more so in most places, it's lucky that the city is covered by a cheap, clean and highly comprehensive public transport system – the subway network is one of the best developed in the world, not least because of the sheer number of workers it has to speed from A to B. Buses dash around the city every which way, and even taxis are cheap enough to be viable for many routes.

Busy roads and noxious emissions mean that **walking** through Seoul is rarely pleasurable, though Insadonggil is closed to traffic on Sundays; the shopping district of Myeongdong and club-heavy Hongdae are so swamped with people that vehicles tend to avoid these areas; and there are innumerable malls and underground shopping arcades around the city. Riding a **bike** is only really advisable on a specially designed route along the Han River; see p.83 for further details.

By subway

With nine lines and counting, and well over two hundred stations, Seoul's **subway system** is one of the most comprehensive on earth – in the area bounded by the circular 2 line, you'll never be more than a short walk or taxi ride from the nearest station, while line 1 runs for a whole third of the country's length, stretching well over 100km from Soyosan in the north to Sinchang in the south. It's also possible to get to Suwon (p.159), Cheonan (p.162) or Incheon (p.154) by subway, and a special extension line finally connected the network to Incheon Airport in 2007; see p.22 for more information. **Fares** are extremely reasonable, starting at W1000 for rides of less than 10km, and very rarely costing more than W2000. **Ticket purchase** has become slightly trickier since station staff were laid off en masse in 2009; unless you've invested in a transport card (highly recommended; see box below), you'll have to buy a single-use card from a machine; though the operating system is a little curious, you should get there in the end. Bafflingly, each card requires a deposit of W500, retrievable from machines outside the turnstiles when you've completed your journey. The subway system itself is very user-friendly: **network maps** are conveniently located around the stations, which are made easily navigable by multi-language signage. You'll be able to find maps of the surrounding area on walls near the station exits, though be warned that north only faces upwards a quarter of the time, since each map is oriented to the direction that it happens to be facing. Running from around 5.30am to midnight (slightly earlier on weekends), trains are extremely frequent but are packed to bursting at rush hour, and often livened up by hawkers selling anything from hand cream to folk music.

By bus

In comparison with the almost idiot-proof subway system, Seoul's **bus network** often proves too complicated for foreign guests – English-language signage is rare, and some of the route numbers would look more at home in a telephone directory (for instance, the #9009-1 to City Hall), the result of a somewhat misguided system "overhaul" in 2004. The buses are split into four coloured categories – **blue** buses travel long distances along major arterial roads, **green** buses are for shorter hops, **red** ones travel way out to the suburbs and **yellow** ones travel tight loop routes. **Fares** start at W1000 for blue and green, W1500 for red and W600 for yellow buses, with prices increasing by distance on longer journeys; cash is still accepted on the bus, alternatively see below for details about travel cards. For more information on routes go to ⓦbus.seoul.go.kr, or call ☎1330.

By taxi

Seoul's taxis are **cheap** and ubiquitous. A W2400 fare covers the first 2km, and goes up in W100 increments every 144 metres – given that bus and subway fares start at W1000, it often works out about the same, and occasionally cheaper, for groups of three or four to travel short distances by cab rather than public transport. Note that a 20 percent **surcharge** is added between midnight and 4am. There are also deluxe *mobeom* cabs, which are black with a yellow stripe; these usually congregate around expensive hotels, charging W4500 for the first 3km and W200 for each

Transport cards

Those staying in the city for anything more than a few days should invest in a **T-money transport card**, available for W3000 at all subway stations and some street-level kiosks. After loading it with credit (easiest at machines in subway station), you'll save W100 on each subway or bus journey, and any remaining balance can be refunded at the end of your stay. These cards make it possible to switch at no extra cost from bus to subway – or vice versa – should a combination be needed to complete your journey; you'll otherwise need two separate tickets. In addition, you can use these handy cards to pay **taxi fares**, make **phone calls** from most streetside booths, and even pay your bill at **convenience stores**.

additional 164 metres. You should never have to wait long for a cab. Drivers do not expect tips, but it's also unlikely that they'll speak any **English** – having your destination written in *hangeul* is the easiest way to get the information across, though many drivers will be both willing and able to call an interpreter on their phone.

Online travel resources

Incheon International Airport ⓦ www.airport.or.kr. Information on flights into and out of Korea's main airport.

Korail ⓦ www.korail.go.kr. Information on train times and passes, including discounted combined train and ferry tickets to Japan.

Korean Airports Corporation ⓦ www.airport.co.kr. Almost identical to the Incheon site, this has details of domestic and international flights for the smaller Korean airports.

Seoul Metropolitan Rapid Transport (SMRT) ⓦ www.smrt.co.kr. Timetables, and a useful best-route subway map.

Tour2Korea ⓦ english.tour2korea.com. Good for bus connections between major cities, and has cursory information on trains and ferries.

The media

The Korean media has come a long way since bursting out of the dictatorial straitjacket of the 1970s and 1980s, but with the country's relatively small number of foreigners and low level of English-language skills, most of it remains inaccessible to all but those versed in Korean.

The two big English-language **newspapers** are the *Korea Times* (ⓦ www.koreatimes.co.kr) and *Korean Herald* (ⓦ www.koreanherald.co.kr), near-identical dailies with near-identical addictions to news agency output and dull business statistics. Neither paper has got the hang of graphic illustration, both usually opting to trot out their parade of cold, hard facts in paragraph form. This said, both have decent listings sections in their weekend editions, which detail the goings-on in Seoul's restaurant, film and club scenes. The *International Herald Tribune* is pretty easy to find in top hotels, served alongside with copies of the *Joongang Daily* (ⓦ joongangdaily.joins.com), an interesting local news supplement. You should also be able to hunt down the previous week's *Time*, *Newsweek* or *Economist* in major bookstores (see p.141). An interesting source of information is *Ohmy News* (ⓦ english.ohmynews.com), a large online compendium of articles written by members of the public that has long been a quirky bee in the bonnet of local politicians and "proper" journalists.

Korean **television** often reveals itself to be exactly what people would expect of Japanese television – a gaudy feast of madcap game shows and soppy period dramas. Foreign viewers are likely to be baffled by most of the output, but there are few more accessible windows into the true nature of Korean society. **Arirang** (ⓦ www.arirang.co.kr) is a 24-hour English-language television network based in Seoul, which promotes the country with occasionally interesting documentaries, and has regular news bulletins.

After years of failed efforts, Seoul now has a few dependable **English-language magazines**. The three main monthlies are **10 Magazine** (ⓦ www.10magazine.asia), a fun publication with good listings sections for Seoul and other Korean cities; **Eloquence;**

and **Seoul** (Ⓦwww.seoulselection.com), a city-sponsored guide that's usually much more interesting than its name may suggest. Its chief author, Robert Koehler, also operates Seoul's most venerated expat blog, the **Marmot's Hole** (Ⓦwww.rjkoehler.com), which is full of interesting snippets about Korean culture and history; the competing

Roboseyo site (Ⓦroboseyo.blogspot.com) is rather more offbeat. Other blogs of note include two related to food: **Seoul Eats** (Ⓦwww.seouleats.com), by Daniel Gray of *O'ngo Culinary School* fame (see p.32), and Joe McPherson's **Zen Kimchi** (Ⓦwww.zenkimchi.com).

Festivals

Most of Seoul's festivals are concentrated around spring and autumn, but a whole host are spread throughout the year. If you're heading to one, don't be shy – the locals love to see foreigners joining in with traditional Korean events, and those who dare to get stuck in may finish the day with a whole troupe of new friends.

It must be said that a large proportion of **Korean festivals** are quite unappealing: many are brazenly commercial in nature, making no bones about being held to "promote the salted seafood industry", for example. Other festivals include those dedicated to agricultural utensils, clean peppers and the "Joy of Rolled Laver" – you'll easily be able to spot the duds. The most interesting events are highlighted below, though bear in mind that celebrations for two of the big national festivals – Seollal, the Lunar New Year, and a Korean version of Thanksgiving named Chuseok – are family affairs that generally take place behind closed doors. As long as you're not in Seoul during the long, cold winter, you'll almost certainly be able to catch a festival of some kind. In addition to the traditional parades and street performances on Insadonggil (usually every Thurs, Fri and Sat), there are a whole host of events, of which a selection is detailed below.

April

Cherry Blossom Though the exact dates are determined by the weather, Seoulites get their picnicking equipment together as soon as the soft pink flowers are fluted through the cherry trees. Yeouido is the most popular place to go – bring a bottle of *soju* and make a bunch of friends.
International Women's Film Festival Ⓦwffis.or.kr. A week-long succession of films that "see the world through women's eyes" (even if they were created by men).

May

Buddha's Birthday With their courtyards strewn with colourful paper lanterns, temples are the place to be at this age-old event, which is also a national holiday. In the evening a huge lantern parade heads to Jogyesa temple along Jongno; get window-space early in one of the cafés overlooking the street. Late May.
Hi Seoul Festival Ⓦhiseoulfest.org. Myriad events take place in this ten-day-long celebration of the coming of summer. From choreographed firework displays and tea ceremonies to men walking across the Han River by tightrope, there's simply no better time to be in Seoul, and the event also incorporates the Seoul World DJ festival.
Jongmyo Daeje Korean kings performed their ancestral rites at the Jongmyo shrine for hundreds of years prior to the end of the monarchy, and it's been carried forward to this day; the event is necessarily sober but very interesting, and is followed by traditional court dances. First Sunday of the month.

Seoul International Cartoon & Animation Festival ⓦ www.sicaf.or.kr. Koreans young and old are major cartoon addicts, but while most of the national fix is sated by Japanese fare, there's still a lot of local talent – *The Simpsons*, *Family Guy* and *Spongebob Squarepants* are among the shows inked and lined here. Screenings take place in several locations. Late May.

June

Dano An age-old event centred around the shamanist rituals still practised by many Koreans, this takes place at locations across the city, but is best experienced in the Namsangol hanok village (see p.70). It's also your best chance to see *ssireum*, a Korean form of wrestling.

Korean Queer Culture Festival ⓦ www.kqcf.org. Not exactly an event trumpeted by the local tourist authorities – in fact, not so long ago the police were still trying to ban it – this is a great way to see Korea crawling out of its Confucian shell. A fortnight-long programme includes a film festival, art exhibitions and the obligatory street parade.

July

Jisan Valley and Pentaport Rock Festivals ⓦ www.valleyrockfestival.com and pentaportrock .com. Two competing European-style music festivals (think tents, mud and portable toilets) which manage to rope in major international acts, though admittedly ones usually on the wane in their homelands. Both events stretch across three alcohol-fuelled nights, the revelry running non-stop.

August

Seoul Fringe Festival ⓦ www.seoulfringefestival .net. This fortnight-long platform for all things alternative is very popular with local students, and its semi-international nature means that certain events will appeal to visitors from overseas, with Hongdae usually the best place to be.

September

Seoul Performing Arts Festival ⓦ www.spaf .or.kr. This increasingly acclaimed event has seen performances from as far afield as Latvia and Israel, though its main aim is to showcase Korean talent. It takes place in various locations around Seoul over a three-week period. Late September and early October.

October

Baekje Festival ⓦ www.baekje.org. This annual event commemorating the Baekje dynasty is held alternately in the old Baekje capitals of Gongju (see p.164) and Buyeo. Early October.

Global Gathering ⓦ globalgatheringkorea.co.kr. The Korean edition of the international electronic music event takes place on the banks of the Hangang, near World Cup Stadium, and should be staying in Korea for some time to come. Early October.

Seoul Drum Festival ⓦ www.drumfestival.org. The crashes and bangs of all things percussive ring out at this annual event, which takes place in the Gwanghwamun area. Early October.

Seoul Fashion Week ⓦ www.seoulfashionweek .org. Since it first opened up in 2000, this has become Asia's largest fashion event, functioning as a great showcase for Seoul's up-and-coming designers.

November

Gimchi Love Festival Get your hands and mouths around the many varieties of spicy fermented cabbage from all over the country – an event surprisingly popular with foreigners. Takes place in the COEX Mall's *gimchi* museum (see p.95).

Pepero Day A crass marketing ploy, but an amusing one nonetheless – like Pocky, their Japanese cousins, Pepero are thin sticks of chocolate-coated biscuit, and on this date in the year when it looks as if four of them are standing together, millions of Koreans say "I love you" by giving a box to their sweethearts, friends, parents or pets. November 11.

Culture and etiquette

You may have mastered the art of the polite bow, worked out how to use the tricky steel chopsticks, and learnt a few words of the Korean language, but beware, you may upset new friends by accepting gifts with your hand in the wrong place. While even seasoned expats receive heartfelt congratulations for getting the easy bits right (some locals are even surprised when foreigners are able to use Korean money), there are still innumerable ways to offend, and unfortunately it's the things that are hardest to guess that are most likely to see you come a cropper.

Korea is often said to be the world's most **Confucian** nation, such values having been instilled for over a thousand years across several dynasties (see, p.181). Elements of Confucianism still linger on today – it's still basically true that anyone older, richer or more important than you (or just male as opposed to female) is simply "better" and deserving of more respect, a fact that becomes sorely clear to many working in Korea. Perhaps most evident to foreigners will be what amounts to a national obsession with **age** – you're likely to be asked how old you are soon after your first meeting with any Korean, and any similarity of birth years is likely to be greeted with a genuine whoop of delight (note that Koreans count years differently from Westerners – children are already 1 when they're born, and gain another digit at Lunar New Year, meaning that those born the day before the Lunar New Year are technically two years old the next day). Women have long been treated as subservient to men, and expected to ditch their job as soon as they give birth to their first child; however, recent years have shown a marked shift towards gender equality, with evidence that men are becoming more forgiving in the home and women more assertive in the workplace. **Foreigners** are largely exempt from the code of conduct that would be required of both parties following their knowledge of age, employment and background, and little is expected of them in such terms, but this does have its drawbacks – in such an ethnically homogenous society, those that aren't Korean will always remain "outsiders", even if they speak the language fluently or have actually spent their whole lives in the country. Conversely, foreigners with Korean blood will be expected to behave as a local would, even if they can't speak a word of the language.

Conduct

The East Asian concept of "face" is very important in Korea, and known here as *gibun*; the main goal is to avoid the **embarrassment** of self or others. Great lengths are usually taken to smooth out awkward situations, and foreigners getting unnecessarily angry are unlikely to invoke much sympathy. This occasionally happens as the result of an embarrassed smile, the traditional Korean retort to an uncomfortable question or incident; remember that they're not laughing at you (even if they've just dropped something on your head), merely trying to show empathy or move the topic onto safer ground. Foreigners may also see Koreans as disrespectful but this is a cultural difference – they simply haven't been introduced to you. Nobody's going to thank you for holding open a door, and you're unlikely to get an apology if bumped into (which is almost inevitable on the subway). **Dressing well** has long been important, but though pretty much anything goes for local girls these days, foreign women may be assumed to be brazen hussies (or, as often happens, Russian prostitutes) if they wear revealing clothing.

Meeting and greeting

Foreigners will see notice Koreans **bowing** all the time, even during telephone conversations. Though doing likewise will do much to endear you to locals, don't go overboard

– a full, right-angled bow would only be appropriate for meeting royalty, and the monarchy fell in 1910. Generally, a short bow with eyes closed and the head directed downwards will do just fine, but it's best to observe the Koreans themselves, and the action will become quite natural after a short time; many visitors find themselves inadvertently maintaining the habit long after they've left. The method of **attracting attention** is also different from what most foreigners are used to – beckoning is done with fingers fluttering beneath a downward-facing palm, rather than with index fingers protruding hook-like from an upturned one.

Koreans are great lovers of **business cards**, and these are exchanged in all meetings that have even a whiff of commerce about them. These humble rectangles garner far greater respect than they do in the West, and folding or stuffing one into a pocket or wallet is a huge *faux pas* – accept your card with profuse thanks, leave it on the table for the duration of the meeting, and file it away with respect (a card-holder is an essential purchase for anyone here on business). Also note that it's seen as incredibly rude to write someone's name in red ink – this colour is reserved for names of those who have died, a practice many Koreans think goes on everywhere in the world.

If you're lucky enough to be invited to a Korean home, try to bring a **gift** – fruit, chocolates and flowers go down well. The offering is likely to be refused at first, and probably on the second attempt too – persevere and it will eventually be accepted with thanks. The manner of receiving is also important – your receiving hand should be held from underneath by the non-receiving one, the distance up or down the arm dependent on exactly how polite you want to be. This will only come with experience and will not be expected of most foreigners, but you will be expected to take your **shoes off** once inside the house or apartment, so try to ensure that your socks are clean and hole-free.

Dining

Korea's Confucian legacy can often be a great boon to foreigners, as it has long been customary for hosts (usually "betters") to **pay** – many English teachers get taken out for regular slap-up meals by their bosses, and don't have to pay a dime. Koreans also tend to make a big show of trying to pay, with the bill passing rapidly from hand to hand until the right person coughs up. Nowadays things are changing slowly – especially among younger folk, "going Dutch" is increasingly common as a payment method, where it would have been unthinkable before. However, there are still innumerable codes of conduct to follow; Koreans will usually guide foreign inductees through the various dos and don'ts. Many surround the use of **chopsticks**, which in Korea are made of stainless steel – essential, given the corrosive red-pepper paste prevalent in most dishes. **Don't use your chopsticks** to point at people or pick your teeth, and try not to spear food with them unless your skills are really poor. It's also bad form, as natural as it may seem, to leave your chopsticks in the bowl: this is said to resemble incense sticks used after a death, but to most Koreans it just looks wrong (just as many Westerners obey unwritten and seemingly meaningless rules governing cutlery positions). Just leave the sticks balanced on the rim of the bowl.

Many Korean meals are group affairs, and this has given rise to a number of rules surrounding who **serves the food** from the communal trays to the individual ones – it's usually the youngest woman on the table. Foreign women finding themselves in this position will be able to mop up a great deal of respect for performing the duty, though as there are particular ways to serve each kind of food, it's probably best to watch first. The **serving of drinks** is a little less formal, though again the minutiae of recommended conduct could fill a small book – basically, you should never refill your own cup or glass, and should endeavour to keep topped up those belonging to others. The position of the hands is important – generally your inactive hand should be resting on the forearm attached to your active one, with the requisite level of Confucian "respect" shown by how close (lots of respect) or far (less respect) the hands are to each other. Watch to see how the Koreans are doing it, both the pourer and the recipient, and you'll be increasing your "face" value in no time.

One big no-no is to **blow your nose** during the meal – preposterously unfair, given the spice level of pretty much every Korean dish. Should you need to do so, make your excuses and head to the toilets. It's also proper form to wait for the **head of the table** – the one who is paying, in other words – to sit down first, as well as allowing them to be the first to stand at the end of the meal. The latter can be quite tricky, as many Korean restaurants are sit-on-the-floor affairs that play havoc on the knees and backs of foreigners unaccustomed to the practice.

All in all, Koreans will tolerate anything viewed as a "mistake" on the part of the foreigner, and offer great encouragement to those who are at least attempting to get things right. This can sometimes go a little too far – you're likely to be praised for your chopstick-handling abilities however long you've been around, and it's almost impossible to avoid the Korean Catch-22: locals love to ask foreigners questions during a meal, but anyone stopping to answer will likely fail to keep pace with the fast-eating Koreans, who will then assume that your dish is not disappearing quickly because you don't like it.

Living and working in Seoul

There are two main subspecies of westerner in Seoul: English teachers and American soldiers. Other jobs are hard to come by, though today's Korea is becoming ever more prominent in global business, with the resulting foreign contingent gradually permeating Seoul's army of suits. It's still fairly easy to land a teaching job, though to do this legally a degree certificate is nigh-on essential; wages are good, and Korea is a popular port of call for those wishing to pay off their student loan quickly while seeing a bit of the world. The cost of living, though rising, is still way below that in most English-speaking countries, and many teachers are able to put financial considerations out of their mind for the duration of their stay – many slowly realize that they've inadvertently been saving more than half of their salary.

Seoul is the most obvious target for those wishing to teach English in Korea, and with the number of **teaching jobs** on offer, it's quite possible to handpick the area of the city you'd like to live in. Doing so may save unnecessary disappointment: those who fail to do their research often end up living in the suburbs (Bundang, for example, has a veritable army of English teachers), which are an hour or so from the city centre. As well as teaching, some come to **study**. Korea has given a number of martial arts to the world, and continues to draw in students keen to learn directly from the horse's mouth; others choose to learn the local language.

Teaching English

Low tax and decent pay cheques make Korea one of the most popular stops on the **English-teaching** circuit. Demand for native speakers is high and still growing; English-teaching qualifications are far from essential, and all that is usually required is a degree certificate, and a copy of your passport – many people have been taken on by a Korean school without so much as a telephone interview. However, **entry procedures** have become more stringent in recent years, though these change like the wind: among those required in the past have been original university transcripts, a police check from your home country, and an HIV test before assuming your job. At the time of writing, the transcripts were not required and the police check was (stamped by a notary), while one foreigner had taken the national government to court over the necessity of the HIV check. Even when you're inside the country, up-to-date information is hard to find: ask as many questions as possible from your school or agent, and don't expect all answers to be correct.

Most new entrants start off by teaching kids at a language school (*hagwon*). Some of the bigger companies are ECC, YBM and Pagoda, and most pay just over W2,000,000 per month, though even for people doing the same job at the same school this may vary depending on nationality and gender – Canadian women usually get the most, British gents the least. After a year or two, many teachers are sick of kids and puny holiday allowances, and make their way to a university teaching post; pay is usually lower and responsibilities higher than at a *hagwon*, though the holiday allowances are hard to resist, often as much as five months per year. It's also possible to teach adults in business or government schools, or you could volunteer for a couple of hours a week at one of the country's many orphanages. Most teachers give their bank balance a nudge in the right direction by offering **private lessons** on the side – an illegal practice, but largely tolerated unless you start organizing them for others. To land a full-time job from outside Korea you'll have to go online, and it's still the best option if you're already in Korea – popular sites include Dave's ESL Café (Ⓦwww.eslcafe .com), ESL Hub (Ⓦwww.eslhub.com) and HiTeacher (Ⓦhiteacher.com), though a thorough web search will yield more.

One of the most regular *hagwon*-related **complaints** is the long hours many teachers have to work – figure on up to 30 per week. This may include Saturdays, or be spread quite liberally across the day from 9am to 9pm – try to find jobs with "no split shift" if possible. Questionable school policies also come in for stick; for example, teachers are often expected to be present at the school for show even if they have no lessons on. Real scare stories are ten-a-penny, too – every teacher knows an unfortunate fellow-foreigner whose school suddenly closed, the manager having ridden off into the sunset with a pay cheque or two. This said, most schools are reputable; you can typically expect them to organize **free accommodation**, and to do the legwork with your **visa** application. Some countries operate Working Holiday visa schemes with Korea, but others will need a full working visa to be legally employed; those unable to collect this in their home country are usually given a plane ticket and directions for a quick visa-run to Japan (the closest embassy is in Fukuoka).

Studying in Seoul

Korea has long been a popular place for the study of **martial arts**, while the country's ever-stronger ties with global business is also prompting many to gain a competitive advantage by studying the Korean language.

Language

Those looking to study **Korean** in Seoul have a full range of options to choose from, depending on what linguistic depth they require and how long they have to attain it. Students desiring fluency may consider attending one of the institutes run by many of the larger **universities**, though even these vary in terms of price, study time, skill level and accommodation. Most of the year-long courses start in March – apply in good time. There's a good list at Ⓦenglish .tour2korea.com, while information on study visas and how to apply for them can be found on the Ministry of Education's website (Ⓦwww.studyinkorea.go.kr). There are **private institutes** dotted around Seoul and other major cities – Ⓦenglish.seoul.go.kr has a list of safe recommendations in the capital, while other official city websites are the best places to look for institutes elsewhere in the country. Those who find themselves working in Korea may have no time for intensive study; in these cases many opt to take language lessons from friends or colleagues.

Cooking schools

Seoul has a range of excellent Korean cooking classes aimed at foreigners, most of whom, of course, will be novices in the field. The best classes are run by **O'ngo** (ⓦwww.ongofood.com), a cooking school just east of Insadonggil; beginner classes include *bulgogi*, *pajeon* and *gimchi* techniques, and cost from W45,000 per person. More refined are the classes at the **Institute of Traditional Korean Food** (ⓦwww.kfr.or.kr) north of Anguk station, who include lessons on royal cuisine (see p.114). At the other end of the scale is **Yoo's Family** (ⓦwww.yoosfamily.com) near Jongmyo, who run simple classes from W20,000.

Martial arts classes

Finding classes for the most popular styles (including **taekwondo**, *hapkido* and *geomdo*) isn't hard, but very few cater for foreigners – it's best to go hunting on the expat circuit. Those looking for something more advanced should seek advice from their home country's own federations, rather than just turning up in Seoul.

Buddhist teachings

Many **temples** around the country offer teaching and templestay programmes for around W50,000 per night, a wonderful opportunity to see Seoul at its most serene (as long as you can stand the early mornings). Some temples are able to provide English-language instruction, and some not – see ⓦeng.templestay.com for more details. In addition, there's the **Ahnkook Zen Academy** (ⓦwww.ahnkookzen.org) north of Anguk station, though this gets mixed reports: the teachings themselves are good, but the awfully ugly building tends to dash any thoughts of true Zen. They run English-language programs every Saturday afternoon. Simpler, but perhaps more enjoyable for some, are the classes run by **Jogyesa** temple (see p.58), who charge W10,000 for a program including Buddhist painting and lotus lantern-making; reserve as far in advance as possible through a tourist office. Lastly, and perhaps most suitable for spiritualism given its out-of-Seoul location, is the **Lotus Lantern Meditation Centre** (ⓦwww.lotuslantern.net) on the island of Ganghwado (see p.157), who run weekend-long meditation programs (W50,000) most weeks.

Travel essentials

Costs

Some people come to Korea expecting it to be a budget destination on a par with the Southeast Asian countries, while others arrive with expectations of Japanese-style levels. The truth is somewhere on the latter side of the scale – those staying at five-star hotels and eating at top restaurants will spend almost as much as they would in other developed countries, though there are numerous ways for budget travellers to make their trip a cheap one. Your biggest outlay is likely to be **accommodation** – Seoul has some grand places to stay for W400,000 and up, and cheaper tourist hotels for around W100,000. Though they're not to everyone's taste, motels (see p.105) usually make acceptable places to stay, costing around W30,000, while the capital also has a fair few backpacker flophouses where costs start at W15,000 for a dorm bed. Real scrimpers can stay at a *jjimjilbang* (see p.145), where overnight entry fees start at around W7000.

Transport is unlikely to make too much of a dent in your wallet – even a taxi ride taking you clean across the city shouldn't cost more than W20,000, and short rides are under W5000. Public transport is even cheaper, usually W1000 per journey. Sightseeing is also affordable, with many sights free, and many more costing a nominal W1000–3000. The easiest thing to splurge on is food: Seoul has an ever-growing number of top-class restaurants, whose prices are generally far lower than they would be in other developed countries. For those fond of Korean cuisine, cheaper restaurants are plentiful, and a good meal can be had for W5000.

By staying in motels or guesthouses and eating at reasonably cheap restaurants, you should be able to survive easily on a daily budget of W40,000 (£22/US$42/€31), or even half this if seriously pushed. After you've added in transport costs and a few entry tickets, a realistic daily figure may be W60,000 (£32/US$63/€46).

Tipping plays almost no part in Korean transactions – try not to leave unwanted change in the hands of a cashier, lest they feel forced to abandon their duties and chase you down the street with it. Exceptions are tourist hotels, most of which tack a ten percent service charge onto the room bill; these are also among the few places in the country to omit **tax** – levied at eleven percent – from their quoted prices.

Crime and personal safety

Korea is one of those countries in which you're far more likely to see someone running towards you with a dropped wallet than away with a stolen one – tales abound of travellers who have left a valuable possession on a restaurant table or park bench and returned hours later to find it in the same place. Though you'd be very unlucky to fall victim to a crime, it's prudent to take a few simple precautions regarding personal safety. One involves the country's awful **road accident** record, the gruesome statistics heightened by the number of vehicles that use pavements as shortcuts or parking spaces. Caution should also be exercised around any **street fights** that you may have the misfortune to come across: since Korean men practise taekwondo to a fairly high level during their compulsory national service, Seoul is not a great place to get caught in a scuffle. In general, female travellers have little to worry about, and though some locals caution

against taking night-time taxi rides alone, you'd be extremely unfortunate to come to harm in this (or indeed, any other) situation.

Electricity

The electrical **current** runs at 220v, 60Hz throughout the country, and requires European-style plugs with two round pins, though some older buildings, including many cheap guesthouses, may still take flat-pinned plugs at 110v.

Entry requirements

Citizens of almost any Western nation can enter Korea visa-free with an onward ticket, though the duration of the permit varies. Most EU nationals qualify for a three-month visa exemption, as do citizens of New Zealand and Australia; Italians and Portuguese are only allowed sixty days, Americans and South Africans just thirty, and Canadians a full six months. If you need more than this, apply before entering Korea. **Overstaying** your visa will result in a large fine (up to W500,000 per day), with exceptions only being made in emergencies such as illness or loss of passport. Getting a new passport is time-consuming and troublesome, though the process will be simplified if your passport has been registered with your embassy in Seoul, or if you can prove your identity with a birth certificate or copy of your old passport.

Work visas, valid for one year and extendable for at least one more, can be applied for before or after entering Korea. Applications can take up to a month to be processed by Korean embassies, but once inside the country it can take as little as a week. Your **employer** will do all the hard work with the authorities then provide you with a visa confirmation slip; the visa must be picked up outside Korea (the nearest consulate is in Fukuoka, Japan; visas here can be issued one working day after application). Visas with the same employer can be extended without leaving Korea. An **alien card** must be applied for at the local immigration office within ninety days of arrival – again, this is usually taken care of by the employer. Work visas are forfeited on leaving Korea, though re-entry visas can be applied for at your provincial immigration office, W30,000 for single entry, W50,000 for multiple. Australians, Canadians and New Zealanders can apply for a **working holiday** visa at their local South Korean embassy.

South Korean embassies and consulates abroad

Australia 113 Empire Circuit, Yarralumla, ACT 2600 ☎02/6270 4100, ⓦwww.korea.org.au.
Canada 150 Boteler St, Ottawa, Ontario K1N 5A6 ☎613/244-5010, ⓦwww.koreanconsulate.on.ca.
China No 3, 4th Avenue East, Sanlitun, Chaoyang District, Beijing 100600 ☎10/6532 0290, ⓦwww.koreanembassy.cn.
Ireland 20 Clyde Rd, Ballsbridge, Dublin 4 ☎01/660 8800.
Japan 1-2-5 Minami-Azabu, 1-chome, Minato-ku, Tokyo 106 ☎03/3452 7611.
New Zealand 11th Floor, ASB Bank Tower, 2 Hunter St, Wellington ☎04/473 9073, ⓦwww.koreanembassy.org.nz.
Singapore 47 Scotts Rd #08-00 Goldbell Towers, Singapore 228233 ☎6256 1188, ⓦwww .koreaembassy.org.sg.
South Africa Green Park Estates, Building 3, 27 George Storrar Drive, Groenkloof, Pretoria ☎012/460 2508.
UK 60 Buckingham Gate, London SW1E 6AJ ☎020/7227 5500, ⓦwww.koreanembassy.org.uk.
US 2450 Massachusetts Ave NW, Washington, DC 20008 ☎202/939-5600, ⓦwww .koreaembassyusa.org.

Gay and lesbian travellers

Despite Goryeo-era evidence suggesting that undisguised homosexuality was common in Royal and Buddhist circles, the **gay community** in today's Korea forms a small, alienated section of society. Indeed, many locals genuinely seem to believe that Korean homosexuality simply does not exist, regarding it instead as a "foreign disease" that instantly gives people AIDS. The prevalent traditional attitudes, together with the lack of a decent gay scene, have been the bane of many a queer expat's life in the country. For Korean homosexuals, the problems are more serious – although the law makes no explicit reference to the legality of sexual intercourse between adults of the same sex, this is less a tacit nod of consent than a refusal of officialdom to discuss such matters, and gay activities may be punishable as sexual harassment, or even, shockingly, "mutual rape" if it takes place in the military. In the early 1990s, the first few gay and lesbian websites were cracked down on by a government that, during the course of the subsequent appeal, made it clear that human rights did not fully apply to homosexuals – all the more reason for the "different people" (*iban-in*), already fearful of losing their jobs, friends and family, to lock themselves firmly in the closet.

Korean society is, however, slowly but surely becoming more liberal, particularly in Seoul. With more and more high-profile homosexuals coming out, a critical mass has been reached, and younger generations are markedly less prejudiced against – and more willing to discuss – the pink issue. Gay clubs and bars, while still generally low-key outside "Homo Hill" in Itaewon (see p.130), can now be found in other parts of the city too; see p.130 for more information about where to go. Finally, the **Korean Queer Culture Festival** takes place over a fortnight in early June at locations across Seoul, see p.27 for more information.

Gay information sources

Buddy ⓦbuddy79.com/htm/foreign-1.htm. A popular gay and lesbian lifestyle magazine.
Chingusai ⓦchingusai.net. Loosely meaning "Among Friends", Chingusai's trailblazing magazine is available at many gay bars in the capital. Though mainly in Korean, the site has some English-language information.
Happy & Safe Most useful for its gay scene city maps; you may come across the odd copy of this little guide on your way around Seoul's bars.
Utopia Asia ⓦwww.utopia-asia.com/tipskor.htm. Site containing useful information about bars, clubs and saunas, much of which goes into their book, *The Utopia Guide to Japan, Korea and Taiwan.*

Health

South Korea is pretty high up in the world rankings as far as **healthcare** goes, and there are no compulsory vaccinations or diseases worth getting too worried about. Hospitals are clean and well staffed, and most doctors can speak English, so the main health concerns for foreign travellers are likely to be financial – without adequate insurance cover, a large bill may rub salt into your healing wounds if you end up in hospital (see p.35). It would be wise to bring along any medicines that you might need, especially for drugs that need to be prescribed – bring a copy of your prescription, as well as the generic name of the drug in question, as brand names may vary from country to country.

Drinking Korean **tap water** is not the best idea, and with free drinking fountains in every restaurant, hotel, supermarket, police station, department store and PC bar in the country, there really should be no need; in addition, the ubiquitous convenience stores sell bottles of water for W700. Restaurant food will almost always be prepared and cooked adequately (and all necessary precautions taken with raw fish), however bad it looks, though it's worth bearing in mind that the incredible amount of red pepper paste consumed by the average Korean has made stomach cancer the country's number one killer.

In an **emergency**, you should first try to ask a local to call for an ambulance. Should you need to do so yourself, the number is ☎119, though it's possible that no English-speaker will be available to take your call. Alternatively, try the tourist information line on ☎1330, or if all else fails dial English directory assistance on ☎080/211-0114. If the problem isn't life-threatening, the local tourist office should be able to point you in the direction of the most suitable doctor or hospital. Once there, you may find it surprisingly hard to get information about what's wrong with you – as in much of East Asia, patients are expected to trust doctors to do their jobs properly, and any sign that this trust is not in place results in a loss of face for the practitioner.

For minor complaints or medical advice, there are **pharmacies** all over the place, usually distinguished by the Korean

character "*yak*" (약) at the entrance, though English-speakers are few and far between. Travellers can also visit a practitioner of **oriental medicine**, who use acupuncture and pressure-point massage, among other techniques. If you have Korean friends, ask around for a personal recommendation in order to find a reputable practitioner.

Medical resources for travellers

Australia, New Zealand and South Africa
Travellers' Medical and Vaccination Centre
☎1300-658844, ⓦwww.tmvc.com.au. Lists travel clinics in Australia, New Zealand and South Africa.
UK and Ireland
British Airways Travel Clinics ☎0845/600 2236, ⓦwww.britishairways.com/travel/healthclinintro /public/en_gb for nearest clinic.
Hospital for Tropical Diseases Travel Clinic ☎0845/155 5000 or 020/7387 4411, ⓦwww.thehtd.org.
MASTA (Medical Advisory Service for Travellers Abroad) ☎0113/238 7575, ⓦwww.masta.org for the nearest clinic.
Tropical Medical Bureau Republic of Ireland ☎1850/487674, ⓦwww.tmb.ie. Has a list of clinics in the Republic of Ireland.
US and Canada
CDC ☎1-877-394-8747, ⓦwww.cdc.gov/travel. Official US government travel health site.
International Society for Travel Medicine ☎1-770-736-7060, ⓦwww.istm.org. Has a full list of travel health clinics.
Canadian Society for International Health ⓦwww .csih.org. Extensive list of travel health centres.

Insurance

The price of hospital treatment in Korea can be quite high and, therefore, it's advisable to take out a decent **travel insurance**

Rough Guides travel insurance

Rough Guides has teamed up with WorldNomads.com to offer great **travel insurance** deals. Policies are available to residents of over 150 countries, with cover for a wide range of **adventure sports**, 24-hour emergency assistance, high levels of medical and evacuation cover and a stream of **travel safety information**. Roughguides.com users can take advantage of their policies online 24/7, from anywhere in the world – even if you're already travelling. And since plans often change when you're on the road, you can extend your policy and even claim online. Roughguides.com users who buy travel insurance with WorldNomads.com can also leave a positive footprint and donate to a community development project. For more information go to ⓦ**www .roughguides.com/shop**.

policy before you go. Keep the emergency number of your insurance company handy in the event of an accident and, as in any country, if you have anything stolen make sure to obtain a copy of the police report, as you will need this to make a claim.

Internet

You should have no problem getting online; South Korea is possibly the most connected nation on the planet. It's a national addiction – **PC rooms** (pronounced "*pishi-bang*") are everywhere, and in any urban area the same rule applies: look around, and you'll see one. These noisy, air-conditioned shrines to the latest computing equipment hide behind neon-lit street signs (the PC in Roman characters; the *bang*, meaning room, in Korean text), and despite their ubiquity can be full to the brim with gamers – you're likely to be the only one checking your mail. These cafés have charged the same price since the dawn of the internet age: an almost uniform W1000 per hour, with a one-hour minimum charge (though it's far more expensive in hotels, and usually free in post offices). Most will have snacks and instant noodles for sale behind the counter and some will offer you a free tea or coffee when you sit down, topping you up every few hours.

Laundry

Almost all tourist hotels provide a **laundry** service, and some of the backpacker hostels will wash your smalls for free, but with public laundries so thin on the ground those staying elsewhere may have to resort to a spot of DIY cleaning. All motels have 24-hour hot water, as well as soap, body lotion and/or shampoo in the bathrooms, and in the winter clothes dry in no time on the heated *ondol* floors. Summer is a different story, with the humidity making it very hard to dry clothes in a hurry. Dry-cleaning is a straightforward, since there'll always be a *setak* (세탁소) within walking distance.

Mail

The Korean postal system is cheap and trustworthy, and there are **post offices** in every district of Seoul. Most are open Monday to Friday 9am–6pm; all should be able to handle international mail, and the larger ones offer free internet access. The main problem facing many travellers is the relative dearth of **postcards** for sale, though if you do track some down postal rates are cheap, at around W400 per card. Letters will cost a little more, though as with **parcels** the tariff will vary depending on their destination – the largest box you can send (20kg) will cost about W150,000 to mail to the UK or US, though this price drops to about W50,000 if you post via **surface mail**, a process that can take up to three months. All post offices have the necessary boxes for sale, and will even do your packing for a small fee.

Maps

Free maps, many of which are available in English, can be picked up at any tourist office or higher-end hotel, as well as most travel terminals. The main drawback with them is that distances and exact street patterns are hard to gauge, though it's a complaint the powers that be are slowly taking on board. Mercifully, maps for Bukhansan National Park are excellent and drawn to scale, and can be bought for W1000 at the park entrances. Those looking for professional maps will find plenty (although mostly in Korean) in the city's major bookshops (see p.141).

Money

The **Korean currency** is the won (W), which comes in notes of W1000, W5000, W10,000 and W50,000, and coins of W10, W50, W100 and W500. Use of credit cards has gone through the roof in recent years – previously it was common to see Koreans paying for expensive household goods with foot-high wads of cash. At the time of writing the **exchange rate** was approximately W1800 to £1, W1500 to €1, and W1100 to US$1.

Travellers occasionally encounter difficulties when attempting to withdraw money from **ATMs** (there are several different systems in operation, even within the same banking chains), but most should be able to withdraw cash using an international debit or credit card. The official advice is to head to an ATM marked "Global", which are easiest to find in branches of KB Bank. Global ATMs and similar machines are also commonplace in the ubiquitous 24-hour convenience stores such as Family Mart, 7-Eleven or LG25. Most machines capable of dealing with foreign cards are able to switch to English-language mode.

Though you shouldn't rely on them, foreign **credit cards** are being accepted in more and more hotels, restaurants and shops. It shouldn't be too hard to **exchange** foreign notes or travellers' cheques for Korean cash once in the country; banks are all over the place, and the only likely problem when dealing in dollars, pounds or euros is time – some places simply won't have exchanged money before. **Leaving Korea** with local currency is not advisable, as it's hard to exchange outside the country – get it changed before you head to the airport if you want a good rate.

Opening hours and public holidays

Until recently, the country was one of the few in the world to have a **six-day working week**; though this has been officially realigned to five, the changes won't filter through to all workers, and Korea's place at the top of the world's "average hours worked per year" table is unlikely to be affected. The number of **national holidays** has fallen, however, in an attempt to make up the slack, and as most of the country's population is forced to take their holiday at the same times, there can be chaos on the roads and rails. Three of the biggest holidays – Lunar New Year, Buddha's birthday and Chuseok – are based on the Lunar calendar, and have no fixed dates.

Korea is one of the world's truest 24-hour societies – **opening hours** are such that almost everything you need is likely to be available when you require it. Most shops and almost all restaurants are open seven days a week, often until late,

South Korean public holidays

Sinjeong (New Year's Day) January 1. Seoul celebrates New Year in much the same fashion as Western countries, with huge crowds gathering around City Hall.

Seollal (Lunar New Year) Usually early February. One of the most important holidays on the calendar, Lunar New Year sees Koreans flock to their home towns for a three-day holiday of relaxed celebration, and many businesses close up.

Independence Movement Day March 1.

Children's Day May 5. Koreans make an even bigger fuss over their kids than usual on this national holiday – expect parks, zoos and amusement parks to be jam-packed.

Memorial Day June 6. Little more than a day off for most Koreans, this day honours those who fell in battle, and is best observed in the National Cemetery (see p.90).

Constitution Day July 17.

Independence Day August 15. The country becomes a sea of Korean flags on this holiday celebrating the end of Japanese rule in 1945.

Chuseok Late September or early October. One of the biggest events on the Korean calendar is this three-day national holiday, similar to Thanksgiving; families head to their home towns to venerate their ancestors in low-key ceremonies, and eat a special crescent-shaped rice-cake.

National Foundation Day October 3. Celebrates the 2333 BC birth of Dangun, the legendary founder of the Korean nation. Shamanist celebrations take place at shrines around Seoul, with the most important on Inwangsan mountain (see p.75).

Christmas Day December 25. Every evening looks like Christmas in neon-drenched Seoul, but on this occasion Santa Haraboji (Grandpa Santa) finally arrives.

as are tourist information offices. Post offices keep more sensible hours (Mon–Fri 9am–6pm), and banks generally open Monday to Friday 9.30am to 4pm. A quite incredible number of establishments are open 24/7, including convenience stores, saunas, internet cafés and some of the busier shops and restaurants.

Phones

With Korea one of the world's most important fonts of **mobile phone** technology, what may qualify as cutting-edge elsewhere may be viewed as passé by Koreans. Getting hold of a phone while you're in the country is easy – there are 24-hour rental booths at Incheon Airport, and some top-class hotels have free-to-hire mobile phones in their rooms. Those who will be in Korea for a while may care to purchase a second-hand mobile phone – these can be as cheap as W15,000, and the pace of change means that even high-quality units may be available for knock-down prices; the best places to look are shopping districts, electrical stores or underground malls – just look for a glassed-off bank of phones. After purchase you'll need to register with a major service provider – KTF and SK Telecom are two of the biggest chains, and so ubiquitous are their stores (named Show and T-Mobile at the time of writing, though subject to frequent change in recent years) that the nearest is likely to be within walking distance. Registration is free (bring your passport), and you can top up pay-as-you-go accounts in increments of W10,000. Despite the prevalence of mobile phones,

you'll still see **payphones** on every major street; these ageing units only take coins, so you'll have to pump in change at a furious pace to avoid the deafening squawks that signal the end of your call-time.

Photography

Photography is a national obsession in Korea – at tourist sights around the country, locals feed their cameras as they would hungry pets, with most of the resulting stash of images ending up on personal homepages. Visitors are little different, since Seoul should keep your camera-finger busy; if you want a personal shot, few locals will mind being photographed, though of course it's polite to ask first. One serious no-no is to go snap-happy on a tour of the DMZ (see p.149) – this can, and has, landed tourists in trouble. You may also see temple-keepers and monks poised at the ready to admonish would-be photographers of sacrosanct areas. Though the digital revolution has scaled back sales of **film**, the regular brands are still available around the country, and getting it processed is cheap and efficient – expect a developing fee of W2000, plus a few hundred won per picture. Most computers, whether in your accommodation or an **internet café**, will be kitted out for the transfer of digital images from memory cards.

Smoking

Most Korean men smoke, as well as a growing number of younger women – no real surprise, with packets of twenty starting

---

Calling home from abroad

Note that the **initial zero is omitted** from the area code when dialling the UK, Ireland, Australia and New Zealand from abroad. Dial 001 to get an international connection. To call Seoul from abroad, use the Korean international dialling code (☏82), followed by 2, then the seven- or eight-digit number.

Australia International access code + 61 + city code.
Ireland International access code + 353 + city code.
New Zealand International access code + 64 + city code.
South Africa International access code + 27 + city code.
UK International access code + 44 + city code.
US and Canada International access code + 1 + area code.

at around W3000 in any convenience store. Larger cafés have dedicated smoking sections, but the same cannot be said for restaurants, which tend to be either completely non-smoking or a free-for-all. Many Koreans retreat to public toilets for a cigarette; curiously, many have both signs on the doors forbidding such activities and ashtrays or paper cups for those who desire to break the rules.

Time

The Korean peninsula shares a **time zone** with Japan – one hour ahead of China, nine hours ahead of Greenwich Mean Time, seven hours ahead of South Africa, fourteen hours ahead of Eastern Standard Time in the US or Canada, and one hour behind Sydney. Bear in mind that daylight saving hours are not observed, so though noon in London will be 9pm in Seoul for much of the year, the difference drops to eight hours during British Summer Time.

Tourist information

The Korean tourist authorities churn out a commendable number of English-language maps, pamphlets and books, which are handed out at hotels and **information booths** around the city. In addition, the city government has installed a number of interactive touchscreen information points in subway stations and tourist centres; at the time of writing, these were in the teething stages and not up to much, but they'll likely be improved before too long.

There are several information booths located on and around Insadonggil (see map, p.55), but the largest by far is in the basement of the **Korea Tourism Organization** building, which sits off the south bank of Cheong-gyecheon. If you can't make it to Insadong, you'll be able to get 24-hour English-language assistance and advice on the dedicated **tourist information line** – dial ☎1330 (or 02/1330 from a mobile) and you'll be put through to helpful call-centre staff who speak a number of languages and can advise on transport, sights, accommodation and much more. The official Seoul **tourist website** (ⓦwww.visitseoul.net) was mercifully given a thorough overhaul in 2009, and is now quite useful.

Travelling with children

Seoul has high standards of **health and hygiene**, low levels of crime and plenty to see and do – bringing children of any age should pose no special problems. Koreans dote upon their children, no real surprise given that the birth rate is among the lowest on earth. Locals make enough fuss over their own kids, but foreign children (particularly those with fair hair) are likely to find themselves the star of plenty of photographs.

Changing facilities are common in public toilets (department stores are particularly good for this), and classier restaurants have highchairs. Unfortunately, baby food labelled in English is almost non-existent. A few hotels provide a babysitting service, though those in need can also ask their concierge for a newspaper with babysitter adverts (see p.25). There are also cinemas (see p.133), theme parks (see p.162) and a zoo or two (see p.99) to keep children amused.

Finally, a few words of warning. It's essential to note that some of the restaurants listed in this guide – especially those serving *galbi*, a self-barbecued meat – have hot-plates or charcoal in the centre of the table, which poses an obvious danger to little hands. Additionally, in a country where it's perfectly normal for cars to drive on the pavements, you may want to exercise a little more caution than normal when walking around town with your children. Note that breastfeeding in public will cause grave offence. For more general advice, check out the *Rough Guide to Travel with Babies and Young Children*.

Travellers with disabilities

Despite its First World status, South Korea can be filed under "developing countries" as far as **disabled accessibility** is concerned, and with rushing traffic and crowded streets, it's never going to be the easiest destination to get around. Until recently, very little attention was paid to those with disabilities, though the past seven or eight years has seen more public discussion of the lot of disabled people in

Korean society. Tolerance is growing and things continue to improve – streets are being made more wheelchair-friendly, and all subway and train stations have been fitted with lifts. Almost all motels and tourist hotels have these too, though at the lower end you'll occasionally come across an entrance that hasn't been built with wheelchairs in mind. Some museums and tourist attractions will be able to provide a helper if necessary.

The City

The City

The Palace District

Seoul was once a much smaller city, bounded by fortress walls erected shortly after it became capital of the nascent **Joseon dynasty** in 1392. While the urban sprawl has since raced mile after mile in every direction, this small area remains the most appealing to visitors, not least on account of the **grand palaces** that once served as home to the kings of Joseon. The dynasty ran for over five centuries, coming to an end in 1910, and during that time no fewer than five palaces served as the country's seat of power; no visit to Seoul would be complete without a visit to at least one or two. By far the most visited is **Gyeongbokgung**, the oldest of the group, though nearby **Changdeokgung** is a little more refined, and the only one to have been added to UNESCO's World Heritage list. Literally a stone's throw away across a perimeter wall is **Changgyeonggung**, which probably has the most interesting history of the five, as well as the most natural setting. Further south are the smaller pair of **Gyeonghuigung** (p.62) and **Deoksugung** (p.63), covered in Chapter 3. For more on Seoul's regal offerings, see the *Traditional Seoul* colour section.

While the palaces are the main draw, there's much more to see in the area, from the cafés and galleries of laid-back **Samcheongdong** to the traditional buildings of **Bukchon Hanok Village**. One popular **day-trip** itinerary is to start the morning at Gyeongbokgung and take in the on-site museums before heading to Samcheongdong for a meal and a cup of coffee; energy thus restored, you can head across hilly Bukchon towards the palace of Changdeokgung.

Gyeongbokgung

The glorious palace of **Gyeongbukgung** (경복궁) is, with good reason, the most popular tourist sight in the city, and a focal point of the country as a whole. The place is quite absorbing, and the chance to stroll the dusty paths between its delicate tile-roofed buildings is one of the most enjoyable experiences Seoul has to offer. Gyeongbokgung was ground zero for Seoul's emergence as a place of power, having been built to house the royal family of the embryonic **Joseon dynasty**, shortly after they transferred their capital here in 1392. The complex has witnessed fires, repeated destruction and even a royal assassination (see History, p.173), but careful reconstruction means that the regal atmosphere of old is still palpable, aided no end by the suitably majestic crags of Bugaksan to the north. A large historical complex with excellent on-site **museums** (see p.48), it can easily eat up

43

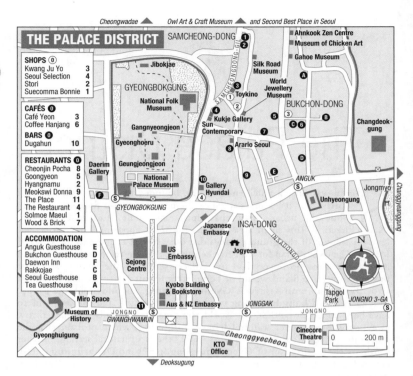

Cheongwadae ▲   *Owl Art & Craft Museum* ▲   *and Second Best Place in Seoul*

THE PALACE DISTRICT   SAMCHEONG-DONG

■ **Ahnkook Zen Centre**
■ **Museum of Chicken Art**
■ **Gahoe Museum**

SHOPS ⊙
Kwang Ju Yo   3
Seoul Selection   4
Stori   2
Suecomma Bonnie   1

CAFÉS ⊙
Café Yeon   3
Coffee Hanjang   6

BARS ⊙
Dugahun   10

RESTAURANTS ⊙
Cheonjin Pocha   8
Goongyeon   5
Hyangnamu   2
Meokswi Donna   9
The Place   11
The Restaurant   4
Solmoe Maeul   1
Wood & Brick   7

ACCOMMODATION
Anguk Guesthouse   E
Bukchon Guesthouse   D
Daewon Inn   F
Rakkojae   C
Seoul Guesthouse   B
Tea Guesthouse   A

■ Jibokjae

GYEONGBOKGUNG

National Folk Museum

Gangnyeongjeon

Gyeonghoeru

Geungjeongjeon

National Palace Museum

Daerim Gallery

Silk Road Museum

Toykino

World Jewellery Museum

BUKCHON-DONG

Kukje Gallery

Sun Contemporary

Arario Seoul

Gallery Hyundai

Changdeok-gung

ANGUK

Unhyeongung

Jongmyo

Japanese Embassy

INSA-DONG

Jogyesa

Sejong Centre

US Embassy

Kyobo Building & Bookstore

Aus & NZ Embassy

JONGGAK

Tapgol Park

JONGNO 3-GA

Miro Space

Museum of History

GWANGHWAMUN

JONGNO

JONGNO

Gyeonghuigung

Cheonggyecheon

KTO Office

Cinecore Theatre

0   200 m

N

▼ *Deoksugung*

the best part of a day (expats and visitors in the know often choose to pop by after visiting hours are over; see box, p.129), and the nearby sights around Insadong (see Chapter 2), Samcheongdong (p.50) and Bukchon Hanok Village (p.50) are all within walking distance.

In 2010 the first phase of substantial **reconstruction** efforts at Gyeongbukgung were completed, begun in earnest in 1989, when the city government embarked on a forty-year campaign to recreate the hundreds of buildings that once filled the palace walls. The Seoul Capitol, which had found use after the war as the Korean National Assembly, then the National Museum, was finally torn down on Liberation Day (see p.37) in 1995. By 2010 around half of Gyeongbokgung's former buildings had been given a new lease of life, in replica form, and the results are extremely pleasing. August of that year also saw the **reopening of Gwanghwamun** – effectively a day of national celebration, since this was the first time Korea's most famous palace gate had been present in its original position, and built with traditional materials, since the fall of Joseon. Further renovations will take place over the coming decades, and are set to make Gyeongbokgung one of Asia's top tourist draws.

To **get to** Gyeongbokgung, take subway line 3 to the station of the same name (exit five); alternatively, it's an easy walk from Insadonggil (p.54). Try to time your visit to coincide with the colourful **changing of the guard** ceremony, which takes place outside the main entrance at 11am, 2pm and 3.30pm, every day except Monday. There are free English-language **tours** of the grounds at 11am, 1.30pm and 3.30pm, although the complex has information boards all over the place, and most visitors choose to go it alone.

Some history

Construction was ordered by **King Taejo** in 1394 and completed in 1399, and the "Palace of Shining Happiness" held the regal throne for over two hundred years. At the peak of its importance, the palace housed over four hundred buildings within its vaguely rectangular perimeter walls, but most were burnt down during the Japanese invasions in the 1590s. Though few Koreans will admit to it, the invaders were not always to blame, however – the arsonists in one major fire were actually a group of local slaves, angered by their living and working conditions, and aware that their records were kept locked up in the palace. The palace was only rebuilt following the coronation of child-king **Gojong** in 1863, but these renovations were destined to be short-lived thanks to the expansionist ideas of contemporary Japan, who in 1895 removed one major obstacle to power by assassinating Gojong's wife, Empress Myeongsong (see box below), in the Gyeongbokgung grounds. Following this murder, the Japanese slowly increased their standing in Korea, before making a formal annexation of the peninsula in 1910. Gyeongbokgung, beating heart of an occupied nation, were first in the line of fire and, all in all, only a dozen of the palace's buildings survived the occupation period.

Under Japanese rule, the palace was used for police interrogation and torture, and numerous structural changes were made in an apparent effort to destroy Korean pride. The front gate, Gwanghwamun, was moved to the east of the complex, destroying the north–south geometric principles followed during the palace's creation, while 1926 saw the construction of the **Seoul Capitol**, a huge Neoclassical Japanese construction that became the city's largest building at the time, dwarfing the former royal structures around it, and making a rather obvious stamp of

Trouble at the palace

Rarely have troubles with the in-laws achieved as much significance as those endured by the Joseon royalty during the latter part of the nineteenth century. Korea was, at the time, ruled by **King Gojong** (r.1863-1907), a weak leader destined to be his country's penultimate monarch. Gojong took the throne when he was just eleven years of age, with his father **Heungseon** acting as regent and de facto ruler of the country. Heungseon was deeply Confucian and suspicious of foreigners: in 1866, he incurred a military invasion from France after ordering the execution of nine French missionaries. King Gojong reached marriageable age at 14, and took **Myeongseong** as a wife. With no powerful relatives, Heungseon assumed that the empress would be as malleable as his son, but the two quickly became enemies – favouring modern-isation, Myeongseong's beliefs ran contrary to those of her father-in-law, and by 1872 she had forced him to retire from the court. Her attempts at reform were stymied by the Japanese, who had their own plans for power in Seoul and ratcheted up their standing on the peninsula during the 1880s and 1890s. Attempting one final hurrah, Heungseon cosied up with the Japanese, but he underestimated the scale of their ambition, which became clear in October 1895. A team of **Japanese agents** entered the palace by force early one morning, murdering Myeongseong and two other ladies. Over fifty men were charged, but none was convicted. An obstacle to the Japanese until the end, it's no surprise that Myeongseong – posthumously made **empress** in 1902, and referred to by the Japanese as "Queen Min" – is now venerated as a national heroine.

Her shady tale has been told in countless movies and soap operas, as well as in *The Last Empress*, Korea's first original musical, the success of which spawned versions in New York and London's West End.

authority. Other insinuations were more subtle – viewed from above, the building's shape was identical to the Japanese written character for "sun" (日). One interesting suggestion, and one certainly not beyond the scope of Japanese thinking at that time, is that Bukhansan mountain to the north resembled the character for "big" (大) and City Hall to the south – also built by the Japanese – that of "root" (本), thereby emblazoning Seoul's most prominent points with the three characters that made up the written name of the **Empire of the Rising Sun** (大日本).

Gyeongbokgung remained a locus of power after the Japanese occupation ended with **World War II** in 1945; the American military received the official Japanese surrender at the Seoul Capitol, and in 1948 **Syngman Rhee**, the first president of Korea, took his oath on the building's front steps. Then, of course, came the Korean War (1950–53, though technically still going on), during which Seoul changed hands four times – it will suffice to say that the palace complex, one of Asia's most wonderful royal abodes just a few decades previously, resembled a bomb site by the time full-scale warfare ceased.

Entering the palace

Most visitors will start their tour at Gwanghwamun (광화문), the palace's southern gate (daily 9am–6pm; Nov–Feb to 5pm, closed Tues; W3000), though there's another small entrance on the eastern side of Gyeongbokgung. Entering through the first courtyard – now minus the Japanese command post – you'll see

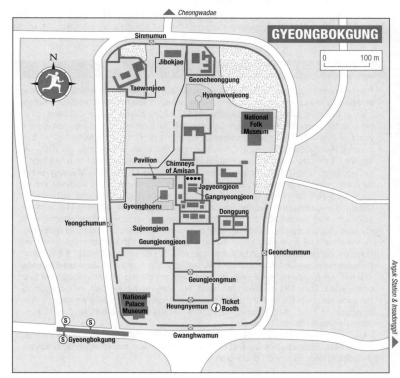

▲ Cheongwadae

GYEONGBOKGUNG

Sinmumun
Jibokjae
Taewonjeon
Geoncheonggung
Hyangwonjeong
National Folk Museum
Pavilion
Chimneys of Amisan
Jagyeongjeon
Gangnyeongjeon
Gyeonghoeru
Donggung
Yeongchumun
Sujeongjeon
Geungjeongjeon
Geonchunmun
Geungjeongmun
National Palace Museum
Heungnyemun ⓘ Ticket Booth
Ⓢ Ⓢ
Ⓢ Gyeongbokgung
Gwanghwamun

0   100 m

N

Anguk Station & Insadong-gil

Geunjeongjeon (근정전), the palace's former throne room, looming ahead. Despite being the largest wooden structure in the country, this two-level construction remains surprisingly graceful, the corners of its gently sloping roof home to lines of tiny guardian figurines, beneath which dangle tiny bells. The central path leading up to the building was once used only by the king, but is now open to all and sundry. However, the best views of Geunjeongjeon's interior are actually from the sides – from here you'll see the golden dragons on the hall ceiling, as well as the throne itself, backed by its traditional folding screen.

The living quarters

After Geunjeongjeon you can take one of a number of routes around the complex. To the east of the throne room are the buildings that once housed **crown princes**, deliberately placed here to give these regal pups the day's first light, while behind is **Gangnyeongjeon** (강녕전), the former living quarters of the king and queen, furnished with replica furniture. Also worth seeking out is **Jagyeongjeon** (자경전), a building backed by a beautiful stone wall, and chimneys decorated with animal figures – these flues were made from pink-red brick, and look slightly incongruous in their surroundings. West of the throne room is **Gyeonghoeru** (경회루), a colossal pavilion looking out over a tranquil **lotus pond** that was a favourite with artists in imperial times, and remains so today. The pond was also used as a ready source of water for the fires that regularly broke out around the palace (an unfortunate by-product of heating buildings using burning wood or charcoal under the floor), while the pavilion itself was used for events as varied as royal banquets and civil service examinations, the latter an integral part of life in the hugely Confucian kingdom of Joseon (see p.181 for more on Confucianism in Korea).

The rear of the complex

To the north again, and past another pond, is **Geoncheonggung** (건청궁), a freshly renovated miniature palace famed as the venue of Empress Myeongseong's assassination (see box, p.45). At the beginning of the twentieth century, there was actually a western-style building on these grounds, providing evidence of how the reclusive "Hermit Kingdom" of Joseon opened up to foreign ideas in its final years. This building, now destroyed, was designed by Russian architect A.S. Seredin-Sabatin, who was visiting at the time of the assassination, and witnessed the murder himself. One foreign-themed building still in existence is **Geoncheonggung** (건청궁), just to the west, a miniature palace constructed in 1888 during the rule of King Gojong to house books and works of art. Designed in the Chinese style that was the height of fashion at the time, this building is markedly different from any other structures around the palace, particularly the two-storey octagonal pavilion on its western end. Geoncheonggung sits right next to the palace's northern exit, but if you still have a little energy to spare, press on further west to **Taewonjeon** (태원전), the palace's newest clutch of buildings, having been opened up in 2010. Though there's little of historical interest here, the area's mountain views and relative dearth of visitors make it the perfect end to a tour around the palace.

The National Folk Museum

On the east of the palace complex is the diverting **National Folk Museum** (국립 민속박물관; 9am–6pm, Nov–Feb to 5pm, open till 7pm weekends; closed Tues, entrance included in palace ticket), a traditionally styled, multi-tier structure that fits in nicely with the palatial buildings. Despite its size, there's only one level, but this is stuffed with dioramas and explanations of Korean ways of life long since gone, from fishing and farming practices to examples of clothing worn during the Three Kingdoms era (c.57 BC – 668 AD). Children may well find the exhibits decidedly more interesting than slogging around the palace buildings, plus there's a gift shop and small café near the entrance, which makes it an excellent pit-stop for those who need to take a break.

From March to October at 3pm on Saturdays there are free **folk performances** outside the museum, usually featuring *pansori* songs (see p.135), and dancing from assorted characters in traditional attire; there are occasionally additional performances at 2pm on Sundays.

The National Palace Museum

At the far southwest of the palace grounds is the **National Palace Museum** (국립 고궁박물관; 9am–6pm, Sat & Sun to 7pm; closed Mon; entry free with palace ticket) – take exit five from Gyeongbokgung subway station. This was once the site of the National Museum (see p.89), until it upped sticks to a large new location in 2005, leaving behind exhibits related to the Seoul palaces. The star of the show here is a **folding screen** which would have once been placed behind the imperial throne, and features the sun, moon and five peaks painted onto a dark blue background, symbolically positioning the seated kings at the nexus of heaven and earth. It's a glorious, significant piece of art that deserves to be better known. Other items in the fascinating display include a jade book belonging to King Taejo, some paraphernalia relating to ancestral rites, and some of the wooden dragons taken from the temple eaves, whose size and detail can be better appreciated when seen up close. Equally meticulous is a map of the heavens engraved onto a stone slab in 1395.

Cheongwadae

What the White House is to Washington, **Cheongwadae** (청와대) is to Seoul. Sitting directly behind Gyeongbokgung and surrounded by mountains, this official presidential residence is sometimes nicknamed the "Blue House" on account of the colour of its roof tiles. In Joseon times, blue roofs were reserved for kings, but the office of president is the nearest modern-day equivalent. This is not without its hazards: in 1968, there was an attempt here to **assassinate** then-President **Park**

Chung-hee (see p.177). Security measures mean that visiting Cheongwadae is a little tricky, and it's only possible to visit on a guided tour (Tues–Fri at 10am, 11am, 2pm & 3pm, free but must be booked at Ⓦenglish.president.go.kr); remember to bring your passport. Unfortunately, tours do not include any of the main buildings, meaning that visitors will have to be content with strolling around the luscious gardens, and popping into the occasional shrine. Tickets can be collected at Gyeongbokgung.

Note that even if you're not visiting Cheongwadae, the road bordering the palace is a high-security area; while you're unlikely to be accused of wanting to assassinate the incumbent head of state, those loitering or straying too close are likely to be questioned.

Samcheongdong and Bukchon Hanok Village

Between the palaces of Gyeongbokgung and Changdeokgung lies a part of Seoul that has recently proved popular with locals, as well as a smattering of in-the-know tourists. **Samcheongdong** and **Bukchon Hanok Village** are two of the city's most characterful areas; despite being just across the road from Insadong and its teeming tourists, they feel a world apart – more traditional,

---

Quirky museums

Samcheongdong and Bukchon are home to countless **tiny museums**, and while none are exactly must-sees, it can be worth popping into one or two on your way around the area – especially if the weather is inclement. Note that all museums listed here are closed on Mondays; they're marked on the map on p.44.

Chicken Art Museum (닭문화관; 10am–6pm; W5000). Impressionism, Art Deco, Bauhaus… chicken art. Focusing solely on the latter school of creation, this is one of Korea's more peculiar museums, and has proven highly popular with international visitors. The greatest surprise is finding out how many countries have produced artists obsessed with the humble chicken.

Gahoe Museum (가회박물관; 10am–6pm; W3000). Housed in one of the area's many *hanok* abodes (see *Traditional Seoul* colour section), the folk art here is suitably traditional. The friendly curators also offer regular hands-on craft programmes.

Owl Art & Craft Museum (부엉이박물관; 10am–7pm; W5000). The result of its founder's quirky (and slightly scary) obsession, this small museum is stuffed to the gills with anything and everything pertaining to owls. There's a small tearoom-cum-café in which you can purchase strigiform trinkets of your very own.

Silk Road Museum (실크로드박물관; 10am–7pm; W5000). A couple of floors' worth of relics from various parts of the famed Silk Road, most specifically Central Asia. You'll get a free cup of tea if you make it all the way to the top.

Toykino (토이키노; 1–7.30pm; W5000). Both a museum and a shop, this popular Samcheongdonggil pit-stop is home to thousands upon thousands of figurines from movies, *anime* and the like.

World Jewellery Museum (세계장신구박물관; 11am–5.30pm; W5000). With a name that's as coldly descriptive as they come, it may come as a surprise that this museum is the most rewarding in the area, with the pieces on display offering great subtlety and variety.

and without the fuss. Samcheongdong is the trendier of the pair, its wine bars, pasta restaurants and shoe shops attracting a discerning (and largely female) crowd. Lined with wooden buildings, hilly Bukchon provides the traditional counterpoint, with tiled rooftops cascading across its slopes.

There are actually several city districts in this tiny area, though such is the confusion of borders that visitors need only be aware of two. The *hanok* village lies immediately north of Anguk subway station (exits 1 or 2), with Samcheongdong a little further uphill the same way, just to the east of Gyeongbokgung (p.43). The area they cover is small, if a little hilly, meaning that in a single afternoon it's quite possible to see the palace, then head north from the east gate to Samcheongdong, before looping back south to Bukchon.

Samcheongdong

The youthful district of **Samcheongdong** (삼청동) is crammed with restaurants, cafés and galleries, most of which have a more contemporary appearance than their counterparts in Insadong. In the years following the turn of the millennium, this was an incredibly well-kept secret given its location between two major palaces, but the area's maze of tiny streets are now regularly jam-packed with camera-toting youngsters seeking content for their blogs. It's still well worth a visit, though fans of peace and quiet may care to head elsewhere on warm weekend afternoons.

The area's charming main drag, Samcheongdonggil (삼청동길), heads off from Gyeongbokgung's northeastern corner, and is a mere five-minute walk from the palace's eastern exit. The road has an almost European air to it, its side streets snaking uphill in a manner reminiscent of Naples or Lisbon. Along these streets you'll find an astonishing number of unusual cafés, clothing boutiques and excellent restaurants – see map, p.44 for the best.

Heading all the way to the top of Samcheongdonggil will bring you to **Samcheong Park** (삼청공원), a small but delightful spot that for some reason never finds itself overrun with visitors, even on the sunniest Sunday of the year. This was actually Korea's first-ever officially designated park, having been awarded said status in 1940, and its leafy, sheltered trails make for fantastic walking. The park can also be used as an entry point for the loftier trails of Bugaksan (p.74).

Bukchon Hanok Village

A few of Samcheongdong's cafés and galleries spill over into **Bukchon Hanok Village** (북촌 한옥 마을), an area characterized by the prevalence of traditional wooden **hanok buildings** – these once covered the whole country, but most were torn down during Korea's economic revolution and replaced with row upon row of fifteen-storey blocks. The city council spared certain parts of this area the wrecking ball, partially from respect due to its proximity to the presidential abode, and partially because of protest movements led by Bukchon locals. As a result there's some delightful walking to be done among this web of quiet, hilly lanes, where tiny restaurants, tearooms and comic book shops line the streets, and children play games on mini arcade machines, creating a pleasant air of indifference hard to find in the capital; a few of the buildings have even been converted into guesthouses (see p.103). The local authorities have produced an excellent booklet to the area; pick one up from a tourist booth.

There are few actual **sights** in the area – Bukchon is best appreciated on an aimless wander, mopping up the odd gallery, café or picturesque view along the way. However, many make a beeline to **Bukchon Hanok Ilgil**, a steep lane with a particularly good view of the *hanok* abodes. From the top of the lane, the high-rise architecture of the City Hall area is impossible to ignore – standing behind such wonderful original structures, this quintessential "tradition-meets-modernity" view certainly poses questions about how Korea may have looked had its progress been a little more gentle. Just north of Anguk station (cross the road from exit 2) is the **Bukchon Cultural Center** (Ⓦbukchon.seoul.go.kr), which hosts regular classes and workshops of traditional art and craft, and functions as a small tourist information centre. There are a number of museums dotted around these lanes, detailed in the box on p.49, while on your stroll you may also come across **Jungang High School**, built in the 1930s along vaguely Tudor architectural lines. The front gates have for years been fronted by stalls selling tat pertaining to soap king Bae Yeon-jun, and a t-shirt, cup or pair of socks with his countenance on it could make for a quirky souvenir. There's no real connection between Bae and the school, but the *hanok* village is highly popular with visitors from Japan, where the actor's work was best received.

Changdeokgung and Changgyeonggung

Three important sights can be found in the small area to the east of Bukchon, all easily visitable on a single loop tour. Sumptuous **Changdeokgung** is, for many, the pick of Seoul's palaces, with immaculate paintwork and carpentry augmenting a palpable sense of history. Just across its eastern wall is **Changgyeonggung**, a palace highly rated by visitors on account of its grassy grounds and fascinating past. It also provides one of Seoul's best-value days out, being connected by footbridge to **Jongmyo**, a historically important shrine – (see p.57).

Changdeokgung

Changdeokgung (창덕궁) is the choice of palace connoisseurs, and also one of the easiest to **access**: its entrance is a short walk from Anguk subway station – take exit three, walk straight up the main road, and it's on your left. Completed in 1412 and home to royalty as recently as 1910, this is the best-preserved palace in Seoul. Entry (₩1000) is regulated to a far greater degree than in other palaces, and for most of the week you'll have no option but to join a **tour** (English-language tours 11.30am, 1.30pm & 3.30pm; palace closed Mon; ₩3000; a night tour is available on the 15th of each month for ₩30,000/person, limited to 100 people/night – contact the tourist office for confirmation before showing up). These last around eighty minutes, during which time a *hanbok*-clad English-speaker guides groups through the complex, but though the information is interesting, you really can't beat the freedom of exploring the palace by yourself. To do this you will need to come on a Thursday (April–Oct 9.15am–6.30pm), and you'll pay more for the privilege – ₩15,000. Note that snacks and drinks are not allowed in the palace.

Some history

Construction of Changdeokgung was completed in 1412, under the reign of King Taejong. Like Gyeongbokgung, it suffered heavy damage during the **Japanese invasions** of the 1590s; Gyeongbokgung was left to fester, but Changdeokgung was rebuilt and in 1618 usurped its older brother as the seat of the **royal family**, an honour it held until 1872. In its later years, the palace became a symbol of Korea's opening up to the rest of the world – King Heonjong (r.1834–49) added distinctively Chinese-style buildings to the complex, and his eventual successor

King Sunjong (r.1907–10) was fond of driving western cars around the grounds. Sunjong was, indeed, the last of Korea's long line of kings; Japanese annexation brought an end to his short rule, but he was allowed to live in Changdeokgung until his death in 1926. This regal lineage still continues today, though claims are contested and the "royals" have no regal rights, claims or titles.

The palace

The huge gate of **Donhwamun** is the first structure you'll come across – dating from 1609, this is the oldest extant palace gate in Seoul. Moving on, Changdeokgung's suitably impressive **throne room** is without doubt the most regal-looking of any Seoul palace – light from outside is filtered through paper doors and windows, bathing in a dim glow the elaborate wooden beam structure, as well as the throne and its folding-screen backdrop. From here, tour groups will be led past a number of buildings pertaining to the various kings who occupied the palace, some of which still have the original furniture inside. One building even contains vintage cars beloved of **King Sunjong**, the Daimler and Cadillac looking more than a little incongruous in their palatial setting. Further on you'll come to **Nakseonjae**. Built during the reign of King Heonjong, the building's Qing-style latticed doors and arched pavilion reveal his taste for foreign cultures; without the paint and decoration typical of Korean palace buildings, the colours of the bare wood are ignited with shades of gold and honey during sunset.

Huwon

The palace's undoubted highlight is **Huwon** (후원), referred to in Seoul's tourist literature as the "Secret Garden". Approached via a suitably mysterious path, this is concealed by an arch of leaves. In the centre is a **lotus pond**, one of Seoul's most photographed sights, and alive with colourful flowers in late June or early July. A small building overlooking the pond served as a library and study room in imperial times, and the tiny gates blocking the entrance path were used as an interesting checking mechanism by the king – needing to crouch to pass through, he'd be reminded of his duty to be humble. This is the last stop on the tour, and most visitors take the opportunity to relax here awhile before exiting the complex.

Changgyeonggung

Separated from Changdeokgung to the west by a perimeter wall, **Changgyeonggung** (창경궁, daily except Tues 9am–5pm; W1000, or accessible on same ticket as Jongmyo; free tours 11.30am & 4pm) tends to split visitors into two camps – those who marvel at its history and the relatively natural beauty of grounds far greener than Seoul's other palaces, and those who feel that there's a little less to see. The Changgyeonggung entrance is awkwardly located on the east side of the complex, and a confusing fifteen-minute walk from Hyehwa, the nearest subway station; it's usually better to take a bus from Anguk station – #150 and #171 are the most frequent. It's also possible to walk here from Changdeokgung or Insadonggil; allow 20–30 minutes. The Jongmyo entrance is far easier to find: it's a short walk east down the main road from Jongno 3-ga subway station – exit eleven is best.

Some history

King Sejong built Changgyeonggung in 1418 as a resting place for his father, the recently abdicated King Taejong. In its heyday the palace had a far greater number of buildings than are visible today, but these were to suffer badly from fires and the

The murder of Crown Prince Sado

In 1762, a sinister event occurred in the grounds of Changgyeonggung, one whose story is, for some reason, omitted from the information boards that dot the palace grounds – a **royal murder**. A young prince named **Sado** was heir to the throne of **King Yeongjo**, but occasionally abused his position of power, as evidenced by the apparently groundless murder of several servants. Fearing dire consequences if the nation's power were placed into his son's hands, Yeongjo escorted Sado to Seonninmun, a gate on the eastern side of the palace, and ordered him to climb into a rice casket; his son obeyed, was locked in, and starved to death. Sado's wife, Hyegyong, held the secret until after Yeongjo's death in 1776, at which point she spilled the beans in a book named *Hanjungnok* (published in English as *The Memoirs of Lady Hyegyong*). Sado's son **Jeongjo** became king on the death of Yeongjo, and built Hwaseong fortress in Suwon (see p.160) to house his father's remains. Jeongjo went on to become one of Korea's most respected rulers.

damage inflicted during the Japanese invasions. Almost the whole of the complex burned down in the Japanese attacks of 1592, and then again during a devastating inferno in 1830, while in 1762 the palace witnessed the murder of a crown prince by his father (see box above). When the Japanese returned in 1907, they turned much of the palace into Korea's first **amusement park**, which included a botanical garden and zoo, as well as a museum – the red brick exterior and pointed steel roof were very much in keeping with the Japanese style of the time, and pictures of this era can still be seen around the palace entrance. Almost all of the Japanese-built features were tolerated by the local government for nearly a century; pretty much everything was finally ripped down in 1983, though the **botanical garden** still remains today (access on palace ticket).

The palace

Considering its turbulent history, the palace is a markedly relaxed place to wander around. The buildings themselves are nowhere near as polished as those in the Gyeongbok or Changdeok palaces, though some feel that they look more authentic as a result; the history of each structure is chronicled on information boards. Be sure to look for **Myeongjeongjeon** (명정전), the oldest main hall of any of Seoul's palaces – it was built in 1616, and somehow escaped the fires that followed. From here, a number of lovely, herb-scented paths wind their way to a pond at the north of the complex. Near the pond are a couple of dedicated **herb gardens**, while also visible are the white-painted lattices of the Japanese-built botanical garden. Those who still have energy after their palace sightseeing can head to the far southwest of the complex, where a footbridge crosses over to Jongmyo shrine (see p.57).

2

Insadong and around

nsadong (인사동) has long been Seoul's main tourist hub, and for good reason: there has been a concerted effort to maintain Korean culture, and the area's small alleyways are filled almost to bursting point with rustic restaurants and secluded tearooms, as well as small shops selling trinkets, art supplies and traditional clothing. If you're only in Seoul for a short time, this is the place to head, especially since the delights of the palace district (see p.43) are within easy walking distance to the north. You could quite happily spend a whole day in Insadong and its surrounding area, and many return again and again during their stay in Seoul, especially to pick up souvenirs before their flight home. Insadong's appeal lies in simply strolling around and taking it all in – most of the commerce here is pleasingly traditional in nature, particularly the food and tea. The galleries also display a fusion of old and contemporary styles very much in keeping with the atmosphere of the place, and there are numerous shops selling paints, calligraphic brushes and handmade paper.

The action is centred on **Insadonggil**, the area's main thoroughfare. At the road's southern end you'll be able to take a well-earned rest at tiny **Tapgol Park**, home to an ancient pagoda. East of Insadonggil are two regal sights: **Jongmyo**, a shrine where ancient ancestral ceremonies are still performed; and the lesser known palace of **Unhyeongung**. Heading west instead will bring you to **Jogyesa**, Seoul's most visited temple, and the newly renovated **Gwanghwamun Plaza**.

The district is surrounded on all sides by subway stations – exit 6 of Anguk station is just 100m from the north end of Insadonggil, with exit 3 of Jonggak station a little further from the south; the middle of the road can be accessed from Jongno 3-ga station (exit 5 is closest).

Insadonggil

Insadonggil (인사동길) is the area's main street, and despite being cramped and people-packed it's still open to traffic – be careful when walking here, as Korean taxis and motorbikes tend to be a law unto themselves. Sunday is the best time to visit, since not only is the street pedestrianized, but (unless the weather's bad) you're likely to see music and dance performances or a traditional parade. The road is best attacked from its northern end, since only a few

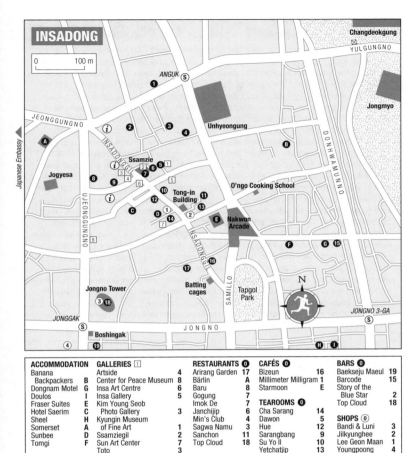

ACCOMMODATION		GALLERIES ☐		RESTAURANTS ❶		CAFÉS ❶		BARS ❶	
Banana		Artside	4	Arirang Garden	17	Bizeun	16	Baekseju Maeul	19
Backpackers	B	Center for Peace Museum	8	Bärlin	A	Millimeter Milligram	1	Barcode	15
Dongnam Motel	G	Insa Art Centre	6	Baru	8	Starmoon	E	Story of the	
Doulos	I	Insa Gallery	5	Gogung	7			Blue Star	2
Fraser Suites	E	Kim Young Seob		Imok De	7	TEAROOMS ❶		Top Cloud	18
Hotel Saerim	C	Photo Gallery	3	Janchijip	6	Cha Sarang	14		
Sheel	H	Kyungin Museum		Min's Club	4	Dawon	5	SHOPS ⓪	
Somerset	A	of Fine Art	1	Sagwa Namu	3	Hue	12	Bandi & Luni	3
Sunbee	D	Ssamziegil	2	Sanchon	11	Sarangbang	9	Jilkyunghee	2
Tomgi	F	Sun Art Center	7	Top Cloud	18	Su Yo Il	10	Lee Geon Maan	1
		Toto	3			Yetchatjip	13	Youngpoong	4

metres in you'll already be in the midst of innumerable galleries (see p.131), restaurants and tearooms. The first actual sight of note is the interesting **Ssamziegil** building, 100m down on the left. One of Seoul's best specimens of modern architecture, this is a spiralling complex of small shops selling traditionally themed paraphernalia: anything and everything from bracelets and earrings to silk clothes and handmade paper. Tiny side streets branch off Insadonggil as you head south along the road, most of which are lined with restaurants serving traditional Korean fare (see p.115 for some of the best). Towards the road's southern end, it segues into the more westernized appearance of "regular" Seoul; look out for the *Starbucks* on the southern reaches of the road, which was the scene of traditionalist protests when it opened – it made a slight concession by having its name spelt in *hangeul* (the first ever time that the chain had represented itself in non-Roman text). These were far from being the area's first **protests** – see the box on p.56 for details.

At certain times, visitors to central Seoul may be forgiven for wondering if they've landed in a police state. The focal point of both city and nation, and home to their leaders, the small area around Insadong is ground zero for **street protests**. Those mounted against the national or city government tend to converge around Gwanghwamun or City Hall, and in the weeks (or even months) surrounding such events, main junctions are manned by police, military personnel and armoured buses. Mercifully, the tear gas that characterized protests through the 1970s and 1980s is no longer used by police, the result of a curious deal struck with protesters, who promised to stop using Molotov cocktails if the police would desist with the tear gas.

The biggest movements in recent times have been the **US beef protests of 2008**, which centred on the decision of president Lee Myung-bak to allow American beef back into the Korean market, after trade ceased in the wake of the 2003 BSE crisis. Blown out of proportion by media scaremongering, the decision led to clashes between police and civilians, and resulted in a slew of burnt-out armoured vehicles, as well as one death by self-immolation (one more than the number of Koreans killed by contaminated American beef). These protests fed off a pool of anti-American sentiment building since 2002, when two schoolgirls were run over by an American army tank – gory pictures of the accident dotted Insadonggil for years afterwards.

While anti-American protests have since subsided, those against the Japanese continue. Each Wednesday at noon a dwindling number of elderly Korean women protest outside the **Japanese embassy** – these are the **"comfort women"** who were forced into sexual slavery during the Japanese occupation of Korea, and are still seeking compensation, or even an apology. "Say you're sorry!" and "You know you did wrong!" are the most popular chants, and with younger protesters joining the cause, the demonstrations seem likely to continue until Tokyo issues an official apology.

Tapgol Park

Insadonggil finishes at small **Tapgol Park** (탑골공원), a small patch of land containing as much concrete as it does grass. It is, however, home to a huge, stunning Joseon-era **stone pagoda,** which sits resplendent at the park's northern end. Grandly titled official "National Treasure Number Two", the pagoda has actually been the de facto number one since the burning down of Sungnyemun (see box, p.65), but sadly the beauty of its ancient design has been hugely diluted by the ugly glass box placed around it for protection – other than surrounding the Mona Lisa with tinsel, it's hard to imagine something less appropriate. The park was the venue for a Declaration of Independence against Japanese rule on March 1, 1919, drawn up by students in a nearby restaurant. A large crowd gathered during the speech, and the ensuing demonstration was countered in brutal fashion by the Japanese, who killed hundreds of Koreans, and arrested thousands more. The independence movement went little further, but in commemoration of the student declaration, 1 March is now a national holiday.

While not terribly attractive in itself, the park does function as a rather interesting window on local society. Groups of old men play chess, drink *soju* and hold lengthy discussions, while office workers and students from the many neighbouring language academies flit in and out on extended cigarette breaks. In addition, the pavement outside the western wall is usually dotted with tent-like booths used by fortune-tellers, still an integral part of Korean society. A less heralded social facet is the gay area to the north and east of the park – homosexuality is still taboo in conservative Korea, but this area is relatively liberal, and gay males both young and old congregate here. See the box on p.130 for more on gay Seoul.

Jongmyo

Along with the palace of Gyeongbokgung, the construction of **Jongmyo shrine** (종묘; 9am–5pm; Nov–Feb to 4.30pm; closed Tues; W1000, or accessible on same ticket as Changgyeonggung) was on King Taejo's manifesto when he inaugurated the Joseon dynasty in 1392. He decreed that dead kings and queens would be honoured here in true Confucian style, with a series of ancestral rites. These ceremonies were performed five times a year – once each season, with an extra one on the winter solstice – when the ruling king would pay his respects to those who died before him by bowing profusely, and explaining pertinent national issues to their **spirit tablets**. These wooden blocks, in which deceased royalty were believed to reside, are still stored in two large wooden buildings that were said to be the biggest in Asia at the time of their construction. Jeongjeon was the first, but such was the span of the Joseon dynasty that another building (Yeongnyeongjeon) had to be added. Though the courtyards are open – take the opportunity to walk on the raised paths that were once reserved for kings – the buildings themselves remain locked for most of the year. The one exception being the first Sunday in May, which is the day of **Jongmyo Daeje** (see p.27), a long, solemn ceremony (9am–3pm) followed by traditional court dances – an absolute must-see if you're in Seoul at the time.

Jongmyo is connected by footbridge to Changgyeonggung palace (p.52), and accessible on the same ticket. The two can be seen in either order, but going north-to-south is recommended, since on exiting the shrine from its main (southern) entrance, you'll find yourself in tiny **Jongmyo Park.** Though not a "park" in the true sense of the word, it nevertheless manages to be one of the most atmospheric places in the capital – on warm days, and even most of the cold ones, it's full of old men selling calligraphy, drinking *soju* and playing *baduk* (a Korean board game). Find a spot to sit, close your eyes and listen to the wooden clack of a thousand game pieces.

Unhyeongung

East of Insadonggil, and very close to Anguk subway station (take exit four) is the tiny palace of **Unhyeongung** (운현궁; 9am–7pm; closed Mon; W700). Never having functioned as an official royal residence, it doesn't qualify as one of Seoul's "big five" palaces; accordingly, it's less showy than the others, but the relative lack of people makes it a pleasant place to visit – the bare wood and paper doors would provide the perfect setting for a Japanese *anime*. Though he never lived here, King Gojong's marriage to the ill-fated Princess Myeongseong (see p.45) took place in Unhyeongung, and during the Joseon period it was also the centre of neo-Confucian thought, which sought to base civil progress on merit rather than lineage: for much of the Joseon dynasty, each Korean was born with a specific limit to what they could achieve in life. One man who railed against such restrictions was Yi Hwang (1501–1570), who ends up in most visitors' pockets – he's the "star" of the W1000 note. Also known as Toegye, he was born in the Korean countryside, but excelled in his studies and was brought to Seoul aged twenty-three, in order to prepare for the notoriously difficult civil service exams. He received this education close to Unhyeonggung (the academy has long since disappeared), and his anti-establishment thought soon permeated the palace.

On the Buddhist trail in Seoul

There's no need for the Buddhist experience to stop with Jogyesa. Indeed, there are a number of Buddhist diversions right outside the temple entrance – here you'll find Buddhist clothing, jewellery, incense and assorted trinkets on sale at dozens of small shops. On the other side of the road is the huge **Templestay Center** (Ⓦeng.templestay.com), where you can book nights at temples across the land – a great chance to get away from city life, though would-be monks should note that a typical temple day starts at around 3am. On an upper floor of the same complex is *Baru* (p.115), a restaurant serving immaculately prepared Buddhist **temple food**. Those who have a little more time on their hands can take a Zen meditation session at the Ahnkook Zen Centre (p.32) north of Anguk station, or head to two wonderful temples on Seoul's periphery – Gapsa, a truly stunning temple in Gyeryongsan National Park; and Bomunsa, which stares over the sea on the island of Seongmodo (p.158).

Jogyesa

Just west of Insadonggil's northern end is **Jogyesa** (조계사), the only major temple in this part of Seoul, and headquarters of the **Jogye sect** – Korea's largest Buddhist denomination. Built in 1910, fronted by a car park and hemmed in by large buildings, the temple has neither history nor beauty to its credit, but for some visitors to Seoul it may represent the only chance to see a Korean temple of such size (see the box above for some more ideas), and its huge main hall is pretty spectacular. The best times to visit Jogyesa are on Buddha's birthday or during the Lotus Lantern festival (see p.26 for more details), when the main courtyard is smothered with a kaleidoscope of paper lanterns; alternatively, turn up for the beating of the drum, which takes place daily at 6am and 6pm. On site is a small information centre (daily 9am–6pm), which is the place to head if you'd like to arrange a session of Buddhist activities (W10,000); this includes lessons on lantern-making and woodblock printing, as well as a traditional serving of green tea. Lastly, adjoining the temple is the new **Central Buddhist Museum** (불교중앙박물관; 9am–6pm, closed Mon; W2000), whose exhibits trace the history and culture of the religion.

The easiest access to Jogyesa is Jonggak station on line 1; take exit 2 and walk straight up the main road for 300m. It's also an easy walk from Gyeongbokgung (p.43).

Gwanghwamun Plaza

Looping back west from Insadong will bring you to **Gwanghwamun** (광화문), an area named after the famed southern gate of Gyeongbokgung (p.43). There's little to see in this business-dominated district, though crowds descend on **Gwanghwamun Plaza**, a large expanse of concrete which reopened in August 2009 after eighteen months of construction. Many locals were disappointed that such extensive, expensive renovations resulted only in water fountains and an uninteresting subterranean information centre, though a seated statue of **King Sejong** – creator of the Korean alphabet (see p.192) – was added shortly afterwards to form a metallic double-team with that of national hero **Admiral Yi Sun-shin**, a famed fourteenth-century naval commander who stands proudly at the plaza's southern end. At the opposite side of the plaza stands **Gwanghwamun** itself, reopened amid much fanfare in 2010 (see opposite); unfortunately, none of the buildings surrounding it match the palatial stylings in any way, shape or form. The most notable of this oversized squadron are the inevitably impenetrable **American embassy**, and the colossal **Sejong Centre for the Performing Arts** (see p.136). Just to the east on the way back to Insadonggil is the unmistakable **Jongno Tower,** one of Seoul's most striking buildings. In 1994 Rafael Viñoly architects added three latticed metal columns to the original tower block, topping them with a storey far divorced from the main building; suspended in mid-air, this oval chunk of metal is now home to the aptly-named *Top Cloud* restaurant (see p.116).

The business district

L ooking north from Gwanghwamun, one can see little but cascading palace roofs, and the mountains beyond. Turn south again and the contrast is almost unbelievably stark. Looming up are the ranked masses of high-rise blocks that announce Seoul's main **business district**, its walkways teeming with black-suited businessfolk. However, there's more to the area than one might expect – two **palaces**, a few major **museums** and **art galleries**, some fine examples of **colonial architecture**, and one of Seoul's most charming roads. In addition, the country's largest **market** and most popular **shopping area** lie within this area, as does **Namsan**, a small mountain in the very centre of the capital.

At the western edge of the business district is **Gyeonghuigung**, Seoul's "forgotten" palace, which has an excellent history museum just outside its main gate. A stroll east along the quiet, tree-lined road of Jeongdonggil will bring you to a second palace, **Deoksugung**, which has a superb art museum within its walls. East again is **Myeongdong**, the country's premier shopping district, followed and counterbalanced by the sprawling arcades of **Dongdaemun** market. Though they're some distance apart, many choose to connect Myeongdong and Dongdaemun on foot, along the pretty walkways flanking **Cheonggyecheon**, a gentrified creek.

Colonial architecture

Seoul's business district is home to the vast majority of its extant colonial architecture, built during the **Japanese occupation** of 1910–45. Although rather unpopular with locals on account of this historical pedigree, many visitors find these old colonial structures to be Seoul's most appealing pieces of architecture. Generally built along **Neoclassical** lines, though there are occasional splashes of Art Deco, these were intentionally designed to be the most dominant structures in what was then a wholly low-rise city; the survivors have been lent a new-found air of humility by the imposing skyscrapers of modern Seoul. Many colonial-era buildings have been destroyed since independence, including the colossal **Seoul Capitol** in Gyeongbokgung (see p.45), demolished in 1995. Others have avoided a similar fate on account of their listed status, including **City Hall** (being refurbished at the time of writing; see p.64), or given a second lease of life as museums or shopping malls. These include **Shinsegae department store** (see p.65) and **Myeongdong Theater**, as well as three notable museums – the **Seoul Museum of Art** off Jeongdonggil (see p.133), the **National Museum for Contemporary Art** inside Deoksugung palace (see p.64), and the **Bank of Korea Museum** opposite Shinsegae (see p.65).

Gyeonghuigung to Deoksugung

Two of Seoul's five royal palaces sit in the centre of the business district, and are both worth hunting out, surrounded as they are by other interesting sights. **Gyeonghuigung** is the most anonymous and least visited of Seoul's Five Grand Palaces (even locals may struggle to point you towards it), but its simplicity tends to strike a chord with its rare guests; just outside its northern wall is the large **Museum of History**. From here, it's a short walk east to **Deoksugung**, a palace notable for a couple of Western-style buildings, one of which houses the **National Museum for Contemporary Art**. Linking the two palaces is Jeongdonggil, a pleasant, ginkgo-tree-lined road with a number of interesting sights on its fringes, including the fantastic **Seoul Museum of Art**.

Gyeonghuigung

Gyeonghuigung (경희궁; 9am–6pm; closed Mon; free), was built in 1616, and became a royal palace by default when Changdeokgung (see p.51) was burned down in 1624. A little forlorn, it's a pretty place nonetheless, and may be the palace for you if crowds, souvenir stands and the necessity of avoiding camera sight-lines aren't to your liking (not to mention false-bearded guards in faux period clothing). Unlike other palaces, you'll be able to enter the throne room – bare but for the throne, but worth a look – before scrambling up to the halls of the upper level, which have a visually pleasing backdrop of grass and rock. While the palace closes down for the evening, its grassy **outer compound** is open all hours, and makes a good place to relax with a few drinks or some snacks – see the boxes on p.129 and p.126 for more alfresco drinking advice.

The Museum of History

You might want to make your trip to Gyeonghuigung coincide with a visit to the **Museum of History** (서울역사박물관; Tues–Fri 9am–10pm, Sat & Sun 10am–7pm; W700), a large building adjacent to the palace. Its blocky, pipe-lined design makes it look something like a leisure centre, but thankfully the museum's contents are far more pleasing to the eye. Certain halls play host to **rotating exhibitions**, which are usually well worth a look, and justify the extra charge (usually W12,000 or so for big names). The **permanent exhibition** is on the third floor and focuses on Joseon-era Seoul. Here you'll find lacquered boxes with mother-of-pearl inlay, porcelain bowls and vases thrown in gentle shapes, and silk gowns with embroidered leaves and dragons; you may be surprised by how much "quintessentially" Japanese design actually started in Korea, or at least passed through here first on its way from China. Another room popular with visitors features a gigantic photographic image of Seoul covering its entire floorspace.

The excellent *Kongdu* restaurant (see p.114) dishes up neo-Korean cuisine down on the museum's first floor, and on exiting keep an eye out for an intriguing piece of art across the road – a 22m-high **metal statue** of a man hammering. Intended by his sculptor, Jonathan Borofsky, to be a mute reminder that life's not all about work, he stands silently mocking the black-suited denizens of the surrounding business district.

Jeongdonggil

Crossing over the road from Gyeonghuigung and the Museum of History, you can continue to Deoksugung along **Jeongdonggil** (정동길), a pretty, shaded side-street whose relative lack of traffic makes it feel a world removed from the bustle of the neighbouring business district. The road is lined with towering **ginkgo trees** (see p.97), each buzzing with cicadas in the summer, and illuminated at night by thousands of tiny lights, which makes it one of Seoul's most romantic places for a stroll. Ironically, this thoroughfare has long been eschewed by courting couples – Seoulites have historically held the superstition that those who walk here will soon break up, since the divorce courts were once present on this road. They have now relocated, and the road is slowly starting to attract camera-toting couples in matching t-shirts. However, Jeongdonggil is more than just strolling territory, as it links two of Seoul's five royal palaces, and features a few interesting sights of its own.

The Russian buildings

Heading east from Gyeonghuigung, the first notable sight you'll hit is the **former Russian legation** (구러시아공관부지), which sits up a side-street to the left. Though only its central tower remains, this is the most interesting of a few structures dotted nearby which prove that Japan was not the only imperial power taking an interest in the Korea of the late 1890s. The UK and Germany were among those to establish legations in Seoul, but Russia and Japan were the two empires with most to gain from Korea, and both vied for dominance. Japanese victory in the Russo-Japanese War of 1904-05 saw them take the upper hand, and the subsequent signing of a **Protectorate Treaty** in the nearby hall of **Jungmyeongjeon** (중면전) – also Russian-designed, and worth a look – ceded Korea's foreign policy-making to Tokyo, a prelude to full-scale annexation five years later.

Cheongdong Theatre and the Seoul Museum of Art

Further east down Jeongdonggil is the **Chongdong Theatre**, which puts on regular performances of *pansori* (see box, p.135) and other traditional Korean arts, and has an excellent on-site restaurant, *Gildeulyeo Jigi* (see p.114). Just along from the theatre and uphill to your right is the large, modern **Seoul Museum of Art** (서울시립미술관), otherwise known as SeMA (see p.133). More gallery than museum, it's well worth popping in for a look at what are invariably high-quality exhibitions of art from around the world.

Deoksugung

Located in the very centre of Seoul's business district, it's no surprise that the palace of **Deoksugung** (덕수궁) receives plenty of visitors, a volume amplified by the compound's relatively small size. The atmosphere here is somewhat different to that of the other royal palaces – Deoksugung's perimeter walls are surrounded by **high-rise tower blocks**, which if nothing else make for a pleasing contrast, as do the **Western-style buildings** found within the complex itself, one of which houses the **National Museum for Contemporary Art**.

The palace entrance lies just outside exit 2 of City Hall subway station, though it's within easy walking distance of surrounding sights including Gyeongbokgung (p.43), Insadong (p.54) and Myeongdong (p.65). There are English-language **tours** of the palace at 10.30am on weekdays and 1.40pm on weekends, and on every day but Monday traditional **changing of the guard** ceremonies take place outside the main entrance at 11am, 2pm and 3.30pm.

Deoksugung was the last palace of Seoul's big five to be built, and it became the country's seat of power almost by default in 1592 when the Japanese destroyed Gyeongbokgung (p.45) and burned all of the other palaces. Its reign was short, however, since only two kings – **Seonjo** (r.1567–1608) and **Gwanghaegun** (r.1608–23) – lived here before the seat of power was transferred to a newly rebuilt Changdeokgung (p.51) in 1618. Deoksugung became the de facto royal residence again after the assassination of Empress Myeongseong in 1895 (see p.45); **King Gojong** fled here after the murder of his wife, then fled to the Russian legation for a short time (picking up an interesting habit on the way; see below) before making a final return to the palace in 1897. Backed up by his new Russian comrades in the face of ever-increasing pressure from the Japanese, he declared the short-lived **Empire of Korea** here that same year. Despite having ceded control to Japan, Gojong remained in Deoksugung until his death in 1919.

The palace

The **palace** (덕수궁; 9am–9pm; last entry 8pm; closed Mon; W1000) is entered through **Daehanmun** (대한문), a gate on the eastern side of the complex – this goes against the tenets of *feng shui*, which usually result in south-facing palace entrances. It's outside this gate that the **changing of the guard** ceremonies take place, the procession eventually heading up Jeongdonggil at a slow pace, amusingly backed up by a few unfortunate cars. Back inside the palace walls, most visitors make a beeline to the main hall, **Junghwajeon** (중화전), whose ceiling sports a pair of immaculate carved dragons. Be sure to check out **Jeonggwanheon** (정관헌), a pavilion used for **coffee-drinking** by King Gojong, who developed something of a taste for said beverage while sequestered at the Russian legation (see p.63) in 1895. Indeed, he almost certainly became the first-ever Korean coffee addict, since even a century later the country had almost no decent cafés. Jeonggwanheon features an intriguing mix of contemporary Western and Korean styles, Gojong having commissioned his Russian architect friend **Aleksey Seredin-Sabatin** to design it.

National Museum for Contemporary Art

Deoksugung contains a couple of other **Western-style buildings**, dating back to when the "Hermit Kingdom" of the latter part of the Joseon dynasty was being forcibly opened up to trade; these incongruous Neoclassical structures are the most notable in the complex. At the end of a gorgeous rose garden is **Seokjojeon** (석조전), which was designed by an English architect and built by the Japanese in 1910; the first Western-style building in the country, it was actually used as the royal home for a short time. It now houses the **National Museum for Contemporary Art** (덕수궁미술관; same times as the palace; W3000), whose exhibits are usually quality works from local artists, more often than not blending elements of traditional Korean styles with those of the modern day. The steps of the museum are a favourite photo-spot for graduating students – in June you may find yourself surrounded by grinning young doctors, accountants or nurses, all dressed up to the nines.

City Hall

Seoul's **City Hall**, (시청) which was built by the Japanese in 1926, sits just east of Deoksugung at the northern side of **Seoul Plaza**, a near-circular patch of grass that hosts free musical performances most summer evenings. Most locals would rather see City Hall torn down, but mercifully, it has been afforded listed status. At the time of writing it was undergoing substantial renovations – the old building was being gutted to make way for a library and exhibition space, while a colossal building of chrome and glass will, by 2012, rise behind to house the new City Hall. Unfortunately, no attempts have been made to integrate the two structures; the shape of the new one, in fact, resembles a tsunami intent on wrecking the old.

Myeongdong

With a justifiable claim to being the most popular shopping area in the whole country, and particularly popular with Japanese visitors, **Myeongdong** (명동) is an intricate lattice of streets that runs from the east–west thoroughfare of Euljiro to the northern slopes of Namsan peak. Though those visiting Myeongdong tend to be primarily concerned with shopping or eating, there are a couple of worthwhile sights in the area.

The Bank of Korea Museum

Down the road from City Hall is the **Bank of Korea Museum** (한국은행화폐 금융박물관; 10am–5pm; closed Mon; free), though the notes and coins on display are less interesting than the building itself, which was designed and built by the Japanese in the first years of their occupation (see box, p.60, for more on colonial architecture). It once served as the headquarters of the now-defunct **Bank of Choson**; a contemporary competitor, the former **Choson Savings Bank**, sits almost directly opposite, alongside the old wing of **Shinsegae** department store (신세계), another colonial structure. Beautifully lit at night, and especially so around Christmas, this was the first of Korea's many department stores, and remains by far the most visually appealing.

These buildings are best accessed by walking south down the main road from exit 7 of Euljiro 1-ga subway station. They're just as close to exit 5 of Myeongdong station, but as this is a noisy and hugely popular meeting spot it can be hard to get your bearings here.

Namdaemun market

Spreading across the area behind Shinsegae department store is **Namdaemun market** (남대문시장), a dense collection of stalls, malls and restaurants second only in size to Dongdaemun market out east (see p.68). Like Dongdaemun, its name is taken from that of a hefty **city gate**, which stood here from the 1390s until it was

---

The death of National Treasure Number 1

Seoul's "Great South Gate", the literal translation of Namdaemun, was built in 1398 by **King Taejo** as a means of glorifying and protecting his embryonic kingdom. This was by no means the only major project to come out of Taejo's first years of rule (see *Traditional Seoul* colour section), but random fires, Japanese invasions and civil war rubbed out the rest over the following centuries. Also known as Sungnyemun and feted as the country's official "**National Treasure Number One**" on account of its age, beauty and importance, Namdaemun was the sole survivor from the Taejo era, which made things all the more harrowing when after six centuries standing proudly over Seoul, it was destroyed in a matter of minutes by a lone **arsonist**, Chae Jong-gi. Chae had noticed that Namdaemun was guarded by nothing but a single set of motion sensors – not the best way to protect one of the oldest wooden structures in the land. Early in the morning on February 10, 2008, he mounted the gate armed with a few bottles of paint thinner – hours later, images of weeping Seoulites were being beamed around the world, all bemoaning the loss of their smouldering city icon. However, Korea's incendiary history means that it has substantial experience of reconstructing its treasures. **Renovation** of Namdaemun got under way in 2010, and work should be completed by 2012.

destroyed by an arsonist in 2008 (see box, p.65). You'll essentially find the same things on offer here as at Dongdaemun, but Namdaemun has found favour among expats as a source of two handy products – cheap **spectacles**, and used **camera equipment**. There's also a pleasing line of **outdoor snack stands** just outside exit 5 of Hoehyeon subway station, which make the best place to chow down and meet the locals; see *Seoul food* colour section for examples of the food on offer.

Myeongdong Cathedral

The hub of Korea's large – and growing – **Catholic** community, **Myeongdong Cathedral** (명동성당) stands proudly over Myeongdong, and is the best-known non-Buddhist religious building in the country. The cathedral was designed in Gothic style by **French missionaries**, and the elegant lines of its red brick exterior are a breath of fresh air in the business district's maze of concrete cuboids. It was completed in 1898 at the bequest of King Gojong, who desired to make up for persecutions witnessed under his predecessors: the site on which the cathedral stands had previously been home to a Catholic faith community, many of whom were executed during the **purges** of 1866 (see p.183). In the 1970s, during the dictatorial rule of Park Chung-hee, the cathedral and its auxiliary buildings were used as a refuge for **political dissidents**, since the police refused to enter this place of worship – a recourse still taken today by occasional fugitives. On the road outside the cathedral, you may come across one of Myeongdong's most famous characters: a zealous gentleman bearing a sandwich-board stating "Lord Jesus Heaven, No Jesus Hell!" (Although further questioning reveals that Protestants, too, will go to hell.) On the same stretch there will usually be locals reading from the Bible through megaphones, and the occasional hymn from a choir – this is by far the best place to witness Korea's recent religious conversion. For more on local Christianity, see p.182.

Chungmuro

Just east of Myeongdong is **Chungmuro** (충무로), a fascinating area that mixes the youthful exuberance of local university students with old-fashioned pleasures more suited to their grandparents. The students cluster in a dense area of cafés and cheap restaurants heading southeast from Chungmuro subway station to Donggook University; heading directly south from the station leads to Namsangol *hanok* village (see p.70). Heading north instead will bring you to the **Jinyang Building** (진양빌딩), erected in the late 1960s and therefore one of Seoul's first high-rise buildings. Unfortunately, it's slated for demolition, but until this happens it should be possible to sneak to the top for one of the best **views of Seoul** – high enough to see the palace and business districts in full, but close enough to feel part of the city. Looking north, one is able to discern a whole line of equally aged buildings (by Seoul standards), sketching a perfect tangent all the way to Jongmyo (p.57), over 1km away. This rare piece of Seoulite urban planning came about during the Korean War, when the whole stretch was levelled as a means of stalling some of the many fires that burned across the city. With nothing but earth to scorch, a large fire would run itself into the ground on one side of the line and only need dousing on the other. In the years following the war, this became prime real estate, and home to the largest development projects of the time – small-fry by today's standards, of course. By 2015, the snake of buildings will be razed to make a long park, the resultant green-belt making it possible to walk (or perhaps even cycle) from Namsan to Bugaksan.

The tiny **side-streets** surrounding this chain of bizarre buildings are of similar vintage and a joy to get lost in, if only to see the contrast between this area and Myeongdong, just to the east. These maze-like streets are home to clutches of cheap restaurants, as well as a fair number of *dabang* – coffee bars popular in the 1970s, but almost extinct in most parts of town. Adding to the area's worn mystique are literally hundreds of **printing presses**, many of which operate late into the night, when their hissing steam and whirring machinery exude a decades-old charm.

Euljiro tunnel

Zigzagging northeast to Gwangjang market, you will pass the entirely pedestrianized **Euljiro tunnel**, which runs under Euljiro (을지로), one of Seoul's most important thoroughfares, for a whopping 4km, making it possible to walk from City Hall all the way to Dongdaemun Design Plaza (a journey of around forty minutes) without having to rise above the surface. The tunnel was a popular shopping area during the 1970s, and the customer base has changed little since, making it a good place to shop for some **unique clothing**, including the trilbies, linen shirts and rhinestone-studded ties popular with elderly local gentlemen, or the lurid floral blouses sported by their female counterparts – great party costumes, at the very least.

Cheonggyecheon

From Myeongdong and the business district, there are two easy ways to head east to Dongdaemun market without being bothered by traffic. One is Euljiro tunnel (see above), while tracing a lazy parallel just to the north is **Cheonggyecheon** (청계천),

Cheonggyecheon's chequered history

Taking a walk along Cheonggyecheon, it's hard to imagine what this small strip of Seoul has been through, even within living memory. The stream's first significant use was as a channel for **royal waste,** after **King Taejo** built Gyeongbokgung palace in 1394. Taejo's wife, Queen Sindeok, was to become part of Cheonggyecheon in a most curious way: King Taejong (r.1400–18), Taejo's son and successor, was said to have used stones from her tomb to construct **Gwangtonggyo**, the first pedestrian bridge you'll come across if walking along Cheonggyecheon from the west.

Now rebuilt, this bridge was knocked down shortly after the **Korean War** (see p.175), the first stage of a process that saw Cheonggyecheon covered entirely with **concrete** and used as a road. The riverbanks were, at that time, home to one of Seoul's largest **shanty towns** – pictures from the postwar era show a level of poverty almost unimaginable today, only eradicated in the late 1970s under the economic reforms of **Park Chung-hee** (see p.177). True to form, Park favoured progress over tradition, and Cheonggyecheon's concrete covering was topped with an **elevated expressway**.

In 2003, **Lee Myung-bak** – then Mayor of Seoul, later President of Korea – announced his plan to tear down the expressway and beautify the stream, only to be met with outrage from his enemies within Korea's hugely influential press, and a public angry at the **near-$1bn** expense of the project – years of neglect had run the stream almost dry, meaning that all water needed to be pumped in. The renovations went ahead, despite some heads rolling on corruption charges in the course of the project (Lee had strong links to the construction industry), and since being completed in 2005 it's become one of Seoul's most popular spots with locals and visitors alike.

a small waterway whose bankside paths make for some of Seoul's best strolling territory. Until recently, Cheonggyecheon was a mucky stream running under an elevated highway, but in 2003 the decision was made to ditch the road and beautify the creek – a far more controversial project than it may sound (see box, p.67). Since completion in 2005 it has served as one of Seoul's most popular **pedestrian thoroughfares**: on descending you'll notice that the capital's ceaseless cacophony has been diluted, and largely replaced by the sound of rushing water; streamside features include **sculptures** and **fountains**, while regular chains of **stepping stones** make it possible to cross from one side to the other. On sunny days, local children (and the young at heart) can't resist the urge to jump in and have a splash around; the water quality is okay (it's all pumped in) but subject to the sullying inevitable when so many people are around, so you may prefer to simply bathe your feet.

Cheonggyecheon starts just southeast of Gwanghwamun Plaza (see p.58), close to exit 5 of Gwanghwamun subway station, at a point marked by a curious piece of **modern art** designed to resemble a snail (you may have another, more cloacal impression) by American husband-and-wife sculptors Claes Oldenburg and Coosje van Bruggen. Most visitors limit their visit to this area, but this is one of the only good chances for a long stroll that Seoul has to offer: the **3km walk** east to Dongdaemun market (see below) is extremely pleasant, and the paths continue on for the same distance again, a stretch used almost exclusively by locals.

Dongdaemun

Cheonggyecheon provides the most pleasurable form of access to **Dongdaemun** (동대문), a famed market area that spreads far and wide on both sides of the creek. It was named after a gigantic **ornamental gate** that still stands here (*dong* means "east", *dae* means "great" and *mun* "gate"). Originally built in 1396, this was once the eastern entrance to a much smaller Seoul, a counterpart to Namdaemun, way to the southwest (see box p.65). This was yet another of the structures added by the incredibly ambitious **King Taejo** in the 1390s (see *Traditional Seoul* colour section), at the dawn of his Joseon dynasty; fires and warfare have taken their inevitable toll, and the present structure is of a mere 1869 vintage.

Dongdaemun is now best known for its **market**, by far the largest in the country, sprawling as it does across several city blocks. Between them, the colossal markets of **Dongdaemun** and **Namdaemun** (see p.65) could quite conceivably feed, and maybe even clothe, the world. Both are deservedly high up on most visitors' sightseeing lists, but very little information on them is available in English. Seoul's tourist offices (see p.39) will be able to furnish you with market maps, and point out the area to aim for if you desire something specific. Just to the south of the market is the new **Dongdaemun Design Plaza**, one of Seoul's most ambitious pieces of modern architecture, and an intriguing district known as "**Russiatown**" to the few expats aware of its presence. This small area is home to tradespeople and businessmen from Central Asia, particularly Uzbekistan and Mongolia, and the sight of occasional shops, offices and hotels marked with **Cyrillic text** is quite a blast. There are also a couple of restaurants serving delicious Russian food (see p.114). To get to this area, take exit 7 from Dongdaemun History & Culture Park subway station.

Dongdaemun market

Hectic Dongdaemun market (동대문시장) is Korea's largest, spread out both open-air and indoors in various locations along the prettified Cheonggyecheon creek (see p.67). It would be impossible to list the whole range of things on sale here — you'll find yourself walking past anything from herbs to *hanbok* (traditional clothing) or pet monkeys to paper lanterns, usually on sale for reasonable prices.

Though each section of the market has its own opening and closing time, the complex as a whole never shuts, so at least part of it will be open whenever you decide to visit. Night-time is when the market is at its most atmospheric, with clothes stores pumping out music into the street at ear-splitting volume, and the air filled with the smell of freshly made food sizzling at street-side stalls. Though some of the fare on offer is utterly unrecognizable to many foreign visitors, it pays to be adventurous; check out the *Seoul Food* colour section for a few mouthwatering — or just downright curious — examples of what's on offer. One segment particularly popular with foreigners is **Gwangjang market** (광장시장), a particularly salty offshoot of Dongdaemun to the northwest, and one of Seoul's most idiosyncratic places to eat in the evening — just look for something tasty and point. During the daytime, it's also the best place in Seoul to buy **secondhand clothes** (see p.139).

The bulk of Dongdaemun market is located around Cheonggyecheon, with Dongdaemun subway station the best point of access. Gwangjang market is to the west — take exit 7 from Jongno 5-ga station, and the main entrance will be on your right.

Dongdaemun Design Plaza

The newest and most notable sight in the Dongdaemun area is the **Dongdaemun Design Plaza** (동대문디자인플라자), a collection of futuristic buildings and grassy walking areas. This gargantuan city project was aimed to give Seoul a new, futuristic look, and provide some much-needed parkland to its citizens. Increasingly referred to as the "DDP", it was under construction at the time of writing and set to open in 2013. The DDP sits on the site of the former **Dongdaemun Stadium**, which was built in 1926 and hosted major football and baseball matches, including the first-ever Korean league games for both sports. It also saw some action during the Olympic Games in 1988, but this event (as well as the World Cup in 2002) saw Korea building larger and better facilities elsewhere, and the stadium fell into disrepair. Following the turn of the millennium, it was used as a flea market, and mostly filled with army surplus clothing, secondhand t-shirts and Chinese sex toys, and was finally torn down in 2008 to make way for the DDP.

Iraq-born architect **Zaha Hadid** won the tender for the new plaza with a design said to echo plumes of smoke — it has since been altered slightly, the new shape being far more proximate to a high-heeled shoe. The reason for the change was the discovery of thousands of **dynastic relics** found in the earth; construction was delayed for over a year, and a **museum** (daily 9am–6pm; free) added to display this bounty. This is open to the public already, as are a small exhibition hall and most outdoor paths; a design library, more exhibition space and a café or two will soon be added to the mix.

Access to the DDP is pretty simple: take exit 2 from the awkwardly named Dongdaemun History & Culture Park subway station.

Namsan

South of Myeongdong station the roads rise up, eventually coming to a stop at the feet of **Namsan** (남산), a mini-mountain in the centre of Seoul. There are spectacular **views** of the city from the 265m-high peak, and yet more from **N Seoul Tower**, a giant hypodermic needle sitting at the summit. On your way up, you may care to stop by at **Namsangol**, a small recreated **folk village** of *hanok* housing.

Namsan's padlocks

You may be slightly confused by the sight of thousands of **padlocks** clustered along the railings, which are placed here by the many young couples who scale Namsan for the romance of the views. The done thing is to scrawl your names or initials on the padlock (preferably inside a love heart; arrow optional), secure it to the railing, then hurl your key over the edge and down the mountain: everlasting love, guaranteed.

Most visitors reach the top by **cable car** (daily 10am–11pm; W5000 one-way, W6500 return), but don't be fooled into thinking you'll be whisked up without a bead of sweat, since the base is an uphill slog south of Myeongdong subway station (although you could get a cab): leave the station through exit three, keep going up and you can't miss it. The mountain is also accessible on the yellow **buses** (W600) that ply local route #2 – the best place to catch these is outside exit four of Chungmuro station. It's also possible to **walk** up in under an hour from Namsangol (see below), Itaewon (p.88) or Seoul station. Thanks to the occasional difficulties encountered by foreigners on local buses, those with a passport or other ID can also access the top by **taxi** (Koreans can jump in the cab too, but at least one foreigner is required).

Namsangol

East of central Myeongdong is **Namsangol** (남산골; closed Tues; 9am–9pm, Nov–March 9am–8pm; free), a small display village of five **traditional hanok buildings**; though a much more interesting and entertaining folk village can be found just south of Seoul (see p.161), this is a more than acceptable solution for those with little time to spare. The complex is particularly enchanting in the evening, when its wooden buildings receive soft illumination from strings of **red-and-blue lanterns**. Further up past the entrance – and past **Namsan Gugakdang**, one of Seoul's best venues for traditional music (p.135) – is a web of grassy walking trails, which eventually head all the way to the top of Namsan.

To get to Namsangol, take exit 3 from Chungmuro subway station, and walk away from the main road.

N Seoul Tower

N Seoul Tower (N서울타워; daily 10am–11pm; W7000; ⓦ www.nseoultower .net) sits proudly on Namsan's crown, the most recent incarnation of Seoul Tower, whose name was clearly not trendy enough to pass the consultancy test that followed the redesigning of its interior in 2005. The five levels of the upper section are now home to a viewing platform, and assorted cafés and restaurants, best of which is *n.Grill* (see p.115). For many, the free views from the tower's base are good enough, and coming here to see the **sunset** is recommended – the grey mass of daytime Seoul turns in no time into a pulsating neon spectacle.

Namsan once marked the natural boundary of a city that has long since swelled over the edges and across the river – some sections of the city wall can still be seen on the mountain, as can the remains of **fire beacons** that formed part of a national communication system during the Joseon period. These were used to relay warnings across the land – one flame lit meant that all was well, while up to five were lit to signify varying degrees of unrest; the message was repeated along chains of beacons that stretched across the peninsula. Namsan's own are located right next to the tower, just above the upper terminal of the cable car.

Northern Seoul

N orth of Gyeongbokgung, Seoul appears to come to a rather abrupt end, with lofty mountains rearing up immediately behind the palace. The city did, indeed, once peter out here, but the "economic miracle" of the 1970s saw its population mushroom, and consequently Seoul's urban sprawl pushed around the mountainsides. Development was, however, not as rampant as in other parts of the city, and Seoul's **northern quarters** maintain a relatively secluded air.

The areas to the northwest of Gyeongbokgung are particularly intriguing. Here you'll find **Buamdong**, a quiet, hilly area becoming increasingly popular thanks to assorted clothing boutiques and swanky restaurants, as well as a couple of superb galleries. The neighbouring district of **Pyeongchangdong** is even steeper and notably affluent, though diversions are largely restricted to its galleries. On the other side of **Bugaksan** mountain lie Seoul's northeastern districts. Flatter terrain has resulted in a far greater population density and therefore more of a bustling atmosphere than the northwest, particularly in the buzzing student district of **Daehangno**, a long-time favourite with visiting backpackers. Better for sightseeing is **Seongbukdong**, just to the north of Daehangno; here you'll find a traditional garden, a secluded temple and an enchanting tearoom, all of which could make credible claims to be the best of their kind in the city.

Finally, there are the peaks of **Bukhansan**, feted as the most visited national park in the world, and possessing a range of historical sites and excellent hiking paths.

The northwest

Though rarely penetrated by international visitors, Seoul's northwest is one of its most appealing corners, and rewards a little detour from the tourist trail. The neighbouring districts of **Buamdong** and **Pyeongchangdong** can easily fill half a day, and it's recommended that you take at least one meal here on your rounds of the area's galleries and intriguing side-streets. Those with a little more energy to burn can use the area as a starting post for a hike across **Bugaksan**, a mountain whose trails provide some superb views of Seoul. Further west is another major peak – **Inwangsan**, whose slopes are home to Seoul's most important shamanist shrines – and an infamous building used as a prison in the occupation period.

This area is not accessible by subway (which may be the main factor behind its relaxed air), but regular **buses** run here from the Gyeongbokgung area. Best is the #1020, which heads to Buamdong from a stop just up the road from exit 2 of Gwanghwamun subway station. There's also a **shuttle bus**, which departs from

▲ Bukhansan National Park

NORTHERN SEOUL

RESTAURANTS & BARS
Art for Life — ❽
Comfort Zone — 2
Dan Vie — 7
Samcheonggak — 1
Sonmandoo — 5
CAFES & TEAROOMS
Club Espresso — ❻
Sammotungi — 3
Suyeon Sanbang — 4

SHOPS ⓢ
Hyojae — 1
Monocollection — 2

ACCOMMODATION
Bong House — B
Golden Pond — C
Inside — A

DAEHANGNO

HANSUNG UNIVERSITY ⓢ

Dongsoong Art Center

Munye Theatre

Marronnier Park

HYEHWA ⓢ

DONGDAEMUN ⓢ

Changgyeonggung

Jongmyo

JONGNO 3-GA ⓢ

Seongnakwon

Gilsangsa

SEONGBUKDONG

Samcheong Park

Changdeokgung

ANGUK ⓢ

Samcheong Park

Sukjeongmun ⊠

Bugaksan (342m) ▲

Gyeongbokgung

GYEONGBOKGUNG ⓢ

BUAMDONG

Whanki Museum

Changuimun ⊠

PYEONGCHANGDONG

▲ Gana Art Centre

Inwangsan (338m) ▲

MUAKJE ⓢ

Guksadang

Seodaemun Prison ⓢ

DONGNIMMUN ⓢ

N

0   500 m

The best of Buamdong

Art Check out the unfortunately titled **Whanki Museum** (p.133), a shrine to a Korean avant-garde master, or the colossal **Gana Art Center** (p.132) just to the north in Pyeongchangdong.

Coffee Sup your latte with a tremendous veranda view of Seoul's northern mountains at **Sanmotungi** (p.122), or take your pick from the remarkably global range of beans on offer at **Club Espresso** (p.121).

Dumplings A delicious cut above their processed brethren, handmade *mandu* are on offer at the minimalist **Sonmandoo** restaurant (p.116).

Fine dining Head to **Art For Life** (p.116), a remarkable restaurant that not only serves up excellent Italian food, but puts on regular jazz nights to boot.

Oriental fabric Modern yet notably Korean in style, the materials sold at **Monocollection** (p.140) are a favourite with expats and visitors alike, while there are more oriental stylings on offer next door at **Hongjo**, a women's clothing store.

Insadong's Insa Art Center (see p.131) on the hour, stopping at various galleries on its way to the Gana Art Center (see p.132) in Pyeongchangdong. Alternatively, the area is a twenty-minute, mountain-skirting walk from Gyeongbokgung station – follow the road flanking the palace's western wall, and keep going straight.

Buamdong

Hidden from central Seoul by the mountain of Bugaksan, **Buamdong** (부암동) is one of the capital's quaintest and calmest corners. Recent years have seen its popularity explode, its fame propelled by modern Korea's number one cultural catalyst, the television drama – ever since the picturesque café *Sanmotungi* (see p.122, and box above) was used as a set in hit drama *The Coffee Prince*, young Seoulites have been heading to the area in ever greater numbers, joined by the odd curious foreigner.

Despite its new-found fame, Buamdong retains a tranquillity that's almost impossible to find in other parts of Seoul, as well as a smattering of galleries and excellent places to eat and drink; see the box above for some special recommendations. The area is perhaps most notable for its lack of high-rise structures, as well as what may be Seoul's greatest concentration of **hangeul typography** – much of what you'll see has changed little since the 1970s, predating the current mania for Roman text. The most famous example by far, and the subject of countless photographs, is the logo of the Hanyang Ricecake Shop, starkly emblazoned in white paint on a plain brick wall; you'll come across it on the way to the superb Whanki Museum (see p.133).

Pyeongchangdong

Just north of Buamdong is **Pyeongchangdong** (평창동), a low-rise district with a high-class air, having served as Seoul's high-roller residential area of choice during the economic boom of the 1970s and 1980s. Most have now upped sticks and moved south of the river to Gangnam, Apgujeong and Jamsil (see Chapter 6 for more information on these areas), but those who favoured tradition over modernity stayed put, and have now been joined by hundreds of writers and artists. Indeed, it's the endeavours of the area's artistic fraternity that now forms its main tourist draw, with dozens of excellent **galleries** to choose from, including the colossal Gana Art Center (see p.132). Art aside, Pyeongchangdong's hilly lanes make for excellent strolling territory, giving the few foreigners who make it here a chance to savour an atmosphere distinctively more relaxed than other parts of Seoul, with low-rise luxury houses, tree-clad hills, and the majestic, ever-present vista of **Bukhansan National Park** and its associate peaks (p.78).

Bugaksan

Rising up directly behind the palace of Gyeongbokgung (p.43) is **Bugaksan** (북악산), one of the most significant mountains in Seoul. It provides some of the most glorious possible views of the capital, but for decades only soldiers were able to take them in, the mountain trails having been rendered off-limits thanks to the rather important building nestling on its southern slopes – Cheongwadae, official home of the country's president (see p.48). These protective measures were not without foundation, as in 1968 Bugaksan was the scene of an **assassination attempt**: a squad of North Korean commandos descended from the mountain with the intention of assassinating then-president **Park Chung-hee** (see box, p.178). You can now follow in their dubious footsteps, since the mountain was finally reopened to the public in 2006. Understandably, there's still a substantial military presence here, and those wishing to take a hike must **register** with officials on arrival.

Hiking practicalities

The **hiking route** across Bugaksan is 3.8km long, and though it gets rather steep at times almost everyone will be able to get up and down in one piece. On the way you'll see remnants of Seoul's fortress wall, which once circled what was then a much smaller city. The first fortifications were built in 1395, at the outset of the **Joseon dynasty** just after the completion of Gyeongbokgung and Jongmyo, with the obvious intent of protecting the new national capital. Most of the wall has now been destroyed, meaning that this is one of the only places in which it can be appreciated.

The Bugaksan hiking route can be accessed from either its eastern or western sides. The latter is found at **Changuimun** in Buamdong (see map, p.72), while the eastern entrance is at Waryong Park, a taxi-ride or ten-minute walk from Anguk station, and also accessible from Samcheong Park (p.50). From this eastern entrance, you'll soon pass the gate of **Sukjeongmun**, beside which is a tree riddled with bullet holes – evidence of the shootout which followed the infamous assassination attempt.

The hiking route is open from 9am, though nobody is allowed to enter after 3pm, and all hikers must be off the mountain by 5pm. You'll have to register at the entrance (either one) – bring your **passport**, or some other form of identification. Also note that photography is not permitted at certain points on the trail.

Seodaemun Prison

The occupied Korea of 1910–45 saw umpteen prisons built across the land to house thousands of activists and those otherwise opposed to Japanese rule (see box opposite, for more on this time). **Seodaemun Prison** was by far the most notorious, and the red-brick wings of its main barracks have now been reopened as a "history hall" (서대문형무소역사관; 9.30am–6pm, closed Mon, W1500). The prison became a symbol of the power of the Japanese, whose brutality during occupation ensured the Korean resistance movement rarely blossomed into anything more than strikes and street protests, though on March 1, 1919, the Declaration of Independence was read out at Tapgol Park (see p.56), an event that achieved nothing concrete but kept the Korean spirit of independence alive.

Japanese occupation

If you've done any sightseeing in Seoul, you'll no doubt have come across information boards telling you when, or how often, certain buildings were burnt down or destroyed by the Japanese. The two countries have been at loggerheads for centuries, but the 1910–45 **occupation period** caused most of the tension that can still be felt today. In this age of empire, Asian territory from Beijing to Borneo suffered systematic rape and torture at the hands of Japanese forces, but only Korea experienced a full-scale assault on its **national identity**. Koreans were forced to use Japanese names and money, books written in *hangeul* text were burnt and the Japanese language was taught in schools. These were merely the most blatant measures of the many employed by the Japanese – others were barely perceptible, and used as subliminal attacks on the Korean psyche. One example was the almost surgical removal of the tallest trees in Korean cities, which were ostensibly chopped down for their wood: straight and strong, they were said to symbolize the Korean mind, and were replaced with willows, which drifted with the wind in a manner more befitting the programme. The most contentious issue remains the use of over 100,000 **comfort women**, who were forced into slave-like prostitution to sate the sexual needs of Japanese soldiers, and are yet to receive compensation or an official apology; see the protest culture box, p.56, for more.

Photos of the prison during occupation fill the rooms and corridors of the barracks, together with written material from the period, and some televised documentaries. Few of these exhibits are in English, but the eerie vibe of the buildings themselves needs no translation, from the tiny vertical booths used for "coffin" torture to the lonely outpost where executions were conducted. The **execution area** has one particularly poignant feature, a pair of **poplar trees**, one inside the compound wall, and one just outside. The latter – termed the "wailing tree", on account of the number of prisoners who clung to it as a last means of resistance – is a large, healthy specimen, as opposed to the tree inside the compound, which is apparently kept short and stunted by the souls of those departed.

One piece of information not conveyed on any signboards, in any language, is the fact that the prison was not only used by the Japanese: though independent, South Korea only became a true democracy in the late 1980s, and until then the prison was used to hold political activists, among others. It was finally closed in 1987, immediately after the first fully democratic elections. Also kept off the information boards is the role played by local collaborators during resistance, or how independence was actually achieved: it was simply part of the package in Japan's surrender to the United States – see p.175.

The prison is a short walk uphill from exit 5 of Dongnimmun station, which lies on subway line 3.

Inwangsan

Just north of Seodaemun Prison rise the craggy peaks of **Inwangsan** (인왕산), which you may have seen flanking the western side of Gyeongbokgung palace (see p.43). While the Bukhansan range (p.78) draws the crowds, less-visited Inwangsan arguably contains more of tourist interest, featuring a number of **temples**, some **Shamanist shrines**, and one of the longest sections of Seoul's old **fortress wall**. It's one of the shrines that forms the main sight here – **Guksadang** (국사당), a boulder-surrounded prayer hall that hosts at least three Shamanist ceremonies (known as *gut*) each day, giving visitors a convenient opportunity to take in this lesser-known facet of Korea's religious make-up.

Guksadang lies a steep twenty-minute walk from Dongnimmun station on line 3 – take an immediate left turn from exit 2, and follow the signs. The **peak** of Inwangsan itself (338m) lies a further 1km hike uphill from the shrine, and from here the massif's spiderweb of routes continues further north. As with other mountain routes in Seoul, everything is well signposted and it's almost impossible to get lost; in dry weather, a sturdy pair of trainers should suffice to reach the peak.

The northeast

A growing number of travellers have been exploring the districts lying northeast of Gyeongbokgung – mostly backpackers seeking to take advantage of the cheap guesthouses in **Daehangno**, a hyperactive student area also home to a number of theatres. Heading further north, pleasures shift from the urban to the urbane in **Seongbukgong**, a quiet area with a couple of sights pertaining to one interesting element of Korean society now consigned to history – the **gisaeng**, female courtesans similar to the Japanese geisha more familiar to westerners (see box opposite).

Daehangno

With an artily sophisticated ambience, a near-total dearth of camera-toting tourists, and some of the cheapest guesthouses in Seoul (see p.104), studenty **Daehangno** (대학로) has become very popular with backpackers in the know. Literally meaning "university street", it's actually the name of the road that heads north from Dongdaemun market, but most of the action takes place in a tightly packed area around Hyehwa subway station on line 4, meaning that it's also a good starting point for a trip to Changgyeonggung palace (p.52).

The area has been one of the city's main student zones ever since the opening of Seoul National University in 1946; while this has since moved south of the river, the presence of at least four more educational institutions keeps this place buzzing. It's almost choked with bars, games rooms and cheap restaurants but has more recently attained national fame for its youthful **theatre scene**. Over thirty establishments big and small can be found dotting the side-streets east of Hyehwa station – take exit one or two – but be warned that very few performances are in English; see listings, p.134, for more on theatre. There are usually free shows in **Marronnier Park** (마로니에공원), an expanse of paving with a distinct lack of greenery which lies a short walk along the road from Hyehwa station's exit two. Here performers make their first tentative steps on their hopeful road to stardom, seeking to drum up custom for later performances or showcase their talents, and you can often catch short bursts of magic, music, comedy or mime, all going on at the same time.

Seongbukdong

Home to much of Seoul's diplomatic corps, the hilly district of **Seongbukdong** (성북동) has a secluded air more in keeping with Buamdong and Pyeongchang-dong in the northwest of the city. Its attractions are low-key, but it's a pleasant place to spend a half-day, and the steep roads will give your calf muscles some definition.

Chief among the sights are **Seongnagwon's** landscaped garden and the Zen temple of **Gilsangsa**; these are both within an uphill pant of Hansung University subway station on line 4 (use exit 6). To hit the furthest sight, an entertainment and dining complex known as **Samcheonggak**, it's best to take one of the free shuttle buses that run from outside *The Plaza* hotel (see p.106) or Kyobo bookstore (p.141); alternatively, it's a short taxi-ride from Hansung University station, Samcheongdong (p.50) or Gyeongbokgung (p.43).

Seongnagwon

It's best to start your tour of the area at **Seongnagwon** (성낙원; closed Sun), a **landscaped garden** that many find to be the equal of Changdeokgung's Huwon (see p.52). Like its more illustrious counterpart, Seongnagwon boasts a picturesque pond, overlooked by a number of ornate pavilions, and Seoul's cacophony of noise is filtered down to leave little but birdsong and the sound of running water. The buildings the garden belongs to were once the home of **Prince Eui** (1877–1955), the fifth son of King Gojong (see p.64); also known as Yi Gang, the prince lived here for much of his long life, and evidently used the tranquil surroundings to good effect, fathering twenty-one children – perhaps quite easy to accomplish when one has fifteen wives.

Gilsangsa

Heading further uphill from Seongnagwon – the labyrinthine network of roads and a dearth of signage mean that it's best to ask for directions – you'll eventually come to the wonderful **Zen temple** of **Gilsangsa** (길상사). This was once one of Seoul's most famous *gisaeng* houses of entertainment (see box below), but was converted into a Seon (Zen) temple in 1997; it now makes one of the most convenient places for visitors to Seoul to experience a **templestay**, though it's only possible on the last

Memoirs of a gisaeng

Many westerners are familiar with the concept of the Japanese geisha, but few are aware that Korea once had something very similar. **Gisaeng** were female courtesans trained to entertain the rich and powerful from the Goryeo dynasty onwards (see History, p.172). Girls chosen to be *gisaeng* received artistic instruction from the age of eight or nine, and though most found themselves retired after their late teens, some went on to become noted experts in **dance**, **music** or **poetry**. *Gisaeng* were employed by the state, and as such were also required to entertain the few foreign dignitaries or businessmen who entered the "Hermit Kingdom". Most were based in Seoul or Pyongyang, cities that were also home to the most reputable *gisaeng* schools, while others found work in regional centres or at inns along major travel arteries.

Despite their frequent interaction with members of the elite, *gisaeng* were technically at the very bottom of the Joseon dynasty's Confucian social ladder, their rank no higher than that of slaves. One of the only opportunities for advancement was to be taken as a **concubine** by a customer, but very few made it this far since *gisaeng* had to be purchased from the government at exorbitant prices. Over the centuries, however, more and more *gisaeng* came under the financial protection of patrons known as **gibu**. During the colonial period, almost all *gisaeng* were under the sponsorship of a *gibu*, but the Korean War and the economic boom which followed took their toll. Though the practice trickled on through the 1970s, it has since faded into history.

Among the most famous *gisaeng* was **Hwang Jin-i**, born in sixteenth-century Kaeson in what is now part of North Korea. Hwang was an entertainer of remarkable beauty and intellect who, in her spare time, created wistful poetry of a Korean style known as *sijo*. To date she has spawned one film, one TV series, and an eponymous novel; the latter is of particular note, having become the first North Korean publication to achieve critical success in the South.

weekend of each month – try to arrange this at one of the city's tourist information booths (see p.39). Gilsangsa's colouration is notably bland compared to most Korean temples, and as a result it looks its best under a thin blanket of winter snow; this is also the best time to take advantage of the little tearoom on the complex (see box, p.123). Almost directly opposite the temple entrance is *Hyojae*, a tiny store selling superb Korean handicrafts (see box, p.73, & p.140).

Samcheonggak

Nestling in the foothills of Bugaksan (see p.74) are the pleasing wooden buildings of the **Samcheonggak** complex (삼청각). This was built surprisingly recently – 1972, to be exact – and in the decades following its opening served as a place of entertainment for politicians, businessmen and other folk from the upper echelons of Seoul society. Here they would wine and dine in style, entertained all the while by *gisaeng* (see box, p.77). The complex was restored in 2000, and now features a teahouse and rather expensive restaurant (see p.116).

Bukhansan National Park

Few major cities can claim to have a national park right on their doorstep, but looming over central Seoul, and forming a natural northern boundary to the city, are the peaks of **BUKHANSAN NATIONAL PARK** (북한산국립공원), spears and spines of off-white granite that burst out of the undulating pine forests. Despite the park's relatively small size at just 80 sq km, its proximity to one of earth's most populated cities makes it the **world's most visited** national park, drawing in upwards of five million visitors per year. While an undeniably beautiful place, its popularity means that trails are often very busy indeed – especially so on warm weekends – and some can be as crowded as shopping mall aisles, hikers literally having to queue up to reach the peaks.

With its position overlooking Seoul, the area has played a significant role in protecting the city. In the second century a **fortress** was built during the capital's earliest days as the hub of the Baekje dynasty. Sizeable fortifications were constructed during the rule of King Sukjong (r.1674–1720), a leader notable for his peacemaking abilities in a time of national and international strife: not only did he pacify the warring factions that threatened to tear the peninsula apart, he negotiated with the Chinese Qing dynasty to define the borders between the two countries as the Yalu and Tumen rivers. These remain in place today, albeit under the control of Pyongyang, rather than Seoul, and it was while the two halves of Korea were jostling for control of the peninsula during the Korean War that much of Bukhansan's fortress was destroyed. Remnants of the wall can still be found, including much of the section that stretched down from the mountains to connect with Seoul's city wall – get off at Dongnimmun station, one stop west of Gyeong-bokgung on subway line 3, to reach the southern terminus of this linking section.

Hiking in Bukhansan

The national park can be split into north and south areas. The southern section – **Bukhansan** proper – overlooks Seoul and is home to the fortress ruins, while 10km to the north is **Dobongsan**, a similar maze of stony peaks and hiking trails. Both offer good day-trip routes which are easy enough to be tackled by most visitors, but still enough of a challenge to provide a good work-out; maps are

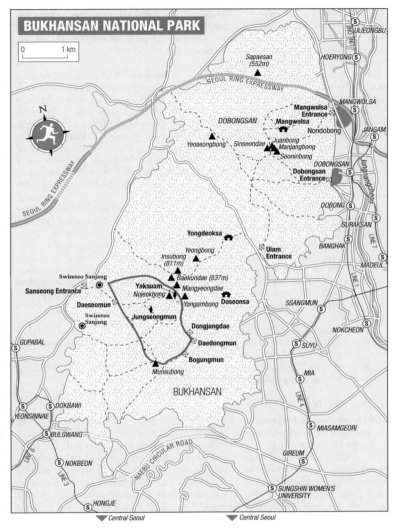

BUKHANSAN NATIONAL PARK

0   1 km

Sapaesan (552m)

SEOUL RING EXPRESSWAY

HOERYONG Ⓢ

UIJEONGBU Ⓢ LINE ONE

MANGWOLSA Ⓢ

Mangwolsa Entrance

Mangwolsa

DOBONGSAN

Nondobong

JANGAM Ⓢ

Yeoseongbong　Sinseondae

Juanbong
Manjangbong

Seoninbong

DOBONGSAN

Dobongsan Entrance ⊠

Ⓢ DOBONGSAN

Jungnangcheon

DOBONG Ⓢ

SURAKSAN Ⓢ

Yongdeoksa

Yeongbong

Insubong (811m)

Baekundae (837m)

Yaksuam
Nojeokbong

Mangyeongdae

Yongambong　Doseonsa

Uiam Entrance

BANGHAK Ⓢ

LINE 7

MADEUL Ⓢ

Swimteo Sanjang

Sanseong Entrance ⊠

Daeseomun

Swimteo Sanjang

Jungseongmun

Dongjangdae

Daedongmun

Bogungmun

Munsubong

BUKHANSAN

SSANGMUN Ⓢ

NOKCHEON Ⓢ

SUYU Ⓢ

MIA Ⓢ

LINE 4

GUPABAL Ⓢ

Ⓢ DOKBAWI

YEONSINNAE Ⓢ

Ⓢ BULGWANG

LINE 6

Ⓢ NOKBEON

LINE 3

Ⓢ HONGJE

NAEBU CIRCULAR ROAD

MIASAMGEORI Ⓢ

GIREUM Ⓢ

Ⓢ SUNGSHIN WOMEN'S UNIVERSITY

▼ Central Seoul　　　　▼ Central Seoul

available at all entrances, and larger versions can be seen at various points en route. Most local hikers choose to wear proper boots, but unless it's rainy a sturdy pair of trainers should suffice. Lastly, you'll have no problem finding a meal after a hike: all entrances are surrounded with restaurants, with *pajeon* (파전; a savoury pancake) the favoured post-hike treat for Koreans.

Southern Bukhansan

The southern half of Bukhansan is best accessed through **Sanseong**, an entry point on the western side of the park. To reach this, head first to Gupabal station on subway line 3 (20min from Gyeongbokgung), and walk from exit one to the small bus stop. From here, bus #704 (10min; W900) makes the run to the park entrance; get off when everyone else does. On the short walk to the clutch of restaurants that surround the entrance, you'll see the park's principal peaks soaring above; unless you're visiting on a weekend, the hustle and bustle of downtown Seoul will already feel a world away.

It's around two hours from the entrance to **Baekundae** (837m), the highest peak in the park, though note that the masses tramping through Bukhansan have resulted in routes being closed off in rotation to allow them time to regenerate – bilingual signs will point the way. Around ten minutes into your walk you'll find yourself at **Daeseomun**, one of the main gates of the fortress wall. From here, it's a long slog up to Baekundae; once you've reached **Yaksuam**, a lofty hermitage, you're almost there (and will doubtless be grateful for the presence of spring-water drinking fountains). Continuing on, the route becomes more precipitous, necessitating the use of steel stairways and fences. Having finally scaled the peak itself, you'll be able to kick off your boots awhile and enjoy the wonderful, panoramic views.

From Baekundae, the easiest route back to the park entrance is along the same route, though there are other options. One trail heads south, squeezing between some neighbouring peaks to Yongammun, another fortress gate. From here – depending on which paths are open – you can head downhill towards Jungseongmun (another gate), then follow the pretty stream to the park entrance, or take a half-hour detour along a ridge further south to Daedongmun gate. Those seeking a sterner challenge can head yet further southwest of Daedongmun to **Munsubong** peak, then take the punishing up-and-down route back to the park entrance – from the entrance, the whole round-trip via Baekundae and Munsubong will be a full-day hike.

It's also possible to exit the park at different locations – from Baekundae, a two-hour route heads east to Uiam entrance via the temple of **Yongdeoksa**; while from Yongammun, a trail heads downhill to **Doseonsa**, the park's principal temple; and from Bogungmun – a gate just south of Daedongmun – a path drops down the **Jeongneung** valley to the entrance of the same name.

Northern Bukhansan

The scenery in the **Dobongsan** area is much the same as around Baekundae to the south – trees, intriguing rock formations and wonderful views at every turn – though the hiking options are less numerous. Most choose to scale the main peak (740m) on a C-shaped route that curls uphill and down between **Mangwolsa** and **Dobongsan**, two subway stations on line 1 (each around 30min from Jongno 3-ga). It's hard to say which direction is better, but most head from Dobongsan. From this station, cross the main road, then go left along the perimeter of a dense network of ramshackle snack bars, then right up the main road. Whichever way you go, it takes just over two hours up to the gathering of peaks at the top; like Baeundae to the south of the park, the upper reaches of the trail are patches of bare rock, and you'll be grateful for the steel ropes on which you can haul yourself up or down. Coming back down, you can take a rest at **Mangwolsa**, a small but rather beautiful temple originally built here in 639, before heading back into Seoul. Mangwolsa roughly translates as "Moon-viewing temple", and was likely used for such purposes by the kings of the Joseon period from the late fourteenth century.

Traditional Seoul

Rarely can a capital have been built so quickly. On the inauguration of his Joseon kingdom in 1392, the ambitious King Taejo immediately set his minions to work on an incredible number of gigantic projects – within the first few years of his rule, Seoul had two stunning palaces, a huge ancestral shrine and gate-studded city walls. Much of this can still be seen today, albeit in reproduction form, since few original structures survived the Japanese occupation and Korean War. Joseon's 500-year rule added yet more palaces, as well as a clutch of fascinating temples, shrines and regal tombs; more numerous are the city's traditional wooden *hanok* houses, some of which function as quintessentially Korean places to stay.

Royal palaces

Most cities would be happy with just the one palace, but Seoul has a remarkable six to choose from, all within walking distance of each other.

Each of the palace complexes contains dozens of wooden buildings, lovingly painted and topped with a gently sloping tile roof – keep your eyes peeled for tiny animal figurines, which sit astride the corners of some roofs. The throne rooms tend to be the most opulent of all, and inside each one you'll see **Ilwolobongdo** (일월오봉도), a beautiful folding screen once placed behind the king. Its name is a summary of its contents: it features the sun (일, representing the king), the moon (월, representing the queen), and five mountain peaks (오봉).

Gyeongbokgung (see p.43) is the oldest and most popular of the palaces, with the craggy mountains behind providing the perfect backdrop to its majestic structures. The palace also contains a couple of pond-side pavilions, used as places of relaxation by Joseon-era royals. There's an even more stunning pond just down the road at the nearby palace of **Changdeokgung** (see p.51), which has an enchanting "Secret Garden" at the back of the complex. On the other side of the eastern wall is **Changgyeonggung** (see p.52), with the grassiest and most natural grounds of the six palaces, as well as a curious secret – in 1762 this was the venue for a royal murder. Further south is **Deoksugung** (see p.63), the most recently used royal palace and home to a few interesting Western-style buildings. Last, but not least, are **Gyeonghuigung** (see p.62) and **Unhyeongung** (see p.57), two palaces whose beauty is accentuated by their relative peace and quiet.

Royal throne and screen at Gyeongbokgung ▲

Hyangwonjeong Pavilion in Gyeongbokgung complex ▼

Colourful palace eaves in Changdeokgung ▼

Buddhist temples

Buddhism was the official religion of the Joseon kingdom, and although most of Seoul's **temples** have fallen prey to the wrecking ball, there are a few beautiful survivors around the city. **Jogyesa** (see p.58) is centrally located and gets the most visitors – you'll find yourself mesmerized by the incredibly ornate interior of the main hall, especially if this is your first Korean temple. However, **Bongeunsa** (see p.95), south of the river, arguably provides a better example of the national style – south-facing, sumptuously painted and built at the foot of a small hill. Again, the main hall is a feast for the eyes, though there are a number of smaller (and no less beautiful) buildings dotted around the gentle surrounding slopes.

▲ Wall painting at Jogyesa

▼ Shoes outside Jogyesa

Shrines

Although Buddhism was the national religion, Joseon was also a deeply **Confucian** kingdom. Ancestor worship was a core tenet of Confucianism, and the gargantuan **Jongmyo** shrine (see p.57) was erected to house the spirits of dead kings. Topped by huge, yet graceful tiled roofs, the two shrine buildings are surrounded by a small forest, whose paths are some of the best places to take a stroll in Seoul. Five times a year, the shrine played host to ancestral ceremonies, and each May you'll be able to take a short trip back in time by watching an absorbing enactment of these rituals.

Smaller shrines stand atop the many mountains encircling Seoul, yet most of these are **Shamanist**, rather than Confucian, in nature – the most spectacular ceremonies take place at Guksadang, a hall that sits atop **Inwangsan** mountain (see p.75).

▼ Royal folding screen in Gyeonghuigung

Seoul's wooden heart

Though it may be hard to believe today, within living memory Seoul was a markedly low-rise city. Its now-ubiquitous skyscrapers all went up in the past few decades, and even as recently as the 1960s there was scarcely a multi-storey building in sight. On the fall of the Joseon kingdom in 1910, almost every Seoulite lived in the traditional form of housing — squat wooden houses now known as **hanokjip** (한옥집), or **hanok** for short. The advent of Western forms of accommodation spawned these terms: the longer version means "Korean house" to distinguish these buildings from their modern counterparts. *Hanokjip* have almost all disappeared, but a few clutches remain, particularly in the charming, hilly neighbourhood of **Bukchondong** (p.50).

Hanokjip are built almost exclusively from local materials — **wood** for the main framework, **stone** for the foundations and courtyard, and **earth** to fill the walls. Earth walls (*hwangteo*, 황터), have long been believed to have health benefits, as well as the practical advantage of insulation.

Like Japanese houses, *hanokjip* make use of hand-made **paper** (*hanji*, 한지), which covers much of the interior — sliding doors and windows are covered with thin sheets and the walls with several layers, and even the flooring is made up of hundreds of sheets, each leaf varnished to produce a yellow-brown sheen mimicked by the yellow linoleum flooring found in most modern Korean apartments.

One feature which sets *hanokjip* apart is their use of underfloor heating, known as **ondol** (온돌). Rooms are raised above the courtyard, providing a space for wood fires; again, this feature has wormed its way into modern Korean housing, though these days gas is used instead of flames.

Hanok house beside new buiilding in Paju Book City ▲

Hanok housing in Namsangol Hanok Village ▼

Suyeon Sanbang teahouse in a traditional *hanok* ▼

5

Along the Hangang

From its source in the Geumgang mountains of North Korea, the Han River – known in Korean as the **Hangang** (한강) – moseys along for over 500km before emptying into the West Sea. Close to its end it passes through Seoul, and cleaves this great city almost perfectly in two. However, despite being the major waterway of one of the world's largest cities, the Hangang is almost entirely devoid of traffic, with nary a vessel to be seen. The reason for this is that part of the river delta, west of Seoul, belongs to **North Korea** – any vessel attempting to make the voyage out to sea would likely be blown to smithereens.

In central Seoul, however, the river continues to play an integral part in daily city life. Despite being a kilometre wide, it's crossed by an astonishing number of **bridges** – 28 and counting in Seoul alone. None is of any historical interest, since in June 1950, at the beginning of the **Korean War**, the few bridges that existed were blown up in an attempt to stymie the North Korean advance. No warning was given, and hundreds of evacuating soldiers and refugees were killed as a result. Most of the bridges seen today were built in the 1970s and 1980s during Seoul's rapid economic and geographic expansion; one unfortunate side-effect is that both river banks – rare pieces of flat, usable land in congested, mountainous Seoul – are now home to colossal **elevated highways**. This may sound like the stuff of urban nightmares, but underneath the concrete and hulking lattices of steel lurks the very heart of Seoul, where half the city seems to spend their evenings (see box, p.83).

The Hangang also lassoes together some of Seoul's most interesting quarters. To the west of the city centre are the university districts, one of which – **Hongdae** – is a pleasantly artsy place by day, then morphs at night into the country's most hectic nightlife zone. South of Hongdae is **Yeouido** island, which has a superb fish market within walking distance, and cosmopolitan **Itaewon**, long Seoul's main base for foreigners and home to the country's most cosmopolitan array of restaurants, as well as a few excellent museums.

Western Seoul

The highlight of western Seoul is the huge **university area** which spreads north from the Hangang – most parts of Korea are hectic and noisy, but imagine what happens if you pour more than **100,000 students** into the one tight band of land. Some studying gets done, of course, but it should come as no surprise to learn that this is the most important nightlife area in the country, with the action going on all through the night, and at its best around Hongdae. The area is admittedly low on tourist attractions, but **World Cup Stadium** to the west draws in more than just footy fans – it's a starting point for the city's best bike ride.

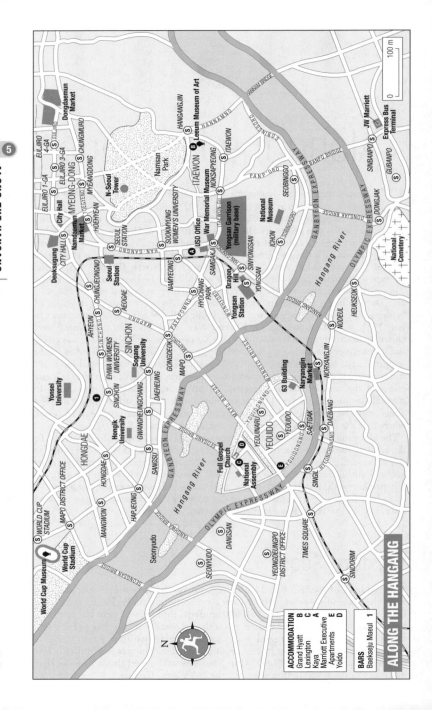

ALONG THE HANGANG

ACCOMMODATION	
Grand Hyatt	B
Lexington	C
Kaya	A
Marriott Executive Apartments	E
Yoido	D

BARS	
Baekseju Maeul	1

Hanging along the Hangang

The banks of the Hangang are a hive of activity, and proof of Seoul's open-all-hours nature: at any time of day or night, you'll see locals riding their **bikes**, puffing and panting on **exercise equipment**, or going for a run. Summertime will provide another peek into Korean culture, since locals flock to the riverbanks for **picnics** – the air can be heavy with the scent of *gimchi* and barbecued meat, and the fact that there's usually a lot of *soju* being knocked back makes this a great place to make new friends. However, the river and its banks also offer up a whole raft of other possibilities, the best of which are detailed below.

Coffee and cocktails. Six bridges – and counting – now have stylish cafés at their northern and southern ends, providing great views of the river and the teeming bridge traffic. They're a little tricky to get to, and are best approached by taxi; all are open daily from 10am to around 2am, making them equally good spots for an evening cocktail. The Dongjak and Hannam bridges (see map opposite) are particularly recommended, since they provide great views of the Banpo bridge fountain shows (see below).

Cycling. The Hangang is the most popular spot for **cycling** in Seoul, and a scoot along the grassy river banks constitutes one of the city's most pleasurable and picturesque activities. The main route runs for a whopping **21km** between **World Cup Stadium** to the west (see below), and **Olympic Park** in the east (p.97). **Rental booths** (generally 9am–sunset) have been around for years, with the main ones just north of Yeouinaru station (W3000 per hour, W6000 for a tandem; kids' bikes also available). At the time of writing the city was putting the final touches to a far more widespread **rental scheme**.

Fountain shows. Banpo bridge, located between the Seobinggo and Express Bus Terminal subway stations, plays host to eye-catching, ten-minute-long fountain shows from April–Oct. Jets of water burst from the bridge at noon, 2pm, 4pm, 8pm and 9pm (more shows on weekends); the night-time shows are particularly recommended, since the fountains are illuminated in eye-catching colours.

River cruises. Evening cruises along the Hangang are quite enchanting, with the most popular routes running from Yeouido's north bank. Schedules change by the day and there's next to no English-language information, so it's best to ask at a tourist office. Hour-long round-trips cost W11,000, or W14,000 including a live music or magic show; special dinnertime services including a buffet meal are also available, and cost W55,000.

Swimming. Seven open-air swimming pools have opened up along the Hangang, with those on Yeouido easiest to reach for foreign visitors. All are open 9am–8pm from Jun–Aug, and entry costs W5000; note that they may be closed during bad weather.

World Cup Stadium

Purpose-built for the World Cup in 2002 (see box, p.84), this superb modern **stadium** (월드컵경기장) is now home to FC Seoul of the **K-League** (see p.143). Football fans here on a non-match day can take a look around the ground, and visit a small **museum** featuring boots and balls from the World Cup (both daily 9am–6pm; W1000). There's an excellent 24-hour **jjimjilbang** (a kind of Korean sauna, see p.145) inside the ground itself (W5000 or W8000 to stay the night); facilities include all manner of hot-tubs, steam rooms and massage benches, though, sadly, there are no views into the stadium. It's also possible to access a **cycle route** from here that runs for 21km to Olympic Park in the east of Seoul, via Yeouido (see box above). World Cup Stadium station is around 20min west of Itaewon on subway line 6.

The university district

Just west of the city centre lies Seoul's greatest concentration of **universities**, but this is no place to be bookish – as with most academic areas around the country, it's

Seoul's World Cup

On May 31, 2002, Seoul hosted the opening ceremony for the **FIFA World Cup**, as well as the tournament's first game. The event was co-hosted with Japan, a country far more familiar to the western media, who initially made it their prime focus. By the end of the tournament, however, most eyes were on Korea, which hosted more of the best games, was blessed with far better weather, and saw its noisy, friendly fans – known as the **Red Devils** – achieve something of a cult status. For games involving the Korean team, over 100,000 people crammed into Seoul Plaza to watch the action on giant screens, in a pulsating sea of red, since almost all were wearing t-shirts bearing the nonsensical slogan **"Be The Reds"**, a design that sold millions but failed to make any money for its creator, who had neglected to patent his idea.

The **football** itself was generally low in quality, but high in shock value: the tournament opener saw Senegal surprise defending-champions France (who exited without scoring a goal), and South Korea made it past Portugal, Spain and Italy to reach the semi-final – the first-ever Asian side to reach the last four.

characterized less by what students do during the day than what they get up to at night, and streets are stuffed to the gills with **bars**, nightclubs, karaoke rooms and cheap restaurants. Though there are precious few tourist sights as such, there's nowhere better to get an understanding of what really makes Korea tick (see the box opposite for more on the local "bang" culture).

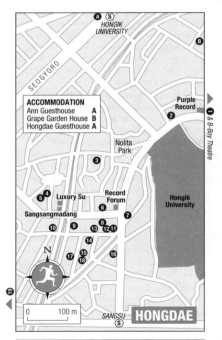

Bound into just a few square kilometres are the universities of Hongik, Yonsei, Ehwa and Sogang. These are located at the peripheries of areas most commonly referred to as Hongdae, Sinchon and Edae, each with a distinctive atmosphere. Hongdae and Edae are colloquial terms for Hongik and Ehwa universities – the Korean tendency is to take the first syllable of the name and add the –*dae* from *daehakkyo*, which means university – and it's these names that you're most likely to hear.

Hongdae

Hongdae (홍대) is one of the edgiest districts in the whole country, teeming with young and trendy people at almost every hour. The area only truly comes into its own after dark, its hundreds of bars and clubs buzzing with activity every night of the week (see p.127). During the daytime, it's fun to

ACCOMMODATION
Ann Guesthouse   A
Grape Garden House   B
Hongdae Guesthouse   A

RESTAURANTS		BARS & CLUBS			
Jopok Deokbokki	9	BricxX	14	Nabi	15
Oyori	18	Chin Chin	2	Oi	3
Samgeori Pocha	7	Club Evans	11	QVo	5
		Club Tool	12	Samgeori Pocha	7
CAFÉS		FF	13	Shain	19
Bau House	10	Flower	1	Tinpan	6 & 8
Café aA	17	M2	4	Vinyl	16

explore the streets lined with small shops selling stylish and secondhand clothing, and there are quirky cafés on every corner. Hongdae university itself specializes in the **arts**, a fact that'll be most evident to the visitor in **Nolita Park** (놀이터공원) – actually a triangular wedge of ground with almost no greenery – which plays host to anything and everything from punk-rock bands to choreographed hip-hop dancing. On weekends there's an interesting flea **market** at which local students sell handmade earrings, bangles and other such **trinkets**.

Exit five from Hongik University subway station will put you in the thick of the daytime action, though most of the clubs and bars are nearer Sangsu station on line 6 – take exit one.

Sinchon and Edae

East of Hongdae, and just one subway stop away on line 2, is **Sinchon** (신촌); like Hongdae, this is a university district, but the atmosphere here is a little earthier.

A banging good time

University areas are a good place to get a grip on the **"bang"** culture that pervades modern Korean life. The term is a suffix meaning "room", and is attached to all sorts of places where locals – and occasional foreigners – like to have fun. Below are a few of the most popular:

DVD-bang (DVD 방) Imagine a small room with wipe-clean sofas, tissue paper on hand and a large television for movies – if it sounds a little sleazy, you'd be absolutely right. Though people do occasionally come to appreciate plot, cinematography or Oscar-winning performances, these places are more often used by couples looking for a cheap bit of privacy – going in by yourself, or with a person of the same sex, would draw some baffled looks. Figure on around W11,000 per movie.

Game-bang (게임방) Filled with all manner of board-games, these rooms underwent a surge in popularity just after the turn of the millennium – a strange development, considering the country's love for digital forms of entertainment – but don't see many foreign guests. Note that they're not really for kids, being café-style places better suited to young couples.

Jjimjilbang (찜질방) Popular with families, teenagers and the occasional budget-minded traveller, these steam rooms have a range of hot and cold pools, sauna rooms, and often a range of services from massage treatment to internet booths. Though they might sound dodgy, the reality is somewhat tamer; most are open all night, making them an incredibly cheap way to get a night's sleep – prices tend to be around W6000. See p.145 for more.

Noraebang (노래방) These "singing rooms" are all over the country, even outside national park entrances, and are wildly popular with people of all ages; if you have any Korean friends, they're bound to invite you to one before long, as *noraebang* are usually *sam-cha* in a Korean night out – the "third step" after meal and drinks. The system is different from what Westerners usually expect of a karaoke room – you don't sing in front of a crowd, but in a small room with your friends, where you'll find sofas, a television, books full of songs to choose from and a couple of maracas or tambourines to play. Foreigners are usually intimidated at first, but after a few drinks it can be tough to get the microphone out of people's hands. Figure on around W15,000 per hour between a group; a good one has been listed on p.136.

PC-bang (PC 방) Even more ubiquitous in Korea are places to get online, which cost an almost uniform W1000 per hour. Despite the sheer number of such places, most of them still contrive to be packed, and incredibly noisy, thanks to the fact that everyone's playing online games – you're likely to be the only one sending emails. See p.36 for more.

Sinchon is best visited at night, when its small side-streets are splashed with neon and filled with barbecue smoke; restaurants here can be incredibly cheap, and since one building in every four seems to house a bar, it makes an interesting nightlife alternative to Hongdae. The main area is situated north of Sinchon subway station – take exit two or three. Sinchon has become the centre of Seoul's small **lesbian** community (see p.130 for more on homosexual Seoul), most likely due to the presence of Ehwa Women's University a few hundred metres to the east; more commonly referred to as "**Edae**", its 20,000-plus students make this the world's largest institution of female learning. It is also the oldest such place in the country, and broke ground by providing Korea's first female doctor and lawyer. The **main campus** itself is also worth a look for its mishmash of **architectural styles** – there are a couple of Gothic-style buildings, augmented by a new wing designed by French architect Dominique Perrault. This wing is largely underground, its open-air access path delving below surface level to reveal floor upon floor of study halls, as well as the odd shop, restaurant and café. Outside the south gate, the area is packed not so much with bars and clubs, as is the case with most universities, but with hundreds of cheap shops selling clothes, shoes, make-up and fashion accessories.

Yeouido and around

The south bank of the Hangang's central stretch contains some notable sights, clustered around the island of **Yeouido**. This forms one of Seoul's main business districts, and as such has some of its largest towers, including the magnificent **63 Building**. Just to the south is **Noryangjin** and its mind-boggling **fish market**, and west along the Hangang is **Seonyudo**, a recently redeveloped islet that has become a popular draw for Seoulites wishing to stroll or cycle.

Yeouido

An island in the Hangang may sound nice, but you'd do well to banish any romantic visions before arriving in **YEOUIDO** (여의도). Meaning something akin to "useless land", it lay barren for years before finally undergoing development during Park Chung-hee's economic reforms in the 1970s. Progress came fast, and little "Sweet Potato Island", as it's nicknamed on account of its shape, is now one of Korea's most important **business districts**, not to mention the home of its National Assembly and the **63 Building**, formerly the tallest structure in Asia. However, as Yeouido is manifestly a place to work, rather than live or go out, on weekends and evenings it has some of the quietest roads in the city. In fact, most of the northern fringe has been turned into a **riverside park**, which is a popular picnicking place for families.

The riverside park

Most of Yeouido's northern flank is devoid of buildings, and this band of **semi-parkland** proves a particularly popular people-magnet on weekends and warm evenings. **Bike riding** is the most popular activity (see p.83). It's also possible to take a **riverboat trip** from near Wonhyo bridge to Jamsil – there are round-trips (90min; W9000) every hour or so. Yeouido's northern shore underwent substantial renovations in 2009, the most notable addition being a few **open-air swimming pools** (9am–6pm; W5000); these are only open in summer months, usually late June to early September.

63 Building

A short walk south of Wonhyo bridge is the **63 Building** (63 빌딩), one of the largest and most notable of Seoul's innumerable towers. A distinctive golden monolith 249m in height, it was the tallest structure in Asia when completed in 1985, though had already lost the title by the time the Olympics rolled into town three years later, and is today struggling to stay in the national top ten. The sixtieth-floor **observation deck** (daily 10am–11pm; W7000) provides predictably good views of Seoul, and is actually at the top of the building, the other three floors from the building's name being basement levels. Down in the basement you'll find **Seaworld** (10am–10pm; W12,000), an aquarium that's apparently home to over twenty thousand sea creatures (there's also a reptile hall), and quite popular with young ones. The same can be said of the **Imax cinema** (10am–8pm; W8000), though both this and the aquarium are somewhat dated.

The Full Gospel Church

Last but not least, Yeouido is also home to the almost sinfully ugly **Full Gospel Church** (순복음교회), by some measures the largest church on earth – it has a membership exceeding one million. Obviously, not all of them pop along for prayers at the same time, but to meet the needs of Seoul's huge Protestant population there are no fewer than seven separate Sunday services, translated into sixteen languages in a dedicated foreigners section. This is quite a trip, whatever your denomination, since most Sunday services see more than ten thousand people pack into the building, creating something of a football crowd atmosphere on the way in. On occasion half of the congregation ends up in tears, as Korean pastors have a habit of ratcheting up the rhetoric, to better exploit the national tendency towards melodrama.

Noryangjin fish market

Dongdaemun (p.68) and Namdaemun (p.65) may be the city's best-known markets, but for **seafood** there's only one winner: **Noryangjin** (노량진), which remains well off the radar for most foreign visitors. During the evening the place is particularly picturesque – under strings of bright lights, you can wander around whole soggy acres of shells, seaworms, spider crabs and other salty fare. Much of the goods on offer will be unfamiliar to the average Western traveller, but fortune favours the brave; unless you have suitable cooking skills and a home to repair to, bag up your goodies and take it up to one of the second-floor restaurants, whose chefs will do the necessary preparations for a surprisingly reasonable price. Prime time at Noryangjin market is between 4am and 6am, when noisy **fish auctions** are held.

The market lies at the other end of a tunnel which heads under the tracks from exit 1 of Noryangjin station.

Seonyudo

A tiny island just west of Yeouido, **Seonyudo** (선유도) was, until recently, the site of a gargantuan water treatment plant. The city authorities felt that the land could be put to better use, and in 2009 a newly gentrified Seonyudo began a new lease of life as a strolling and picnicking place. It has since become extremely popular, especially on weekends, when you'll see Seoulites arriving in their hundreds for a spot of cycling, rollerblading, or a family meal; stay until evening time to see **Seonyugyo** – a bridge that links Seonyudo to the north and south banks of the Hangang – lit up in pretty colours. Unless you're walking here on said bridge, the island is best reached by taking a short walk north from exit 3 of Seonyudo station.

Itaewon and around

One of Seoul's most famed quarters, **Itaewon** (이태원) is something of an enigma. It has, for years, been popular with American soldiers, thanks to the major military base situated nearby. Expat businessmen and visiting foreigners have followed suit, and until English teachers started pouring into Korea by the planeload it was one of the only places in the country in which you could buy "Western" items such as leather jackets, deodorant, tampons or Hershey's Kisses. While it remains a great place to shop for shoes and cheap **tailored suits** (see p.139), Itaewon's popularity also made it a byword for transactions of a more sexual nature – **hostess bars** sprung up all over the place, particularly south of the *Hamilton*, a hotel that marks the centre of the area, on the affectionately named "Hooker Hill" (actually more of a steep road). Times are changing, however. Western goods are now available in cities across the country, and the gradual withdrawal of American troops has coincided with the opening of an ever more cosmopolitan array of restaurants (see p.118), possibly the hippest in the city outside ultra-fashionable Apgujeong. The area also heaves with clubbers on weekends, and from Hooker Hill sprouts a second road, "Homo Hill", Seoul's main **gay area**. For more details on Itaewon's bars and clubs, see p.128; for some information on the city's gay scene go to p.130.

However, there's more to Itaewon than eating, drinking and having suits made. Within walking distance are two major **museums**, one crammed with fine art, the other with items pertaining to the **Korean War**. The country's **National Museum** is also just a short cab-ride away.

War Memorial Museum

To the west of central Itaewon is the **War Memorial Museum** (전쟁기념관; 9.30am–5.30pm; closed Mon; W3000), a huge venue that charts the history of Korean warfare from ancient stones and arrows to more modern machinery. You

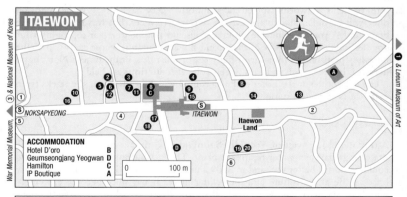

ITAEWON

ACCOMMODATION
Hotel D'oro **B**
Geumseongjang Yeogwan **D**
Hamilton **C**
IP Boutique **A**

0   100 m

RESTAURANTS ●		BARS ●				SHOPS ●	
Above	8	La Plancha	5	All That Jazz	16	Gecko's Terrace	17	Curious Curious	1
Ashoka	C	Le Saint-ex	6	Always Homme	14	Nashville Sports	15	Foreign Book Store	3
Buddha's Belly	7	OK Kitchen	10	B1	11	Queen	20	Hahn's Custom Tailoring	5
Gecko's Garden	3	Passion 5	1	Bar Nana	12	Spy	15	Hamilton Shirts	4
Macaroni Market	13	The Wolfhound	18	Bungalow	4	Trance	19	Royal Antiques	2
My Thai	9	Zelen	2	Function	13			What the Book	6

don't even need a ticket to see the larger sights, as the museum's park-like periphery is riddled with B-52 bombers and other flying machines; with some, you'll be able to clamber up ladders to cockpit windows for a look inside. Before entering the main building itself, look for the names written on the outer wall: these are the names of every known member of Allied forces who died in the Korean War, and the list seems to go on forever. This is particularly heart-wrenching when you consider the fact that a far greater number of people, unmarked here, died on the Chinese and North Korean side – in total, the war claimed over two million souls. After all this, the main hall itself is a little disappointing, but you'll find plenty of exhibits and video displays relaying (incredibly one-sided) information about the **Korean War**; see Contexts, p.175, for an account of the conflict. To get to the museum, take exit twelve from Samgakji subway station, or walk downhill from Itaewon.

Leeum Museum of Art

The excellent **Leeum Museum of Art** (리움미술관; 10.30am–6pm; closed Mon; W10,000) is not so much a museum as one of the most esteemed galleries in the country. It's split into several halls, each with a distinctive and original design; one, built in black concrete, was designed by acclaimed Dutch architect Rem Koolhaas, who has since busied himself on the fantastic CCTV headquarters in Beijing. The museum hosts the occasional special exhibition of world famous artists, both past and present – works from such luminaries as Mark Rothko and Damien Hirst have been displayed here. It's within walking distance from Itaewon, about fifteen minutes east of the subway station, but access is slightly faster from exit one of Hangangjin station – follow the road uphill towards Itaewon for 200m, and take the (signed) turn right.

National Museum of Korea

The **National Museum of Korea** (국립중앙박물관; ⓦwww.museum.go.kr; 9am–6pm, Wed & Sat to 9pm, Sun to 7pm; closed Mon; W2000) used to be based in Gyeongbokgung (p.43), but was moved in 2005 to a huge, ugly building just north of the Han. Although it may look like something from *Star Trek*, it's a Seoul must-see for anyone interested in Korean history, and houses over eleven thousand artefacts from the museum's collection, including an incredible 94 official National Treasures, though only a fraction of these will be on show at any one time. Among the many rooms on the ground level are exhibitions from the **Three Kingdoms** period, which showcase the incredible skill of the artisans during that time – gold, silver and bronze have been cast into ornate shapes, the highlight being a fifth-century crown and belt set that once belonged to a Silla king.

Moving up a floor the focus shifts to paintings, calligraphy and wooden art, and there's usually a colossal **Buddhist scroll** or two, over ten metres high; some were hung behind the Buddha statue in temples' main halls, while others were used to pray for rain and other such purposes. The museum owns quite a few, but due to the fragility of the material, they're put on a rota system and displays are changed regularly. The uppermost floor contains countless metal sculptures and a beautiful assortment of pots – some of these are over a thousand years old, though look as if they were made yesterday. There are also interesting collections from other Asian countries, the large Chinese and Japanese displays supplemented by relics from Turkestan, Sri Lanka and more. From this floor you'll also get the best view of the museum's pride and joy, a ten-storey stone **pagoda** that is situated in the main hall of the museum on the ground level, and stretches almost all the way to the top floor. It's in remarkable condition for something that was taken apart by the Japanese in 1907, hauled to Tokyo then all the way back some years later; from on high, you'll be able to appreciate more fully its true size, and the difficulties this must have posed for the people who built it.

Elsewhere in the complex there's a **children's museum** and library, as well as a food court and café; the wide, green area around the museum also has some pleasant walking paths and a lake – great for a picnic. The museum is best accessed from Ichon subway station – take exit two then walk up the main road for 100m, and the museum will be on your left.

National Cemetery

A **graveyard** may sound like a rather morbid tourist sight, but **Seoul's National Cemetery** (국립현충원; daily 8am–6pm) merits a visit, both for its historical importance and paths that, somewhat surprisingly, make for some of the most pleasant strolling territory that the capital has to offer. With gravestones stretching across an area 2km square, the place is gigantic and notably free of people – a rare oasis of calm in this hectic city. Despite its size, the bowl-shape formed by the surrounding mountains makes it very easy to orientate yourself and work your way back to the exit, located on the eastern side of the complex.

This is the final resting place of thousands of Korean **war veterans**, as well as **three presidents**. These are **Rhee Syngman**, the first president of an independent South Korea (see p.177); **Park Chung-hee**, the autocratic military general whose sweeping economic changes essentially shaped the country you see today (see p.177); and **Kim Dae-jung**, leader of the opposition during Park's rule and at one point sentenced to death, though he later became the country's first democratically-elected president and won the **Nobel Peace Prize** to boot (see p.178). Each of the presidents lies interred in a **grassy hill-tomb**, similar to those used to house the remains of kings and queens in pre-presidential Korea; the fallen soldiers surrounding them have to make do with simple plaques. With signage in Korean only, these tombs are a little hard to find, tucked away towards the rear of the huge complex. Near the cemetery entrance are a few large halls detailing the histories of the Korean War and the three dead presidents with photographs and film, but they're old-fashioned and not really worth bothering with.

To get to the cemetery, take exit 8 from Dongjak subway station, and the main entrance will be just up the road to your left.

6

Southern Seoul

The Korean capital is a city of two distinct halves. Seoul proper once stopped north of the Hangang, and almost all of its historical sights are located there. Development then spilled over the river during the heady days of the 1970s, giving rise to an almost entirely new part of town. The area immediately **south of the Hangang** is known as Gangnam, which since that era of economic expansion has become the **wealthiest** area in the land, and indeed one of the richest urban zones in the whole of Asia. Seoulites have relocated here in their millions, creating a distinct **north–south divide**: northerners tend to find those from the south money-obsessed and self-centred, while southerners find the north relatively lacking in modern sophistication.

While the north wins hands-down in sightseeing terms, there's still a fair amount to see down south: **Bongeunsa** is Seoul's most enchanting major temple, while just down the road are the **royal tombs** in **Samneung Park**, the grassy resting place of a few dynastic kings and queens. Moving into the modern day there's **COEX**, a large underground shopping mall, and **Lotte World**, a simply colossal theme park. The area also sheds light on Seoul's artistic scene, with several prominent galleries and performance halls, most notably those in and around the Seoul Arts Center; there are even a few in **Olympic Park**, an area that provides a glimpse into the Seoul of the 1980s. However, southern Seoul is perhaps best viewed as a window into **modern Korean society** – the teeming streets surrounding Gangnam station are simply pulsating with neon and noise, with innumerable tower blocks rising into the heavens. In addition, the restaurants, cafés and **boutique shops** of the classy **Apgujeong** district are without doubt the costliest and most exclusive in the land.

Gangnam

Literally meaning "South of the River", **Gangnam** (강 남) is the name for a huge swathe of land south of the Hangang, and an all-encompassing term for several distinct city districts. However, it's most commonly used to describe the area around **Gangnam subway station**, a relatively flat district almost entirely built since the 1970s. This zone is easy to get around, its grid of perfectly straight streets served by a number of bus and subway lines. While almost entirely devoid of traditional tourist sights, this is an absorbing place to walk around; these streets – especially to the northeast of the station – are hugely popular with young Koreans, and crammed full of cafés and cheap restaurants. Recent years have seen the local city district adding huge LED displays, full-building octaves

SOUTHERN SEOUL

ACCOMMODATION
Blue Pearl — B
Ellui — A
Imperial Palace — E
Jelly — I
Novotel — F
Ambassador — H
Park Hyatt — D
Richmond — G
Ritz-Carlton — C
Riviera —

RESTAURANTS
Arte — 8
Asian Live — 3
Marco Polo — 1
La Trouvaille — 9
Pasha — 7

CAFÉS
Kring — 5
The Lounge — H

BARS & CLUBS
Blush — 3
Club Eden — 4
Club Heaven — 6
Marcie — 2

0 _____ 1 km

Jaebeol society

Korean society is dominated by a string of gargantuan conglomerates known as the **jaebeol** (재벌). Many of these are household names around the world, although poor international marketing means that surprisingly few people realize that these companies hail from Korea; **Hyundai** cars race around more than one hundred countries (with **Daewoo** and **Kia**, a Hyundai subsidiary, not far behind), while homes around the world feature electronic goods from **Samsung** and **LG**. Consumer goods are just the tip of the iceberg. In the 1970s, for example, colossal **shipyards** built by Samsung and Daewoo sounded the death knell for such business in the UK, at that time the world leader – Korea now has 25 percent of the global industry, the UK around three percent.

In Korea itself, these businesses have their fingers in almost everything: construction, insurance, telecommunications, heavy industries and much more besides. Indeed, some locals say that the president of Samsung, the largest of the *jaebeol*, is actually more powerful than the head of the country. Many of these companies have even meddled directly in politics – prominent company heads have, on occasion, successfully run for governmental roles, while in the late 1990s Hyundai was at the forefront of the **Sunshine Policy** (a North–South thaw; see p.178), transferring business across the North Korean border and actually buying a whole chunk of land in the Geumgang mountains for South Korean tourist use. This led to allegations of money laundering and the suicide of the company founder's son; subsequent governmental investigations into widespread **corruption** led to yet more high-level suicides at other *jaebeol*, and the enforced break-up of Hyundai, Samsung and other large conglomerates into more easily manageable (and policeable) chunks. Smaller in size they may be, but the *jaebeol* remain a hugely influential element of modern Korean culture.

of neon and all sorts of other technological gizmos to the roadsides, which, in addition to the massed ranks of high-rise, bring something of a *Blade Runner* feel to the area. A short journey away west from Gangnam station will bring you to **Seorae Maeul**, a curious little Frenchified neighbourhood, and the superb **Seoul Arts Centre**.

Samsung d'light

The Samsung Electronics arm has transformed the lower levels of its towering Gangnam headquarters into a sharply designed and highly appealing showroom; named **Samsung d'light** (daily 9am–9pm), this is the place to come if you want a sneak preview of the gadgets that will be racing around the world in the near future. Samsung is the largest of Korea's many **jaebeol**, colossal conglomerates which permeate most spheres of local society (see box above). The company is also better known abroad than its Korean rivals, largely thanks to its success in the electronic goods market. Exhibitions at its showroom change as often as the products themselves, but there's a clear emphasis on nature – water trickles down some walls, while others are festooned with (fake) greenery, and there's a notable use of natural and ambient lighting, rather than the neon soaking the streets of Gangnam outside. The complex connects directly to exit 4 of Gangnam station.

Kukkiwon

Just up the hill from Gangnam station is **Kukkiwon** (국기원; Mon–Fri 9am–5pm; free), a brutalist structure that functions as the headquarters of the **World Taekwondo** federation. **Demonstration events** are occasionally held here, as well as the odd competition, but at most times it stands empty. There are other options in Seoul if you're itching to have a go yourself – see p.145 for details.

Seorae Maeul

One interesting place near Gangnam station, and one that doesn't feature on many tourist brochures, is **Seorae Maeul** (서래마을), a peculiar place that many locals refer to as **"Frenchtown"**. Here live some of Seoul's more moneyed European expats, many drawn by the French school just up the way. Bar a couple of restaurants (see p.119), there's precious little here that's truly French, though the area's tranquil, cosmopolitan air is markedly different from most other Seoul districts. Essentially a residential area, most of its buildings are low-rise in nature, and there are a few charming brick structures dotting the lanes; those visiting in the evening will be able to take their pick from over a dozen pleasant bars. Seorae Maeul is a little hard to track down, but it's within walking distance of the Express Bus Terminal subway station – take exit 5, cross the main road and head right past the *Palace Hotel* until you see a footbridge. Cross this and head a little further up the road; Seorae Maeul will be on your left.

Seoul Arts Center and around

Hugging a mountainside southwest of Gangnam station are a number of buildings catering to myriad forms of the arts. Largest is the **Seoul Arts Center** (예술의전당; ⓦwww.sac.or.kr), made up of five different buildings. The delights on offer here include opera, ballet and orchestral performances – see p.136 for more. It also houses the **Seoul Calligraphy Art Museum** (daily 11am–7pm; free), which looks at calligraphic works both ancient and contemporary. Nearby is the **National Center for Korean Traditional Performing Arts** (국립국악원악기연구소; ⓦwww.gugak.go.kr), which hosts performances largely musical in nature, and is affiliated to the Gugakdang near Namsan (p.135). The closest subway station to the area is Nambu Bus Terminal, though it's still a fair walk away – head straight on from exit 6, and turn left at the T-junction.

Samneung Park

During the Three Kingdoms period and beyond, deceased Korean royalty were buried in highly distinctive **grass mounds**. While these are more numerous elsewhere in Korea – notably the former Silla capital Gyeongju way down in the southeast of the country, or the Baekje capitals of Gongju (p.164) and Buyeo closer to the capital, Seoul has a few of its own. The easiest to reach are in **Samneung Park** (삼릉공원; 6am–4.30pm; closed Mon; W1000), just to the north of Seolleung subway station – take exit eight and walk straight up the road for a few minutes. The park's name means "Three Mounds". One was for **King Seongjong** (r.1469–94), an esteemed leader who (unusually) invited political opponents to have a say in national government. Two of his sons went on to rule; **Yeonsangun** (r.1494–1506) undid much of his father's hard work in a system of revenge-driven purges, and was overthrown to leave his half-brother **Jungjong** (r.1506–44) in control. Jungjong's mound can also be found in the park, as can one created to house one of Seongjong's wives.

For all the history, it's the prettiness of the park itself that appeals to many visitors, a green refuge from grey Seoul crisscrossed by gorgeous tree-shaded **pathways**. The area is popular with workers from nearby offices as a lunch spot, many of whom come here to munch a sandwich or go for a jog. Its early opening times mean that you'll be able to visit at daybreak, which can be a rather atmospheric experience; dew sits on the grass and the morning mist occludes nearby buildings.

COEX and around

Within walking distance of Gangnam, the **COEX** complex is a huge assortment of shopping, dining and office space. Inclement weather sees Seoulites heading here in droves – its large underground **mall** area is one of the only sizeable covered spaces in the whole city. Also part of the complex are a couple of five-star hotels (see p.108 & p.109), which house some of Seoul's best restaurants (p.119). The area around COEX also boasts a number of interesting sights, including the pretty temple of **Bongeunsa**.

COEX Mall

This huge underground **shopping mall** is a popular place for tourists to spend a rainy day. The mass of shops, restaurants and wall-to-wall people can be quite bewildering, but there are a couple of tourist attractions on site. One of these is the **Gimchi Museum** (김치박물관; daily 10am–5pm, Sat & Sun from 1pm; W3000), the only facility in the land dedicated to this national dish; after a look through the exhibits you'll be able to differentiate some of the many varieties available, and there's usually some for tasting. The **COEX Aquarium** (10am–8pm; W16,500) sees far more visitors and has been designed with flair – this must be the only aquarium in the world to use toilets as goldfish tanks, though mercifully there are normal facilities for public use. Sharks, manta rays and colourful shoals of smaller fish are on display, while other activities within the mall include a pool hall, a board-game café and a large multiscreen cinema.

Bongeunsa

Sitting directly across from the north face of COEX is **Bongeunsa** (봉은사), the most appealing major temple in Seoul. Despite an incongruous location amidst a plethora of skyscrapers, this is a fairly decent rendition of a Korean temple; like Jogyesa, its uglier sibling to the north of the river (see p.58), it's affiliated to the **Jogye sect**, the largest Buddhist denomination in Korea. There has been a temple here since the late eighth century, but assorted fires and invasions mean that all of its buildings are of fairly recent vintage; still, it's worth peeking at its gorgeous main hall and clutch of small yet appealing outer buildings. See p.180 for more on Buddhism in Korea, and p.58 for information about Buddhist sights and experiences in Seoul.

Kring

Just to the south of COEX itself is **Kring**, an intriguing complex that's one of Seoul's only decent pieces of modern architecture (see Contexts, p.178, for more on this dearth). The building is covered with circles of all sizes, both inside and out – its metallic exterior gives way to a squeaky-clean inside that's something like a space station set from a sci-fi film. It does, indeed, feature an **art-house cinema**, as well as a **contemporary art gallery** and one of Seoul's best **cafés** (p.121).

Apgujeong

Seoulites refer to **Apgujeong** (압구정) as "Korea's Beverly Hills", and the comparison is not far off the mark – if Louis Vuitton bags are your thing, look no further. Boutique clothing stores (see p.139), chic restaurants and European-style outdoor cafés line streets frequented by a disproportionate number of Seoul's young and beautiful, but bear in mind that their good looks may not be entirely natural – this is also Korea's plastic surgery capital, and clinics are ubiquitous. Though there are no real sights as such, Apgujeong is one of the most interesting places in Seoul to sit down with a latte and people-watch.

The best restaurants (see p.119) huddle in a pleasantly relaxed, leafy area outside the main entrance to **Dosan Park** (도산공원), a pleasant quadrant of grass and trees but nothing more. Heading further north, past the clothes shops and plastic surgeons, you'll eventually come out onto Apgujeongno, the area's main road, which features the most exclusive clothes shops and department stores in Korea (see p.138). Notable for its visual appeal alone is the gargantuan **Galleria department store**, whose west wing had its exterior remodelled in 2004 by Dutch design team UN Studios. It now finds itself cloaked from head to toe with thousands of perspex discs, which are illuminated at night in a kaleidoscope of vivid colour – something like a marooned spaceship. Heading west of Dosan Park, though actually far closer to exit 8 of Sinsa station (turn

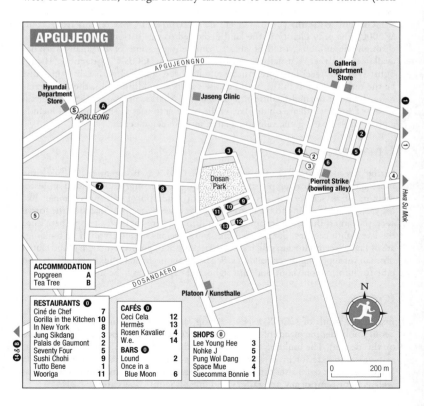

APGUJEONG

APGUJEONGNO

Galleria Department Store

Hyundai Department Store

Ⓢ APGUJEONG Ⓐ

Jaseng Clinic

Dosan Park

Pierrot Strike (bowling alley)

Hwa Sul Mok

DOSANDAERO

Platoon / Kunsthalle

N

ACCOMMODATION
Popgreen	A
Tea Tree	B

RESTAURANTS Ⓞ
Ciné de Chef	7
Gorilla in the Kitchen	10
In New York	8
Jung Sikdang	3
Palais de Gaumont	2
Seventy Four	5
Sushi Chohi	9
Tutto Bene	1
Wooriga	11

CAFÉS Ⓞ
Ceci Cela	12
Hermès	13
Rosen Kavalier	4
W.e.	14

BARS Ⓞ
Lound	2
Once in a Blue Moon	6

SHOPS Ⓞ
Lee Young Hee	3
Nohke J	5
Pung Wol Dang	2
Space Mue	4
Suecomma Bonnie	1

0   200 m

Ginkgo trees

Growing up to 50m in height, the **ginkgo biloba** is one of East Asia's most characteristic species of tree. Long heralded as a symbol of longevity, since they themselves can live for over 2,000 years, they're found on mountainsides and outside temples throughout Korea, and known locally as *eunhaeng-namu* (은행나무) - *eunhaeng* means "bank", as *ginko* does in Japanese, on account of the magical golden hue the tree's leaves assume in autumn. Unfortunately, at this time the ginkgo also release their juicy seeds, which when trampled underfoot release a smell somewhat akin to dog excrement; saved in time and roasted, they're quite delicious – keep an eye out for old ladies selling paper cupfuls of what look like green beads.

left after 200m), there's **Garosugil**, a particularly trendy street studded with hip cafés and sharp designer boutiques. Its name literally means "tree-lined street", bestowed on account of the roadside lines of gorgeous **ginkgo trees** (see box above), whose spectacular golden fall foliage makes Garosugil a superb place to stroll in Seoul's all-too-short autumn.

Olympic Park

Built for the **1988 Summer Olympics**, (see box, p.98), this large **park** (올림픽 공원; 24hr) remains a popular picnicking place for Seoul families, and hosts a regular roster of small-scale municipal festivals; you're likely to see one if you turn up on a weekend. It's a very large place around 2km square, but mercifully everything is well signposted, and it's possible to rent bikes at the two main entrances (₩3000 per hour).

Near the eastern entrance to the park (take subway line 5 to Olympic Park station) are a number of facilities that remain from the games, including a couple of gymnasiums and the indoor swimming pool, though very few are actually open for public use. There's a general air of decay about the place but it's all part of the appeal; the order of play from the Olympics is still in place outside the ground, and through the peeling paint you can see the routes that Miroslav Macir and Steffi Graf took to their gold medals. On the way into the park, you'll pass by buildings and sculptures displaying the rather Stalinist themes that were in vogue in 1980s Seoul – some of this would look quite at home in Pyongyang, and those with interests in art and architecture may find the area quite absorbing.

The main concentration of sights run along the south of the park, and it's best to stick to these paths. West of the tennis courts, you'll pass the Olympic velodrome, a popular gambling venue where elderly Seoulites come to bet on bike races in summer months (technically illegal, but tolerated by the government). A few minutes' walk away is **SOMA** (10am–8pm; closed Mon; ₩3000), a small art centre split into an outdoor sculpture garden and indoor modern art gallery. The **Papertainer Museum** (daily 10am–6pm; ₩10,000) is just down the way, housed inside an interesting structure made from old steel containers and paper tubes; the exhibits inside focus on such themes as 'marketing as art', shedding new light on the purposes of corporate logos and the like. The gallery, museum and velodrome are all best accessed from Mongcheontoseong

Seoul's hosting of the **Olympic Games** in 1988 was a tremendous success, bringing pride not just to the city, but to the whole nation. In fact, it did much to make Korea the country that it is today, and has even been credited with bringing democracy to the nation. President **Park Chung-hee** had been first to toy with the idea of bidding for the games in the 1970s, seemingly wishing to win international approval for his authoritarian running of the country; he was assassinated in 1979, but the bid went ahead. However, large-scale protests against the government in the years running up to the games brought a hitherto unprecedented level of international scrutiny, and direct elections took place in 1987.

The games themselves were no less interesting, and produced several moments which have become part of sporting folklore. This is where American diver **Greg Louganis** won gold despite bloodying the pool by walloping his head on the dive-board, and where steroid use saw Canadian sprinter Ben Johnson stripped of first place and his 100m world record. A lesser-known tale is that of Canadian sailor **Lawrence Lemieux,** who sacrificed a probable medal to race to the aid of two Singaporean competitors who had been thrown into the water in treacherous conditions.

subway station on line 8, as is the **Olympic Museum** (10am–5pm; closed Mon; W3000), which may appeal to sports buffs – there's a collection of Olympic torches from various games, as well as an exhibit showing just how terrifying Olympic mascots have been through the years (Atlanta's "Izzy", a thoroughly repulsive character of indeterminate species, and Barcelona's "Cobi", the cubist Catalan sheepdog, being just two examples). Outside the museum, flags from the 159 countries that competed in the games stand in a semi-circle; though several countries have since merged, split or changed their flags, the authorities have decided to leave the originals as a symbol of what the world was like at the time – the Soviet and Yugoslav flags remain, but there's no South Africa, the country at that time having been banned from competing. The **Olympic Stadium** itself is actually a few subway stops to the west (immediately north of Sports Complex station), and can usually still be entered during the day for a nose around.

Lotte World

This local version of Disneyland is incredibly popular – the complex receives over five million visitors per year, and it's hard to find a Korean child, or even an adult, who hasn't been here at some point. While it may not be quite what some are looking for on their visit to "The Land of Morning Calm", **Lotte World** (롯데월드; Ⓦ www.lotteworld.com; daily 9.30am–11pm; day-tickets W37,000 adults, W28,000 children; less after 4pm) can be a lot of fun, particularly for those travelling with children. It comprises two theme parks: indoor Lotte World Adventure and outdoor Magic Island, the latter in the middle of a lake and accessed by monorail from the former. Also within the complex is a bowling alley (9am–midnight; W3000 plus shoe rental), an overpriced ice rink (10am–9pm; W12,000 plus skate rental), and a large swimming pool (noon–7pm, Sat & Sun to 8pm; W8000). The complex is an easy walk from Jamsil subway station; you'll see signs pointing the way from the ticket gates.

Seoul Grand Park

Seven subway stops south of the Hangang on line 4 is **Seoul Grand Park** (서울대공원; ⓦgrandpark.seoul.go.kr; daily 9.30am–9pm), one of the largest expanses of greenery in Seoul, and one of the best places to take children for a fun day out. The highlight is its **zoo** (9am–6pm; W3000); home to animals from around the world, it puts on special dolphin shows (W1500) at least four times per day, as well as other animal performances. In 2005, six elephants escaped during one of these events, and were only caught hours later after trashing a restaurant and wading through a nearby resident's garden; needless to say, security has been tightened, and a repeat pachyderm performance is unlikely. To get to Seoul Grand Park, take exit two from the subway station of the same name. The entrance is just fifteen minutes' walk away and well signed, or you can take a tram train (W800) or a chairlift (W4500).

Other attractions in the park area are **Seoul Land** (서울랜드; ⓦeng.seoulland .co.kr; 9am–6pm, later in peak season; entry W16,000, day-pass for rides W30,000), a large amusement park with an abundance of roller coasters and spinning rides, and the **National Museum of Contemporary Art** (March–Oct Mon–Fri 10am–6pm, Sat & Sun to 9pm; Nov–Feb to 5pm, Sat & Sun to 8pm; closed Mon; W1000), an excellent collection of works by some of the biggest movers and shakers in the Korean modern art scene.

Listings

Listings

7

Accommodation

S eoul has by far the best range of **accommodation** in the country, with everything from five-star hotels to cheap-and-cheerful hostels. Those seeking high-quality accommodation have a great wealth of places to choose from, particularly around Myeongdong and City Hall on the north of the river, and Gangnam to the south. At the lower end of the price spectrum are Seoul's ballooning number of **backpacker guesthouses**. One interesting option popular with foreign travellers is to stay in **traditional wooden guesthouses** north of Anguk station. At around the same price, though different in character, **motels** form a cheap alternative to official tourist hotels, sometimes having rooms of comparable size and quality. It's hard to book these in advance, except for those listed on the excellent Innostel website (Ⓦinnostel.visitseoul.net), which also features an ever-growing number of cheap hotels.

Traditional guesthouses

In the surprisingly tranquil city sector north of Anguk subway station (right next to Insadonggil) lie some of Seoul's most interesting places to stay – here you can spend the night in traditional Korean housing known as **hanok** (see *Traditional Seoul* colour section). These are wooden buildings with tiled roofs, set around a dirt courtyard, a style that once blanketed the nation, but is rarely seen in today's high-rise Korea. The generally bed-less rooms – you'll be sleeping Korean-style in a sandwich of blankets – are kept deliberately rustic and heated in the winter with the underfloor *ondol* system; all, however, provide modern indoor toilets and internet access.

Anguk Guesthouse Angukdong ☎02/736-8304, Ⓦwww.anguk-house.com. There are just five rooms at this tiny guesthouse, where breakfast is included. The owner speaks excellent English and is full of information about the area; though his place is tucked away down some small side-alleys, the website has good directions. W70,000.

Bukchon Guesthouse Gyedong ☎02/743-8530, Ⓦwww.bukchon72.com. Simple yet comfortable rooms set around a pleasingly authentic courtyard, within easy walking distance of two palaces and Insadonggil. The friendly owners will even pick you up at nearby Anguk subway station if you phone ahead; if you feel like walking, take exit three and

continue straight up the main road, then take the first left, and the guesthouse will be on your left after five minutes or so. W60,000.

Rakkojae Gyedong ☎02/742-3410, Ⓦwww.rkj.co.kr. The most authentic of the bunch, character-wise. Not only is the *hanok* an 1870s original, but the owners serve traditional food for dinner: a little like a Japanese *ryokan*. Studded with maple and pine trees, the courtyard is divine, featuring precious few concessions to the modern day; it's best appreciated at night, when soft light pours through the paper doors. W250,000.

Seoul Guesthouse Gyedong ☎02/745-0057, Ⓦwww.seoul110.com. Seoul by name but not by nature. For somewhere so close to the centre, the atmosphere here is astonishingly farm-like – they do actually grow crops in the garden. There are no beds, though the simple rooms do come with wi-fi internet connections. W50,000.

Tea Guesthouse Bukchondong ☏02/3675-9877, ⓦwww.teaguesthouse .com. More expensive than most traditional guesthouses in the area, but the owners put in a lot of effort to introduce Korean traditions to their guests – if there are enough people around, you may find yourself making (and eating) *gimchi* or *pajeon*. The owners also have an endearing habit of chalking up information, such as the day's weather, on a tiny blackboard. W90,000.

Backpacker guesthouses

Just a few years ago, there were only a handful of backpacker hostels in Seoul, but there are now dozens to choose from, almost all of them in the most interesting parts of the city. There are a few places in and around **Insadong**, and a couple of cheapies in the student area of **Daehangno**, but a whole bunch have recently sprouted up in **Hongdae**, meaning that it's now the most popular area to stay for backpackers. All of the following have private rooms available for around W35,000; motel rooms are larger and better value, but for some the chance to meet fellow travellers is adequate compensation.

Ann Guesthouse Seogyodong ☏070/8279-0835, ⓦwww .annguesthouse.co.kr. Terrific location, peering over Hongdae subway station. Despite being in the centre of Seoul nightlife, it's a quiet and relaxed place, presided over by a friendly couple. If it's full, there's another decent hostel (*Hongdae Guesthouse*) in the same building. Free laundry service. Dorms W20,000.

Banana Backpackers Angukdong ☏02/3672-1972, ⓦwww.bananabackpackers .com. One of the oldest hostels in the city, this is an easy walk from Insadonggil; it has free internet, laundry and cooking facilities, and a common area that's great for making new mates. There's bread and jam to tuck into in the morning, as well as free tea and coffee throughout the day. Take exit four from Anguk subway station, head straight past the palace and turn left, then right at the crossroads; if it's full, there's a sister hostel around the corner. Dorms W20,000.

Bong House Daehangno ☏02/6080-3346, ⓦwww.bonghouse.net. Sprightly owner Bong tries his best to make guests feel at home – the free can of beer waiting on arrival is an especially nice touch. Dorms (W17,000) are simple but do the job, private rooms are by the month for a similar daily rate, and the surrounding area is a pleasing slice of retro Seoul.

Daewon Inn Gyeongbokgung Yeok-ap ☏02/735-7891. In a prime location just west of Gyeongbokgung – take exit four from the station – this is one of Seoul's longest-serving backpacker guesthouses, and though a little long in the tooth still makes an agreeable place to stay. Rooms are clustered around a small courtyard. Dorms W19,000.

Grape Garden House Seogyodong ☏010/4278-9808, ⓦwww.grapegardenhouse .com. In the heart of the Hongdae nightlife area, this new place is something of a party spot: there are regular barbecues on the outside patio, and shindigs on the balcony almost every night. Don't expect to do too much sightseeing while you're here. Dorms W17,000.

Golden Pond Guesthouse Daehangno ☏02/741-5621, ⓦwww.goldenpond.co.kr. Highly popular with western backpackers and those seeking work in Seoul, this is the cleanest and most secure guesthouse in the area; it's small and very often full. Dorm beds go for as little as W17,000, and drop another couple of thousand if you stay for more than a night.

Inside Daehangno ☏02/3672-1120, ⓦguesthouseinsideseoul.com. A great place to stay in studenty Daehangno. The owners try as hard as possible to please their guests, even down to laying out computer games when the weather's bad. Dorms are colourfully decorated and cheap at W17,000.

Motels

Seoul has a seemingly infinite range of **motels**, mostly used by local couples searching for a degree of much-needed privacy. However, they also suffice for many travellers on a budget: any seediness goes on behind closed doors and can be roundly ignored, save for the free contraceptives that tend to be waiting on the table. Rooms are kept immaculately clean, and internet-ready computer terminals are becoming the norm in newer establishments. **Prices** vary from W25,000 for a simple, old-fashioned room to over W100,000 for the trendiest new ones. Note that two of the most popular nightlife areas have a shockingly poor range of motel accommodation: the few in and around Hongdae are vastly overpriced, while Itaewon has almost no such establishments (and those that exist are best avoided, since they're generally used by off-duty soldiers and their night-time companions). Note that almost none of these establishments will take reservations; indeed, few have functional phone lines.

Hotel D'Oro Hannamdong ☎02/749-6525. Itaewon station, see map, p.88. Highly recommended mid-range establishment on Itaewon's main drag, and rare value for money in a notoriously poor area for accommodation. Free wi-fi and minibar, and standards of service more akin to a hotel. W120,000.

Dongnam Motel Jongnodong. Jongno 3-ga station, see map, p.55. Though often used by amorous couples, this is a cheap and acceptable motel within sniffing distance of Insadonggil and its delights – take exit three from Jongno 3-ga subway station, and the motel entrance is right there. Rooms have comfy beds and a/c, and free sachets of coffee for the morning pick-me-up. W35,000.

Geumseongjang Yeogwan Itaewondong. Itaewon station, see map, p.88. A grubby but cheap place for Itaewon party-goers to crash, a short walk south of the subway station from the main crossroads. Though the rooms are small, there's enough space for contraceptive vending machines on the walls. W20,000.

Jelly Hotel Yeoksamdong ☎02/553-4737, ⓦwww.jellyhotel.com. Yeoksam station, see map, p.92. A hip and extremely interesting love hotel that has achieved cult status with young Seoulites, some of whom come to couple up (a "rest" is half the price of a night's stay), others to party

with a group of friends. The hotel is possibly home to the most idiosyncratic rooms in the city – some contain pool tables, jacuzzis or karaoke systems, making them popular with young groups wanting a night out. W80,000.

Hotel Kaya Galwoldong ☎02/798-5101, ⓦwww.kayahotel.net. Namyeong station, see map, p.82. Far more professional and less seedy than your average motel, this is as close as you'll get to the USO base if you're going on one of their early-starting tours of the DMZ (see p.149). Try to get a room at the back if possible – the views aren't great, but at least you'll get some light. W50,000.

Sheel Jongnodong ☎02/466-3330. Jongno 3-ga station, see map, p.55. Like the Jelly, this is something of a "high-end" motel, filling its rooms with all sorts of interesting quirks. Lace curtains billow over the ceilings, projectors fill whole walls with computer or televisual output, and some bathrooms are decked out in the style of a sauna. W70,000.

Tomgi Nagwondong ☎02/742-6660. Jongno 3-ga station, see map, p.55. Rooms at this pleasantly seedy love motel are excellent value for the area, and come in a variety of fresh styles, some of which include whirlpool baths. Just choose from the panel at reception: those not illuminated are taken (or just "busy"). Take exit four from Jongno 3-ga subway station. W55,000.

Hotels

Official tourist hotels are graded from two to five stars. Those at the higher levels usually have on-site restaurants, fitness and business centres, currency exchange and cafés, but even at these establishments many foreign guests are disappointed by the small size and impersonal nature of the rooms. Most top-end places will have wi-fi or an in-room **internet connection**, and many even provide computers; some do so for free, while others charge ridiculous rates of over W20,000 per day – be sure to check beforehand. Hotels are also the only forms of accommodation which regularly omit **tax and service charges** – around ten percent each – from their quoted prices.

City Hall

A number of five-star hotels can be found around Seoul Plaza and City Hall, near Deoksugung palace; it's also convenient for the Myeongdong shopping area. All are within walking distance of City Hall or Euljiro 1-ga subway stations, and can be found on the map on p.61.

Koreana Hotel Taepyeongno ☎02/2171-7000, ⓦ www.koreanahotel.com. Half the price of some of its competitors, but with similar rooms and service standards. It's worth paying a little extra for the larger "Prestige" rooms – try to nab one from the eleventh to the fifteenth floors, which have been renovated. W210,000.

Lotte Hotel Sogongdong ☎02/771-1000, ⓦ www .lottehotel.co.kr. Like others in the chain, the *Lotte* sits on top of a busy shopping mall. The hotel has two wings – the older one, though cheaper, is truly dire, with rooms no better than the average motel, while those in the new wing are far bigger and better value for money. W425,000.

Metro Hotel Euljiro 2-ga ☎02/752-1112, ⓦ www.metrohotel.co.kr. A modern, squeaky-clean hotel away from the bustling Myeongdong main roads, where the staff are friendly and breakfast is included. Rooms are fresh and have free internet connections, though views are generally poor – ask to see a few. Come out of Euljiro 1-ga subway station, turn right off the main road then right again. W100,000.

Millennium Seoul Hilton Namdaemunno ☎02/753-7788, ⓦ www.hilton.co.kr. Up on the Namsan slopes above Seoul Station, this top hotel is a regular on the international conference circuit. Views are excellent whichever side of the building you end up staying in, and the on-site restaurants nothing short of superb. In addition, Seoul's best wine bar, *Naos Nova* (p.129), is just up the road. W330,000.

The Plaza City Hall ☎02/771-2200, ⓦ www .hoteltheplaza.com. Directly facing City Hall

and adjacent to Deoksugung, you could hardly wish for a more central location. In addition, a thorough overhaul in 2010 made its interior one of the most attractive in the city, with immaculate rooms and superb on-site restaurants. Try to grab a room on one of the north-facing upper floors for some wonderfully Manhattanesque views. W440,000.

Westin Chosun Sogongdong ☎02/771-0500, ⓦ www.echosunhotel.com. Serious effort has been put into making this the most appealing hotel in central Seoul – an energetic group of knowledgeable staff preside over rooms that eschew the typical Korean concrete blockiness for splashes of lime, plush carpets and curved sofas. Even the bathrooms are graced with modern art, and a free mobile phone will be yours for the duration of your stay. Prices often fall to W250,000 off-season. W460,000.

Myeongdong

Seoul's busy shopping area has a wide range of accommodation, from flophouses to five-star. All are marked on the map, p.61.

Astoria Hotel Namhakdong ☎02/2268-7111. Chungmuro station. Set away from the bustle of central Myeongdong (though still on a main road), the gently decaying *Astoria* has rooms that are acceptable but totally devoid of frills; try to nab one with a view of Namsan to the south. W150,000.

Doulos Gwangsudong ☎02/2266-2244, ⓦ www.douloshotel.com. Jongno 3-ga station. Excellent value, comfy rooms, friendly staff and a convenient location... this mid-range hotel ticks all the boxes, even if it's a little tricky to find: take a few steps south of Jongno and you should be able to make out its sign. There's usually a W20,000 discount if you book online. W100,000.

Ibis Ambassador Myeongdong ☎02/3454-1101, ⓦ www.ibishotel.com. Euljiro 1-ga station. Mid-range hotel right in the centre of Myeongdong, with clean and present-able rooms. Staff make a concerted effort, and are particularly adept at dispensing advice to those fresh off the plane: handy, since the airport bus stops right outside. W190,000.

Pacific Hotel Namsandong ☎02/752-5101. **Myeongdong station.** Excellent value when off-season discounts kick in, this hotel tries its best to look like a five-star, with a wide range of on-site services including a tailor and bakery. Some rooms have views of Namsan or central Myeongdong. W220,000.

PJ Hotel Inhyeondong ☎02/2280-7013. **Euljiro 3-ga station.** This mid-ranger is the only modern link in a bizarre chain of 1960s structures that stretches all the way from Chungmuro to Jongmyo (see p.57). Rooms here are larger than at most competing hotels, and though facilities are as modern as they come, the surrounding area provides a fascinating peek into 1960s Seoul. W140,000.

Sejong Hotel Chungmuro ☎02/773-6000, Ⓦwww.sejong.co.kr. **Myeongdong station.** This large, expensive Myeongdong landmark seems to attract most of the city's Japanese tourists, and is extremely busy for much of the year. Rooms are perfectly adequate, and some have great views of Namsan and its tower. Access to the hotel is easy, since there's an airport limousine bus stop right outside the entrance. W270,000.

Seoul Royal Hotel Myeongdong ☎02/756-1112, Ⓦwww.seoulroyal.co.kr. **Euljiro 3-ga station.** Golden hues and comfy beds make rooms rather appealing at this towering hotel, which rises near the cathedral at the centre of Myeongdong's sprawling shopping district. Rooms are cosy, the grill and buffet bars on the 21st floor are great places to eat, and there are free shuttle buses to and from the airport. W220,000.

🏃 **The Shilla Namsandong** ☎02/2233-3310, Ⓦwww.shilla.net. Tucked away in a quiet area on the eastern access road to Namsan, this hotel is characterized by the traditional style of its rooms and exterior. The lobby and restaurants are a luscious shade of brown, as if they've been dunked in tea, though the common areas can often be a little busy – this is one of Seoul's most popular conference venues. The rooms themselves are five-star quality, if a little overpriced, and feature genuine Joseon-era antiques. W480,000.

Insadong and around

Despite Insadong's status as a tourist magnet, accommodation here is firmly in the cheap-to-midrange bracket – the nearest places with decent tourist facilities are around City Hall, while the best cheapies are listed in the motels section. The three most useful subway stations are Anguk, Jonggak and Jongno 3-ga; on the below can be found on the map on p.55.

Hotel Saerim Gwanhundong ☎02/739-3377. Whatever its titular claims, this is a motel through and through. Some rooms have huge televisions and internet, making it extremely good value for the area. W50,000.

Sunbee Gwanhundong ☎02/730-3451. Tucked into a side-street near Insadonggil, rooms here are moderately sized, quirkily designed and good value; all have internet and large televisions, and staff will bring you free toast in the morning. W50,000.

Itaewon

Given the area's popularity with foreigners, it's somewhat surprising that there aren't that many places to stay in Itaewon; note that some cheaper alternatives have been listed in the motels section. All are a short walk from Itaewon subway station, and unless otherwise stated are marked on the area map, p.88.

Grand Hyatt Hannamdong ☎02/797-1234, Ⓦwww.seoul.grand.hyatt.com. **See map, p.82.** A favourite of visiting dignitaries, this is one of Seoul's top hotels in more ways than one – perched on a hill overlooking Itaewon, almost every room has a fantastic view through floor-to-ceiling windows. There's a fitness centre, an ice rink and squash courts, as well as swimming pools, indoors and out. W390,000.

Hamilton Hotel Itaewondong ☎02/794-0171, Ⓦwww.hamilton.co.kr. More of an Itaewon landmark than a decent place to stay, but countless foreigners do regardless. Despite dated rooms and patchy service, this remains the only real high-end option on the strip, and guests can make use of an outdoor pool in warmer months. W180,000.

IP Boutique Hannamdong ☎02/3702-8000, Ⓦwww.ipboutiquehotel.com. Korea's first genuine stab at the boutique hotel concept, though sadly a little flawed. Rooms have all been individually decorated, with different colour schemes for each floor, and are mercifully a lot better than the nightmarish lobby: something like a giant handbag with a few swing-chairs and medieval statues. W220,000.

Yeouido

Though unlikely to be a venue of choice for the casual visitor, Yeouido has a few hotels to cater to its population of travelling businessmen; they're not near the subway line, but cabs will cost less than W3000 from Yeouinaru station. Both of these recommendations are marked on the map on p.82.

Lexington Hotel Yeouidodong ☎02/6670-7000, ⓦwww.thelexington.co.kr. By far the best hotel on Yeouido island, with stylish communal areas, immaculate rooms and an airport limousine bus stop directly outside. Discounts of thirty percent are not uncommon, and it's easy to wangle free breakfast at all but the busiest times. W240,000.

Hotel Yoido Yeouidodong ☎02/782-0121. Eschews the usual Korean tourist hotel decor for frosted glass in the lobby, zebra-print carpets in the corridors and airy rooms, all of which have computer terminals; some of the doubles have pretty views over the Han. Staff are extremely amiable, and breakfast is free. W130,000.

Gwanjangdong

Though these interconnected hotels are among the best in the country, they're inconveniently located far to the east of town, in a nondescript area near Gwangnaru subway station on subway line 5. From here a cab will cost W2000, or there are free shuttle buses every twenty minutes.

Sheraton Grande Walkerhill Gwanjangdong ☎02/455-5000, ⓦwww.sheratonwalkerhill .co.kr. With scented, plush-carpeted corridors and muted-tone rooms, it's not as showy as the W next door, but the views are rarely as good, but it's immaculately designed nonetheless. There are some wonderful restaurants within the complex (you can also use those in the W), and the

hotel contains the most expensive rooms in the country – up to a colossal W15,000,000 per night. W480,000.

W Seoul Walkerhill Gwanjangdong ☎02/465-2222, ⓦwww.starwoodhotels .com/whotels. The W is the most distinctive hotel in Korea. With artfully designed furniture in the rooms, neon gym rings in the elevators, sharp-suited staff and a loungey beat pulsing through the lobby, every inch of it is achingly trendy – not to everyone's tastes. Particularly popular with Korean honeymooners, rooms range in style – many have their own whirlpool and views over the river – while there's also a gym, a juice bar and a great swimming pool within the complex. On-site restaurants are excellent, as is the *Woo Bar* (see p.129), where the city's *nouveaux riches* come to slurp fifteen-dollar cocktails. W570,000.

Gangnam, Apgujeong and Jamsil

There are a great number of places to stay in Gangnam, mostly lining Bongeunsaro, the road one kilometre north of Gangnam subway station, though there are a few motels closer to the station exits. Apgujeong, Seoul's fashion capital, has surprisingly few places to stay, and those that exist tend to be overpriced.

Blue Pearl Cheongdamdong ☎02/3015-7712. Apgujeong station; see map, p.92. Mid-range hotel that's poor value compared to similar hotels north of the river, but just about acceptable if you have to stay in the Apgujeong area. Try to go for a room with a view of the teeming traffic outside, which can be quite spectacular in the evening; mercifully, double-glazed windows keep out the noise. W230,000.

COEX Intercontinental COEX complex ☎02/3452-2500, ⓦwww.seoul.intercontinental .com. Samseong station; see map, p.92. One of a pair sitting at opposite ends of the COEX mall, this is newer and marginally less expensive than the *Grand*, and though also slightly less inviting it still has high service standards and admirable restaurants. W420,000.

Ellui Cheongdamdong ☎02/574-3535, ⓦwww .ellui.com. Apgujeong station; see map, p.92. Despite being near the centre of Seoul's most affluent and stylish area, this hotel has a pleasing 1970s style. Some rooms overlook the Hangang, and these are the ones to aim for. W220,000.

Grand InterContinental COEX complex ☎02/555-5656, ⓦwww.seoul.intercontinental.com. **Samseong station; see map, p.92.** Designed with exceptional attention to detail, this hotel belies its age with regular overhauls. Rooms are fresh and tastefully decorated in pleasing tones, with modern furniture. Some of the city's best restaurants can be found on the lower floors (see p.119), and guests have access to a gym and indoor swimming pool. W450,000.

Imperial Palace Nonhyeondong ☎02/3440-8000, ⓦwww.imperialpalace.co.kr. **Hakdong station; see map, p.92.** One of the most eye-catching hotels in all Korea. Don't be fooled by the cheesy stylings of the lobby; rooms are almost unbearably opulent, filled with antique lamps, oil paintings and other mementos of the owner's (evidently numerous) trips abroad. Best are the duplex rooms, which allow you to bathe upstairs before climbing down to bed. The only weak point is its rather uninteresting location. W360,000.

JW Marriott Hotel Banpodong ☎02/6282-6262, ⓦwww.marriott.com. **Express Bus Terminal station; see map, p.82.** Though the hotel towers over the express bus terminal, confusing signs make access a little problematic. It proudly claims to have the biggest bathrooms in Korea, though the rooms are otherwise bland, and occasionally patchy service means that they're not really worth the money unless you're doing business around Jamsil, or in cities accessible from the bus terminal. W380,000.

Novotel Ambassador Yeoksamdong ☎02/567-1101, ⓦwww.ambatel.com. **Sinnonhyeon station; see map, p.92.** More of a base for business travellers than tourists, rooms here are accordingly more practical than aesthetically pleasing. There's a health club on site, as well as a buffet restaurant, and the friendly staff will be more than happy to give travel advice. W330,000.

Park Hyatt COEX ☎02/2016-1234, ⓦseoul.park.hyatt.com. **Samseong station; see map, p.92.** First things first: this is Seoul's best hotel. Designed in its entirety by Japanese firm Super Potato, its class will already be evident by the time you've entered the lobby, which is actually on the top floor. Rooms employ an almost Zen-like use of space, and the hewed-granite bathrooms were voted "Asia's best place to be naked" by *Time* magazine. Staff are experts at making themselves available only when needed, and those on a repeat visit will find their preferred room temperature, TV channels and light level all ready and waiting. Bliss. W520,000.

Popgreen Sinsadong ☎02/5446-6237. **Apgujeong station; see map, p.96.** For years a favourite with first-time visitors to Seoul, this hotel is located on trendy Apgujeongno, a mere stroll from dozens of brand-name showrooms. Rooms are a little on the small side, though, and note that many have bathrooms that are visible from the bedroom: better not share with someone you don't know intimately. W140,000.

Richmond Yeoksamdong ☎02/562-2151, ⓦwww.hotel-richmond.co.kr. **Sinnonhyeon station; see map, p.92.** A fantastic budget option in an area whose establishments usually pride themselves on valet parking and other five-star facilities. Rooms come with free internet access and large TVs, and the more expensive ones are at least as big as those in the nearby *Ritz*. W80,000.

Ritz-Carlton Yeoksamdong ☎02/3451-8000, ⓦwww.ritzcarltonseoul.com. **Sinnonhyeon station; see map, p.92.** Service here is as professional as you'd expect from the chain, and no effort has been spared to make this one of Seoul's top hotels. The on-site bakery and restaurants are excellent (including a leafy outdoor area for warmer months), and though the rooms aren't terribly spacious, there are wonderful views from those that face north. W430,000.

Riviera Cheongdamdong ☎02/541-3111, ⓦwww.riviera.co.kr. **Apgujeong station; see map, p.92.** Very convenient for Apgujeong's classy shopping strip, though the twelve-lane road outside is a conduit for traffic rampaging over the Han, rooms are so quiet that you'll barely notice. Ask to be placed in the newer building, which has bigger and airier rooms than those in the old block; some doubles have great views over the river. W270,000.

Teatree Garosugil ☎02/542-9954. **Sinsa station; see map, p.96.** Small, boutique-style hotel that's very good value for a south-of-the-river establishment, especially given its location on fashionable Garosugil. Some ground-floor rooms come with cute mini-gardens, which are ideal places to drain a coffee. W100,000.

Serviced apartments

Seoul has a range of **serviced residences**, which prove particularly popular with its ever-increasing number of business visitors. All have daily rates, though of course there are considerable savings for those staying for a month or more.

Fraser Suites Nagwondong ☏02/6262-8282, ⓦseoul.frasershospitality.com. The plushest residence in Seoul, with rack rates starting at W6,500,000 per month for a single room. Also on site are a gym and swimming pool, as well as a rooftop driving range for golfers. The location, just off Insadonggil, is hard to beat.

Marriott Executive Apartments Yeouidodong ☏02/2090-8000, ⓦwww.marriott.com. A good choice for those who have business to do in Yeouido, with immaculate rooms and a good on-site restaurant. Rates start at around W230,000 per day.

Somerset Suseongdong ☏02/6730-8888, ⓦwww.somerset.com. The venue of choice for long-term expats, thanks to impeccable service and wonderful on-site facilities. Some rooms have views of Gyeongbokgung (see p.43), though you'll be paying a premium; rack rates start at W6,000,000 per month.

8

Eating

With much of the national cuisine alien to most foreign guests, a good place to start may be the **food courts** in department stores and shopping malls, where you can see plastic versions of the dishes. Single travellers may quickly discover that Korean meals are usually for sharing; it's possible to take solace in one of the many cheap **fast food chains** (see below), which are also perfect for those on a budget. Whether you're eating at a snack shack or high-class restaurant, almost all Korean meals come with free water and **side dishes** known as *banchan* (반찬). *Gimchi* and pickled radish are all you'll get at the lower end of the scale, while at more salubrious venues there may be over a dozen plates, largely centred on roots and vegetables.

Seoul's excellent choice of **restaurants** is growing more cosmopolitan with each passing year. They run the full gamut from super-polished establishments in five-star hotels to local eateries where stomachs can be filled for just a few thousand won; even in the cheapest places, you may be surprised by the quality of the food. **Reservations** and tipping are unheard of at all but the classiest places (which tend to tack a ten percent service charge onto the bill), and English-language menus are quite common, though note that romanization is woefully inconsistent. For example, *gimchi jjigae* can be rendered as *kimchi zzigae* and *gimchee chige,* and other versions besides.

Many parts of Seoul have their own particular culinary flavour. Most popular with tourists are the streets around **Insadonggil**, where restaurants serve traditional Korean food in a suitably fitting atmosphere. At the other end of the scale is **Itaewon**, where local restaurants are outnumbered by those serving Indian, Japanese, Thai or Italian food, among others. Student areas such as **Hongdae**, **Sinchon** and **Daehangno** are filled with cheap restaurants, and the establishments of trendy **Apgujeong** cater to the fashionistas.

Fast food

Such is the pace at which Seoulites live their lives that many find it impossible to spare time for a leisurely meal, so it should come as no surprise that their city's streets are packed with **fast food outlets**.

Korean fast food is something of a misnomer: fast it may well be, but the local offerings are far healthier than their western equivalents – you could eat them every day and never get fat. One slight problem for travellers is that few of these cheap places are used to dealing with foreigners, so don't expect English-language menus or service; you'll find a menu reader on p.200.

Dishes are cheaper versions of local staples, and largely revolve around rice or noodles. **Rice dishes** include *bibimbap* (비빔밥), rice topped with a mix of veggies; bubbling broths known as *jjigae* (찌개); and either broiled beef (*bulgogi*; 불고기), spicy squid (*ojingeo*; 오징어) or curry (*kare*; 카레) served on rice (*deop-bap*; 덥밥). Also of note are seaweed-wrapped rice rolls known as *gimbap* (김밥), which come with a wide variety of fillings and can be made to take away. **Noodle dishes** tend to revolve around simple from-the-packet creations called *ramyeon* (라면), though some choose to throw cheese or rice-cake into the mix. **Dumplings** known as *mandu* (만두) are popular with foreigners, either fried (*gun-mandu*; 군만두) or boiled with *gimchi* (김치) or processed meat (*gogi*; 고기) fillings.

Below is a selection of the outlets you're most likely to come across as you explore the city.

Bongchu Jjimdak (봉추찜닭) *Jjimdak* is steamed chicken, mixed with potatoes and other vegetables in a delicious, aromatic stew. A W22,000 serving – one chicken – should be enough for two, and be sure to don one of the bibs provided, as there's bound to be some splashback.

Gimbap Cheonguk (김밥천국) In Seoul street-space terms, this ubiquitous orange-fronted franchise is rivalled only by internet bars and the more prominent convenience store chains. The concept is pretty miraculous – almost all basic Korean meals are served here for around W5000 per dish, and despite the variety on offer you'll usually be eating within minutes of sitting down. They also do *gimbap* from W1500, and these can be made to go: perfect if you're off on a hike. Other similar chains include *Gimbap Nara* and *Jongno Gimbap*; you'll never be more than a minute's walk from one.

Isaac Toast (이삭토스트) Toast, but not as you know it. The Korean variety is made on a huge hot-plate– first your perfectly square bread will be fried and smeared with kiwi jam, then joined by perfect squares of spam and/or fried egg (or even a burger, for those to whom the word "cholesterol" means nothing), and the whole lot injected with two sauces, one spicy and one brown. No, it's not healthy, but it makes a tasty breakfast; prices start at W1500.

Kim Ga Ne (김家네) A slightly more upmarket version of *Gimbap Cheonguk* (see above), serving more or less the same things with a few snazzy "fusion" additions. Most branches have their menu on the walls in pictorial form, handy if you don't speak Korean. Dishes W3000–7000.

Lotteria (롯데리아) Unlike the similarly omnipresent *McDonald's* outlets, at least this is a Korean burger chain, a fact made evident by local takes on the simple Big Mac: witness the delicious *bulgogi* burger (W4500), made with marinated beef (at least in theory), or the meatless *gimchi* one served between two slabs of rice, rather than a bun.

Paris Baguette (파리바게트) & **Tous Les Jours** (뚜레주르) A pair of near-identical bakery chains, whose offerings may satisfy those who require something devoid of spice or rice for breakfast; many branches are also able to whip up a passable coffee. Baked goods start at around W1500, but note that in Korea, even the savoury-looking ones are usually extremely sugary. You'll find branches all over the place; harder to spot is *Paris Croissant*, a slightly more upmarket version, one of which is inside Anguk station near Insadong-gil.

Shimpo Woori Mandoo (심포우리만두) w A good selection of cheap dumplings (*mandu*), as well as a few Korean staple meals, and a few from Japan. Meals from W3000 to W8000.

Yu Ga Ne (유가네) This chain serves tasty barbecued meat, cooked at your table by an apron-wearing attendant. Unlike most barbecue joints, there are dishes for those dining alone, such as the delectable *dakgalbi bokkeumbap*, which is something like a chicken kebab fried up with rice. W10,000 should be enough to get a bellyful.

Street food and market food

Those who favour something more rustic can go for some of Seoul's wide variety of **street food**. Most prevalent are stalls serving *deokbokki* (떡볶이), which consists of rice-cake pieces in a thick, spicy sauce. Rice-cake tends to be a bit

Culinary curiosities

While even "regular" Korean food may be utterly alien to most visitors, there are a few edibles that deserve special attention; you'll find some of the following at restaurants, but street stalls and markets are the best places to go hunting.

Baem soju (뱀 소주) Not strictly a food, but interesting nonetheless – this is regular *soju* with a snake (*baem*) marinating in the bottle, which is said to be extremely healthy, especially for the back muscles. Though many may feel that the bottles would make wonderful souvenirs, particularly with the larger serpents inside, be warned that international customs officials aren't too fond of them.

Beonddegi (번데기) In colder months, stalls selling this local delicacy – silkworm larvae – set up on pavements and riverbanks across the whole country. The smell of these mites boiled up in a broth is so disgusting that it may well breach international law. The treat is also served as bar snacks in many *hof*s, bursting in the mouth to release a grimy juice – perfect drinking game material.

Dak-pal (닭발) So you've learnt the word for "chicken" in Korean (*dak*), spotted it on the menu and ordered a dish. Unfortunately, with this particular meal the suffix means "foot", and that's just what you get – dozens of sauced-up chicken feet on a plate, with not an ounce of meat in sight.

Gaegogi (개 고기) This is dog meat, but let it be known that – contrary to the expectations of many a traveller – it rarely features on Korean menus: you're not going to get it on your plate unless you go to a dedicated restaurant. It's usually served in a soup: *yeongyangtang* and *bosintang* are its most common incarnations.

Pojangmacha (포장마차) Plastic chairs to sit on, tables littered with *soju* bottles, and a cackling *ajumma* serving you food that's still half-alive – these are the delights of the *pojangmacha*, mobile tent-like stalls that congregate on many a Korean street. They're usually distinguishable by their orange, tent-like covering; one good area to find them in Seoul is outside exits three to six of Jongno 3-ga subway station. Just watch out for the octopus tentacles – every year, people die of suffocation when their still-wriggling prey makes a last bid for freedom.

Sundae (순대) Don't let the romanization fool you – this is nothing whatsoever to do with ice cream. In Korea, it's actually a sausage made with intestinal lining, and stuffed with clear noodles. Head to the nearest market to try some.

---

bland and textureless for foreign tastes, so many choose to have battered, refried comestibles known as *twigim* (튀김) thrown into the mix: sweet potato, dumplings and squid are among the items on offer. Wintertime sees similar booths doling out *hoddeok* (호떡), delicious sweet pancakes filled with cinnamon and melted brown sugar. **Markets** such as Namdaemun and Dongdaemun have a wide range of earthy fare available; see the *Seoul Food* colour section for details of a few dishes you may encounter. Also worth a mention are tent-like shacks known as *pojangmacha* (포장마차); see box above for details.

Restaurants

A favourite with foreigners are **barbecue houses** known as *gogijip* (고기집), at which you barbecue pork, beef or chicken at your own table. Emanating from charcoal briquettes or gas burners, the open flames would contravene safety regulations in most western nations, but the sight, sound and smell of the juices fizzing away is one of the richest experiences Korea can throw at you; see the *Seoul Food* insert for more. Most opt for marinated beef known as *galbi*, with a choice of beef (*so-galbi*; 소갈비) or pork (*dwaeji-galbi*; 돼지갈비), or fattier pork belly roll (*samgyeopsal*; 삼겹살). Chicken *galbi* (*dak-galbi*; 닭갈비) is only available at dedicated restaurants, and prepared slightly differently in a large pan. **Vegetarians** often have a hard time in Seoul: very few Koreans make this particular lifestyle choice, and the few meals that do not contain meat are unlikely to be prepared in a meat-free environment. Delicious solace can be found in a couple of Insadong restaurants serving **Buddhist temple food**. In the same area, you'll find a few restaurants specializing in **dynastic cuisine** (*hanjeongsik*; 한정식); a couple of places have taken the traditional concept further, and lay on **royal sets** approximating those once eaten by Joseon-era kings and queens; meat dishes will be included, but most of the meal will be vegetarian in nature. *Bibimbap*, a delicious Korean staple dish of vegetables on rice, can usually be made without meat.

"Fusion" restaurants mixing Korean and western tastes have now become ubiquitous, with the very best now eschewing what has become a *passé* term to serve **neo-Korean** cuisine; see colour section for more information on this trend. For those looking to take knowledge of the local cuisine back home plenty of **cooking classes** are available; see p.31 for details.

The business district

The following are marked on the map on p.61.

Benigni Sinmunno 2-ga ☎02/3210-3351. Gwanghwamun station. A classy Italian restaurant on the ground floor of the Miro Space complex. The menu concentrates on Tuscan specialties, including pasta and risotto dishes (W14,000–16,000), as well as assorted meat steaks for around double the price; another highlight is the baked sea bass with fennel. 11.30am–10pm.

Bulgogi Brothers Myeongdong ☎02/319-3351. Myeongdong station. The barbecuing of raw meat at your table is one of the quintessential Korean experiences, but new arrivals can find it hard to jump straight in at the deep end. This elegant venue is the easiest place to learn the ropes, and the meat is always of exceptional quality. Around W30,000 per person, including side dishes and drinks. 10am–11pm.

Gildeulyeo Jigi (길들여지기) Jeongdong ☎02/319-7083. City Hall station. The name is a quote from the Korean translation of *The Little Prince*, and the decoration here is accordingly esoteric. Diners often call in here on their way out of Chongdong Theatre (see p.134) underneath, to feast on spaghetti or grilled meat. Alternatively, the salmon with herb pepper sauce is particularly recommended. Mains from W20,000. 11am–10pm.

🏃 **Gostiniy Dvor** Daehogil ☎02/2275-7501. Dongdaemun History & Culture Park station. By far the best restaurant in Dongdaemun's curious little Russiatown. Its owners are Uzbek but the food is typical Russian, including meaty mains (W10,000), filling soups (W6000) and delicious salads (W5000). The total lack of any sort of Korean atmosphere (and Korean people) can come as quite a surprise if you've been in Seoul a while: the restaurant's furniture, crockery and decoration are quite unique, and the Russian beer (W5000) goes down nicely. Noon–2am.

Kenzo Ramen Myeongdong. Euljiro 1-ga station. This place serves Japanese *ramen* noodles for W5000 and up. There's no English-language menu but pictures of the dishes should do the trick – *shoyu*, *shio* and *miso* are the most popular, washed down with an Asahi beer. 9.30am–10.30pm.

Kongdu (콩두) Seoul Museum of History ☎02/722-0272. Gwanghwamun station. Located on the ground floor of the history museum (p.62), this high-end restaurant prides itself on neo-Korean cuisine: basic ingredients with a modern twist, such as fish with pumpkin sauce or tofu ice cream. Come in the evening and you'll be able to sample some of their home-made *makkeolli*. (see p.126). 10am–10pm.

🏃 **Korea House** Toegyero ☎02/2266-9101, ⓦwww.koreahouse.or.kr. Chungmuro station. Exquisite is not the word – meals here have been modelled on the court cuisine enjoyed by the kings of the Joseon dynasty. Dinner sets go for W68,000 and up (lunch ones are smaller and cheaper), and are made up of at least fifteen separate components, usually including broiled eel, ginseng in honey, grilled sliced beef and a royal hotpot. For W50,000 extra you'll be able to enjoy a performance of traditional song and dance after dinner. Reservations recommended. Lunch noon–2pm; dinner 5.30–7pm & 7.20–8.50pm.

Myeongdong Gyoja (명동교자) **Myeongdong** ☏02/776-5348. **Myeongdong station.** Everything's W6000 at this wildly popular restaurant, which is often full to the brim with hungry visitors jostling to try some of the famous meat dumplings. Noodle dishes are also available. 10am–10pm.

N Grill Namsan ☏02/3455-9298, ⓦwww .nseoultower.net. Expensive steakhouse perched atop the N Seoul Tower (see p.70). You won't get much change from W100,000 per person, but the steaks are top-class, and there are few better views of Seoul. See p.70 for details of how to get to the top of the mountain. 11am–11pm.

Pierre Gagnaire à Seoul Euljiro ☏02/317-7181, ⓦwww.pierregagnaire.co.kr. **Euljiro 1-ga station.** Molecular gastronomy hits Seoul: the unique creations of Michelin-starred French megachef Pierre Gagnaire are tickling tastebuds atop the otherwise awful *Lotte Hotel*. The menu has a discernable Korean twist, with ingredients such as ginger, sesame leaves and "five-flavoured" *omija* berries letting off little flavour bombs in certain dishes. Lunch menu W130,000, dinner W180,000 and up; reservations essential. Noon–3pm & 5–11pm.

🏃 **Potala Myeongdong. Euljiro 1-ga station.** Run by a Nepali–Korean couple and just downhill from the cathedral, this charmingly decorated second-floor restaurant serves simple specialities from Nepal, Tibet and India. Prices are incredibly reasonable; go in a small group and you should get change from W10,000 per head. One highly recommended dish is the *samosa chat* – three large samosas served with chopped green onion, chickpeas, curry sauce and sour cream (W7000). 11am–11pm.

Sanchaejip (산채집) **Namsan. Myeongdong station.** The most pleasant of a small, slightly overpriced clutch of restaurants near the Namsan Cable Car entrance. Pork cutlet, *bibimbap* (both W7000) and set meals are on the menu – some for cooking at your own table. 10am–9pm.

Taj Myeongdong ☏02/776-0677. **Euljiro 1-ga station.** The best Indian restaurant in Seoul, according to many an expat. You'll be

paying far more than you would for Korean food, but dishes are well made and absolutely delicious. Curries start at W17,000 and dinner sets are around double that, though from noon–3pm on weekdays there are bargain lunch deals for just W10,000. Noon–3pm & 6–10pm.

Woo Rae Oak (우래옥) **Jugyodong** ☏02/2265-0151. **Euljiro 4-ga station.** This meat-house and its elegant, hotel lobby-like atrium have been here since 1946: only one year less than Korea itself. The customer base seems to have changed little in decades, and the sight of septuagenarians munching away in their Sunday best is rather charming. Most are here for the meat (W20,000 or so per head), though they also serve superb *naengmyeon*, cold buckwheat noodles similar to Japanese *soba* (W9000). 11am–10.30pm.

Insadong and around

The following are marked on the Insadong map, p.55; all are within walking distance of Anguk, Jonggak and Jongno 3-ga stations.

Arirang Garden Insadong. Traditional courtyard restaurant set back from Insadonggil, and illuminated in the evenings by fairy lights. The beef *galbi* sets (W24,000) are colossal and will feed two, with a similar pork option for just W11,000. Single diners can try one of the *jjigae* stews (W5000), which come with rice and a few side dishes. 10.30am–9.30pm.

Bärlin Susongdong ☏02/722-5622, ⓦwww .baerlin.co.kr. Those hankering for a bit of bratwurst or sauerkraut should hunt down this upmarket German restaurant in the Somerset complex (see p.110). Schnitzels can be made in three different styles (all around W27,000), the raw beef tartare on rye is delectable (W25,000) and there's herring on the menu – extremely rare in Korea. 11.30am–11.30pm.

🏃 **Baru** (바루) **Gyeonjidong** ☏02/2031-2081, ⓦwww.baru.or.kr. Overlooking Jogyesa temple (see p.58), this is quite simply one of the best places to eat in Seoul, particularly for vegetarians. The huge set meals are consummately prepared approximations of Buddhist temple food, and the balance of colour, texture, shape and taste is beyond reproach. Mung-bean pancakes, acorn jelly, sweet pumpkin tofu and sticky rice with ginkgo nuts are among the dozens of items that may appear on your table. Sets W25,000–50,000; lunch Noon–1.30pm or 1.30–3pm, dinner 6–9pm.

Gogung (고궁) **Gwanhundong** T02/736-3211. Next to a gallery on the basement floor of the Ssamzie complex, the decor here is accordingly quirky, with walls festooned with threads and tie-dye. The food is traditional Korean – best is the *Jeonju bibimbap* (W10,000), a tasty regional take on the Korean staple. 11am–10pm.

Imok De (이목데) **Gwanhundong.** Like *Gogung*, this is located in the Ssamzie complex, but on the roof rather than in the basement. The *bibimbap* (W7000) is perhaps the most delicious of the many Korean staples on offer, and there are pretty views of the building's open-air interior. 11am–10pm.

Janchijip (잔치집) **Gwanhundong.** Tucked away behind Ssamzie, this rambling den is a real jack of Insadong trades – here you can devour traditional Korean food (such as the savoury *pajeon* pancakes; W7000), sup traditional teas (W5000) or get drunk the traditional way with delicious *dongdongju*, a ginseng-infused rice wine. Noon–10pm.

Min's Club Gyeongundong T02/733-2966. This restaurant is a little piece of history. Named after Queen Min (see box, p.45), it was built in the 1930s to house one of her descendants. While the place may look traditionally Korean, this was actually one of the country's earliest "modern" structures, and the first to have a flushing indoor toilet. The menu is largely French, though Korean dishes such as barbecued beef and pumpkin congee also make an appearance; figure on around W50,000 per head. In addition, the wine list one of the best in Seoul. Noon–2.30pm & 6–11.30pm.

The Place Sinmunno. Swanky Western-oriented place popular with staff from the local banks and embassies. Pasta meals go from W8000, while the mini pizzas (W5000) are good for something light. Waffles and cakes are available for dessert, and there are plenty of coffee styles to choose from. 8.30am–10pm.

Sagwa Namu (사과나무) **Insadong.** Something different in traditional Insadong: this cosy hideaway serves plates of tasty bangers and mash, which you can eat in the courtyard under the apple trees the place is named after. Portions (W13,000) are on the small

side, but so tasty you won't be grumbling. 11am–10.30pm.

Sanchon (산촌) **Insadong** T02/735-0312. One of the most famous restaurants in the area, serving a slightly modern take on Buddhist temple food: great for vegetarians. The set meals (W20,000–35,000) are prepared with consummate attention, and the temple-styled interior makes this a lovely place to eat. 11.30am–10pm.

Top Cloud Jongno Tower T02/2230-3000, W www.topcloud.co.kr. Though the tower itself is only 24 storeys high, this restaurant contrives to be on the 33rd floor – it's hoisted high on a barricade of steel. The views are tremendous, of course, and are almost equalled by the largely French food on offer; the duck dishes are particularly recommended, as is tiramisu for dessert. Lunch noon–2.30pm (sets from W50,000), dinner 6–10pm (from W72,000).

Northern Seoul

The following are marked on the Northern Seoul map, p.72. None is particularly close to a subway station; see p.71 and p.77 for travel information.

Art for Life Buamdong T02/3217-9364. The hustle and bustle of Seoul feels very far away at this artsy, out-of-the-way lair. There are pleasingly authentic pizza and pasta meals (W20,000 plus), and on Saturday evenings feature live jazz from some of Seoul's top musicians. 11.30am–11pm.

Samcheonggak (삼청각) **Seongbukdong** T02/765-3700. This mountainside venue was once a *gisaeng* house of some repute (see box, p.77), and used by luminaries such as president Park Chung-hee as a secluded place of pleasure. It has since been converted into a traditionally styled restaurant serving a take on Korean royal cuisine, and still hosts occasional shows of traditional song and dance. Set meals W50,000–150,000. 10am–11pm.

Sonmandoo (손만두) **Buamdong** T02/379-2648. Dumplings known as *mandu* are a cheap Korean staple, but unlike the regular processed fare, the handmade versions made here are utterly delectable, filled with chunks of quality beef, radish, shitake mushrooms and the like. The setting is just as pleasant, a minimalist space with mountain views. Dishes from W10,000. 10am–10pm.

North of Anguk Station

The following are marked on the Palace district map, p.44, and best accessed via Anguk subway station.

🏃 **Cheonjin Pocha** (천진포차) **Sogyeok-dong.** Almost permanently packed, this small, steamy restaurant is so popular that you may have to take a number and wait outside while the Chinese chef doles out portion after portion of his famed Tianjin dumplings to hungry diners. Around W4000 per meal. 10am–10pm.

🏃 **Goongyeon** (궁연) **Gahoedong**
☎02/3673-1104, ⊛www.goongyeon.com.
Food literally fit for a king: the head chef at this restaurant is the only person schooled in the art of Korean court cuisine, and has been handed the singularly unromantic title of National Intangible Cultural Asset #38. The immaculately designed set menus showcase a subtlety and balance largely lost in modern Korean cuisine, and cost W28,000–130,000: a small price to pay for what may well be the best food in Seoul. In warmer months, you can eat in the garden area outside. 11am–10pm.

Hyangnamu (향나무) **Samcheongdong.** An airy second-floor *galbi* joint overlooking Samcheongdonggil, the most popular dish here is *moksal-sogeumgui* (W6000 per portion): this is pork from pigs bred on a special diet, which you get to fry yourself at the table and wrap in leaves before chowing down. There's also good tofu *jjigae* – a spicy broth – for just W5000. 10.30am–10pm.

Meokswi Donna (먹쉬돈나) **Angukdong.** In Korea, when places get popular, they get really popular – there's often a queue of people outside this plain-looking restaurant, waiting to get their teeth around some *deokbokki*. This rice-cake smothered in a red-hot sauce is available all over the country, but *Meokswi* was the first place to experiment with ingredients such as seafood, cheese and *bulgogi*. Dishes W3000 and up. 11am–9pm.

The Restaurant Sogyeokdong ☎02/735-8441. Connected to the excellent Kukje Gallery (see p.132), and within easy walking distance of Gyeongbokgung, this Italian restaurant is perfectly placed for those sightseeing in the area. Pasta dishes go for W15,000 and up, while for visitors just needing a snack there are desserts and baked goods on offer – the tiramisu is heavenly – as well as good coffee. 10.30am–10.30pm.

🏃 **Second Best Place in Seoul Samcheong-dong.** A rarity on cosmopolitan and fast-changing Samcheongdonggil, in that it has not only been here for decades, but serves traditional fare. The menu is short and sweet, with an assortment of Korean teas and snacks. Best is the *patjuk* (W4000), something like a viscous red bean fondue containing all manner of ingredients from cinnamon to chestnut chunks. 10am–9pm.

Solmoe Maeul (솔뫼마을) **Samcheongdong.** A sure-fire contender for the "Best Side Dishes in Seoul" award, should it ever come into being – you'll be in danger of filling up before the main course arrives. Traditional Korean sets (*jeongsik*) go from W18,000 per person, while *ssambap* meals (consisting of side dishes, with leaves to wrap them in) are only marginally smaller and cost W8000. Try to nab one of the window tables if you don't fancy sitting Korean-style on the floor. It's on the second floor, overlooking Samcheong-donggil. 10am–10pm.

Wood & Brick Gahoedong. This classy restaurant-cum-deli dishes out scrump-tious Italian food from W20,000 a dish, though many are here to take advantage of the excellent wine menu, or the produce of the in-house bakery or deli counter. Lunch sets go for W35,000 and up, and typically feature pasta or grilled meat, as well as a choice of cake. Noon–10pm.

Hongdae

The following are marked on the Hongdae map, p.84, and best accessed via Sangsu subway station.

Jopok Deokbokki (조폭떡볶이) **Seogyodong.** A dish of rice-cakes in spicy sauce, *deokbokki* is available at street-stands all across the city, though this small sit-down restaurant is by far the most famous venue, since its staff are rumoured to be connected to the local mafia (*jopok*). Whether fact or fib, the food's pretty good, especially if you have a few refried treats (*twigim*) thrown on top: just point at what you'd like. W2000 for four *twigim*. Opening times vary; usually 2pm–2am.

🏃 **Oyori Seogyodong** ☎02/332-5525. One has to admire the thinking behind this restaurant, which not only gives employment to single mothers from other Asian countries, but uses the profit to send their children to kindergarten. The various nationalities working here take it in turns to enrich the menu, which contains Malaysian stir-fries, Japanese noodles, Burmese curry and Russian desserts. Benevolence aside, the food is excellent, and the setting surprisingly stylish thanks to connections with a local art society. 11am–11pm.

Samgeori Pocha (삼거리포차) **Seogyodong.**
Nights out in Hongdae usually end late, meaning that this rustic raw fish restaurant can be heaving with drunken students at 6am: it's an integral part of the nightlife scene, and one of the most atmospheric places to be of a weekend. Having a bit of *soju* for Dutch courage makes it easier to handle the house speciality, *sannakji* (W15,000, feeds two) – this is chopped-up baby octopus that, while not exactly alive, is so fresh that it's still writhing on your plate when served. Open till late.

Itaewon

The following are marked on the Itaewon map, p.88, and with the exception of *Passion 5* are best accessed via Itaewon subway station.

Above Itaewondong ☏02/749-0717. The mainly Korean customer base makes this stylish, dimly lit restaurant a rather refreshing change in foreigner-heavy Itaewon. The menu is extremely varied, and contains dishes such as Spanish omelette, Belgian mussels (W20,000 or so) and Polish cucumber salad, while there's a special evening dinner menu to complement the excellent wine list. 11am–2am.

Ashoka Itaewondong ☏02/792-0117.
Capturing the feel of an English curry-house perfectly, this has long been a favourite with hungry expats, and sits on the third floor of the *Hamilton Hotel*. Tandoori meals are still the Rajasthani owner's pride and joy, but local competition for the curry dollar has seen renewed effort put into all the dishes. There's also a daily buffet lunch (W15,000). Noon–3pm & 6–10.30pm.

Buddha's Belly Itaewondong ☏02/796-9330. All of your favourite Thai dishes from green curry and *pad thai* to chicken coconut soup (all around W14,000) are lovingly prepared at this spick-and-span restaurant, and

served in a wonderfully laid-back atmosphere – the comfy seating will tempt you to stay on for a glass of wine or two. 11am–1am.

Gecko's Garden Itaewondong ☏02/790-0540. Not to be confused with *Gecko's Terrace*, an expat bar just down the way, this rambling restaurant is fenced off from Itaewon by a line of trees, and feels a world removed from smoky Seoul. The silver bistro tables impart a vaguely European air to the courtyard and the menu follows suit with pastas and risottos (from W17,000), while on weekends chefs will grill your choice of meat on an open barbecue. Noon–midnight.

La Plancha Itaewondong ☏02/790-0063.
There's meat, meat and more meat on the menu at this Spanish restaurant, whose walls have been painted a pretty Andalucian pink. Beefy *combos* are W16,000 per person, while the same amount will buy four plates of tapas. It's located at the western end of the restaurant-filled road that runs behind the *Hamilton Hotel*. 11am–11pm.

🏃 **Le Saint-Ex** Itaewondong ☏02/795-2465. Check out the blackboard for the daily specials at this French bistro; which generally include steaks (W27,000) and hearty salads. Teasingly set out near the exit, the desserts are hard to resist, and there's a good wine list. Lunch noon–3pm; dinner 6pm–midnight (last orders 9.30pm).

🏃 **Macaroni Market** Hannamdong ☏02/749-9181. This swanky second-floor Italian restaurant has all bases covered. In the morning, try something from the deli counter, and wash it down with a latte. Coming for lunch? Head to a windowside table for a sandwich or salad. Dinner instead? Move a little further around and order a pasta or steak (W15,000 –30,000), served with bread, olive oil and balsamic vinegar. The popping of wine corks heralds the arrival of evening, and customers who fancy a dance can head to *Function*, an adjoining bar (see p.128). 10am–11pm.

OK Kitchen Itaewondong ☏02/797-6420. All of the veggies and most of the meat used in this restaurant come from the Okinawan chef's own patch of farmland, located far away near the North Korean border. A mix of French, Japanese and Korean food, dishes change both with the season and the whim of the chef: in the mornings, he can often be seen at Noryangjin fish market (see p.87) piecing together components for the perfect meal. Three-course lunch sets are a bargain at W20,000, while mains cost around the same for dinner. Noon–3pm & 5–9pm.

Passion 5 Hannamdong ☎02/2071-9505. **Hangangjin station.** Precious few places in Seoul can whip up a decent Eggs Benedict, which makes this venue a valuable addition to Itaewon's culinary scene. Salads, pasta and an international range of coffees are also on the menu, with prices around W15,000 per person. The restaurant sits atop a superb bakery, from which customers are welcome to bring up a few treats for dessert. 9am–9pm.

The Wolfhound Itaewondong ☎02/749-7971, Ⓦwolfhoundpub.com. This may be an Irish pub, but it's also notable for an authentic selection of pub grub, including burgers, fish & chips and shepherd's pie. Best, however, are the fried breakfasts, which cost from W9000 including a tea or coffee, and slide down quite nicely. Open from Noon.

Zelen Itaewondong ☎02/749-0600. Itaewon now has a Bulgarian restaurant, tangible proof of the area's successful graduation from safe Italian and Indian fare. Bulgarian cuisine is one of the culinary world's best kept secrets, taking hearty meat and veg dishes from the Slavic lands to the west, and fusing them with kebabs and breads from the Turkic east; meals here are well prepared, though best may be the gigantic "couple" *shashlik* kebab (W34,000). 11am–3pm & 6–11pm.

Gangnam

Unless otherwise stated, the following are marked on the Southern Seoul map, p.92.

Arte Banpodong ☎02/532-0990. **Express Bus Terminal station.** Seoul's quirky little Frenchtown has – surprisingly – a fair share of Italian restaurants, of which this is the best. They're proud of their sautéed salmon with mushrooms, the steaks are succulent and spaghetti dishes are good value at W17,000. Noon–9pm.

🏃 **Asian Live COEX complex** ☎02/3130-8620. **Samseong station.** Despite the rather tacky-sounding name, this is one of the city's top hotel restaurants, sitting pretty on the second floor of the *COEX InterContinental*

(p.108). The kitchens are visible from many tables, meaning that you get to see the chefs whipping up what will be invariably excellent Indian, Chinese, Japanese or Korean food – set meals are usually the best value, starting at around W70,000 per person. 11.30am–2.30pm & 5.30–10pm.

La Trouvaille Banpodong ☎02/534-0255. **Express Bus Terminal station.** The best restaurant in Seorae Maeul (see p.94), *La Trouvaille* has a pleasingly authentic European atmosphere. Friendly hosts dish out cuisine such as duck breast with gnocchi in a raspberry sauce – you'd have to look hard to find better-prepared food. Dishes W30,000 and up. Noon–9pm.

Marco Polo COEX complex ☎02/559-7620. **Samseong station.** Seoul's top restaurant – in a literal sense, at least, sitting as it does on the fifty-second floor of the World Trade Center, which rises from the centre of COEX. It's split into two halves: one serving Mediterranean cuisine and one Chinese, with prices slightly cheaper at the former. Either way, you'll be paying about W40,000 for lunch, and double that for dinner. Views are, of course, superb. 11.30am–1am, Sunday to 11.30pm.

🏃 **Pasha Seochodong** ☎02/593-8484. **Gangnam station.** Style and substance mix perfectly at this Turkish kebab house, whose attractive interior sets it apart from its dowdier counterparts in Itaewon. The meals (generally W15,000) are filling, with the familiar *döner* and *köfte* dishes supplemented by more unusual fish meals. *Pide* – a kind of Turkish pizza – is best washed down with some sour *ayran* yoghurt. Noon–midnight.

Apgujeong

The following are marked on the Apgujeong map, p.96, and just about within walking distance (or a W3000 taxi ride) of Apgujeong subway station.

Ciné de Chef Sinsadong ☎02/3446-0541. Immaculate Italian restaurant located in the bowels of the CGV cinema complex. The place is only really for couples, since dinner sets (from W70,000 per head, and usually including soup, a steak or pasta dish and dessert) include tickets to a private movie theatre, featuring just 30 comfy chairs laid out in couple formation; here you can watch the latest Hollywood blockbuster over a bottle of wine. 3–11pm.

Gorilla in the Kitchen Sinsadong ☎02/3442-1688. Glass and chrome interior, all-white furniture and surgical-uniformed waitresses – this place has an air of arty European about it, but the calorie listings will serve as a reminder that you are, indeed, in waistline-conscious Apgujeong. The food here is innovative and delicious, with temptations including turkey steak with berry sauce, rice-covered tofu salad in sesame dressing, and peppered chicken breast on black rice, but prices aren't extortionate, and lunch sets go as low as W27,000. 11am–11pm.

In New York Sinsadong ☎02/541-1373. A great place to head for a romantic dinner: this restaurant has just the one table, which makes it a popular place for anniversaries or marriage proposals. Those lucky enough to have made a reservation will be feasting on Italian food, and have their choice of "flower course": a bouquet of roses, roses served with a cake, or rose petals covering the floor. Usually W150,000 per head; open by reservation only.

Jung Sikdang (정식당) Sinsadong ☎02/517-4654, ⊛www.jungsikdang.com. Another purveyor of neo-Korean cuisine, this restaurant had to relocate in 2009 due to an escalation in popularity. Korean ingredients are prepared with French techniques and a few non-native herbs and veggies, and the result is rather mouth-watering: the prawn salad is recommended, served with melon balls on wafer-thin lime jelly. Figure on at least W60,000 per head for a meal. Noon–4pm & 6pm–late; Sun lunch only.

🏃 **Palais de Gaumont** Cheongdamdong ☎02/546-8877. A firm favourite with local fashionistas, this may well be the most visually appealing restaurant in the whole country. Gigantic angled mirrors reflect the light of a dozen large chandeliers, while floor-to-ceiling windows bring the outdoor maple trees into the fray. The food is superbly crafted Parisian fare, though it doesn't come cheap – set meals start at W100,000 per head. Noon–3pm & 6–10pm.

Seventy Four Cheongdamdong ☎02/542-7412. Affiliated to Lound, one of Seoul's best cocktail bars (see p.129), this rambling venue serves up excellent brunches and light meals (from W20,000). Come early to grab a window seat, and watch bag-laden shoppers trooping up and down one of the most fashionable streets in the country. 10am–1am.

🏃 **Sushi Chohi** Sinsadong ☎02/545-8422. Sushi fans will be in their element at this pine-lined restaurant, overlooking Dosan Park. Absolutely no concessions are made regarding the fish or its preparation: the blades and chopping boards cost upwards of $1000 each, while each fish is selected from the best possible place, whether it be southwestern Korea or northern Japan. The head chef speaks English, and if you're seated at the main bar he will be happy to discourse on the merits of each creature as he performs his magic upon them. Sets from W50,000. 11am–10pm.

Tutto Bene Cheongdamdong ☎02/546-1489. Connected by walkway to *Palais de Gaumont* (see opposite) and under the same ownership, this serves Italian dishes and is slightly cheaper than its neighbour. Again, the setting is utterly gorgeous, its Orient Express-like wooden panelling offset by amber and honey-yellow lighting, and the scent of freshly cut flowers mingling with the creations of the chef. Pasta dishes are most popular (W25,000 and up), but don't overlook the seafood menu – sourced from remote islands off Korea's west coast, the oysters are superb. Noon–Midnight.

🏃 **Wooriga** (우리가) Sinsadong ☎02/3442-2288. Some meals are presented so beautifully that it seems a sin to destroy them, and that's certainly the case at this sparsely decorated neo-Korean hideaway. Whether you're here for lunch (sets from W40,000) or dinner (from W100,000), each dish is served as a work of art, and even the sweets and *omija* tea (see p.123) to finish provide gentle flavour explosions. Superb. Open by reservation only.

Cafés

Seoul's **café** society has come a long way since the turn of the millennium. Back then it was tough to find anything but repulsive brews infused with hazelnut, but now good coffee is available on almost every corner, at almost any hour. There are a number of major chains knocking around, including *Pascucci*, *Starbucks* and *The Coffee Bean and Tea Leaf*. In theory, all have **wi-fi access**, but you may need a Korean ID number to get online; with no such identity restrictions and power sockets aplenty, branches of *Tom & Toms* are best for the internet-hungry, though the coffee itself is poor. Far more interesting for the visitor are the thousands of privately run ventures, which reach heights of quirky individuality around Hongdae and Samcheongdong. **Prices** tend to be W3000–5000 per cup, though you can usually double this south of the river. There are also a number of cafés on the bridges crossing the Hangang itself. Opening hours for cafés are generally 9am to 11pm.

Bau House Seogyodong. Sangsu station. See Hongdae map, p.84. Koreans are more famed abroad for eating dogs than owning them, but this café should show where the balance lies these days. Over a dozen cuddly pooches are on hand to greet customers, who are encouraged to bring their own dogs along. The coffee's good too, but in such a bizarre atmosphere you may barely notice the taste.

Bizeun (비쥰) Insadong. Anguk station. See Insadong map, p.55. Waffles and ice cream are the regular snacks in Korean cafés, but here you'll be able to chow down on something more traditional: sweet rice-cakes, known as *ddeok*, which come in a wonderful kaleidoscope of colours, with flavours running the gamut from pumpkin to black sesame.

Cafe aA Seogyodong. Sangsu station. See Hongdae map, p.84. Several things set this place apart from the regular Korean café. For a start, there's the huge, church-like front door, and a ceiling at least three times higher than the national average. Most notable, however, is a range of chairs imported from Europe; the upstairs floor functions as a sort of furniture museum, featuring examples from luminaries such as Jean Prouvé and Salvador Dalí. Art aside, the coffee here is excellent, as are the various cakes.

Café Yeon Samcheongdong. Anguk station. See Palace district map, p.44. Set around a tiny traditional courtyard on a hillside above trendy Samcheongdonggil, this café's relaxed vibe will doubtless appeal to backpackers. Vietnamese coffee, hydrangea tea and banana lassi are on the drinks list, and food is also available.

Ceci Cela Sinsadong. Apgujeong station. See Apgujeong map, p.96. An Apgujeong institution, this is permanently full of young, fashionable females somehow keeping their waistlines intact while chowing down waffles, panini or slabs of cheesecake. Coffees and vitamin juices are also available, as are thick milkshakes.

Club Espresso Buamdong. See Northern Seoul map, p.72. If you're living in Seoul, this is where to buy your beans. The range of single-plantation Java is huge and truly global, from Zambian Munama Ndola to Brazilian Santo Antonio, and the pine interior is a pleasant place to compare and contrast a few samples.

Hermès Sinsadong. Apgujeong station. See Apgujeong map, p.96. The Hermès flagship store has a café discreetly tucked away on the basement level, and W10,000 will be enough to get you coffee. All cutlery, cups and glasses – plus the tables and chairs – are Hermès originals, and a fair proportion of the customers are local celebrities. There's no cheaper way to buy your way into high society, but dress smartly.

Kring Daechidong. Samseong station. See Southern Seoul map, p.92. This superbly designed artistic complex (see p.95) features a space-age café, where there's a pay-what-you-like policy for the uniformly excellent coffees.

The Lounge Daechidong. Samseong station. See Southern Seoul map, p.92. Sitting atop the *Park Hyatt* (p.109) alongside the infinity pool of the hotel's fitness centre, this is a superb place for a coffee or light snack. Better still are a range of smoothies designed by David Beckham's nutritionist, Patricia Teixeira: well worth the W15,000 splurge.

Millimeter Milligram Angukdong. Anguk station. See Insadong map, p.55. Also known as MMMG, Millimeter Milligram are a local design team producing arty stationery, postcards and other such items. This is the best place to buy their products –

even the cup your coffee's served in will be available for sale.

O'Sulloc Teahouse Myeongdong ☎ 02/774-5460. **Euljiro 1-ga station.** O'Sulloc is Korea's largest producer of green tea, but don't let that fool you into thinking that people come to their flagship tearoom to drink the stuff. Instead, this is a café and dessert bar *par excellence*, since the precious leaves have been blended into tiramisu, ice cream, lattes and chocolates (all W5000 or so). There's another branch on Insadonggil. 9am–11pm.

Rosen Cavalier Sinsadong. Apgujeong station. See Apgujeong map, p.96. Decked out like a 1930s Viennese café, right down to the starched shirt of the waiter, the delicious cakes on offer. *Rosen's* refined atmosphere is further enhanced by the

tunes humming across from the classical music shop next door.

Sanmotungi (산모퉁기) **Buamdong. See Northern Seoul map, p.72.** Made famous by its use as a set in Korean drama *The Coffee Prince*, this remote coffee house is worth a visit for the fresh air and mountain views on offer from its upper level.

🏃 **W.e. Off Garosugil. Sinsa station. See Apgujeong map, p.96.** At last, a place willing to shun the American café norms and inject a rare bit of Korean culture. Here you can take your pick of quirky lattes such as ginseng, sweet pumpkin or green tea; those who fancy a little something extra can go for black sesame pudding, or delicious pancakes known as *hoddeok*, filled with cinnamon and burnt brown sugar, and served with Haagen-Dazs ice cream.

Tearooms

Insadonggil and its surrounding alleyways are studded with **tearooms**, typically decorated in a traditional style and therefore much in keeping with the area. You'll be paying W5000 or more for a cup, but most people come away feeling that they've got value for money – these are high-quality products made with natural ingredients, and are likely to come with a small plate of traditional Korean sweets. Some of the teas available are detailed in the box opposite. With the exception of *Suyeon Sanbang*, all the places listed below are marked on the Insadong map, p.55, and within walking distance of Anguk, Jonggak and Jongno 3-ga stations. All are open from around 9am–9pm.

Cha Sarang (차사랑) Swankier and more polished than others in the area, this multi-floor tearoom nevertheless manages to retain a warm, traditional style. Teas go from W5500.

Dawon (다원) Located in the grounds of the *Kyung-In Museum of Fine Art* (see p.132), in warm weather you can sit outside in the courtyard, while inside you'll find traditionally styled rooms where guests are encouraged to add their musings to the graffiti-filled walls. Teas from W6000 are on the menu, alongside information about their purported health benefits.

Hue (휴) With an exterior seemingly fashioned from broken tiles, this looks a little like a Korean temple roof that has fallen down and been compressed into four floors of tearoom. Inside, you'll find interesting varieties such as medicinal herb and pomegranate, as well as a number of fruit juices and shakes. There's a great view from the fifth-floor terrace.

Sarangbang (사랑방) On the second floor of an unassuming building west of Insadonggil, this small tearoom is run by a Korean man and his Japanese wife, a friendly pair who are full of local information and money-saving tips.

🏃 **Suyeon Sanbang** (수연산방) **Sogyeok-dong. See Northern Seoul map, p.72.** Though a little out of the way and hard to find, this secluded *hanok* tearoom is highly recommended for those looking for a piece of old-world Seoul. Built in the 1930s, it exudes the charm of a bygone age, turning down the volume button of modern Seoul to leave only the sounds of bird chatter and running water.

Su Yo II (수요일) Built in a similar style to *Cha Sarang* across the road, though here the opportunity to see and be seen on the balconies overlooking Insadonggil pushes prices a little higher. In addition to the Korean options, they also offer Earl Grey, Darjeeling and other more familiar teas.

Korean teas

Tea is no longer the national drink in this coffee-crazed country, which is a tremendous shame considering the wonderful concoctions available here. The following are particularly recommended:

Bori Cha (보리차) This barley tea is served with meals at many Korean restaurants, and is replenishable at no extra cost.

Daechu Cha (대추차) Apparently good for relieving muscle pain, this warming tea is made from the jujube, a type of oriental date.

Insam Cha (인삼차) Korea is the world's largest producer of ginseng, so it's no surprise to find that they make tea from the stuff. This hugely healthy drink is also available in powdered form at convenience stores, and many hotel lobbies.

Maesil Cha (매실차) Tea made from the Korean plum, and usually very sugary. Many Koreans make the stuff at home, and an alcoholic variety is available at most convenience stores.

Nok Cha (녹차) Korea's version of green tea, usually grown on the south coast or Jeju island, and available in many different varieties.

Omija Cha (오미자차) Shocking pink in colour, this tangy tea is made from the *omija* berry, whose name literally means "five tastes". Particularly good served cold as a refreshing summer drink.

Saenggang Cha (생강차) Made from ginger root, this throat-warming tea tastes just like a Chinese pharmacy smells, and is perfect for chasing away coughs or colds. Not to everyone's tastes, though for others it's the best of the bunch.

Yuja Cha (유자차) A citrus tea usually made with honey, and perfect if you've got a cold coming on. Unlike most other teas listed here, this one's pretty easy to make yourself – jars of condensed *yuja cha* are available in any convenience store, so all you'll need is hot water.

Yetchatjip (옛찻집) Though a little hard to find, this small upstairs tearoom is well worth hunting out, since it's quite simply one of the most pleasant spots in Seoul. The comfy, soft-lit setting is agreeable, but it's the team of amiable finches who happily chirp their way from wall to wall, occasionally stopping by to tilt a curious head at the guests that make this place so special. The tea's not bad, either.

Self-catering

Eating out is such good value for money that there's precious little need to make your own meals – even those staying at the cheapest guesthouses tend to eat out each day of their stay. In addition, 24-hour convenience stores such as 7-Eleven, Family Mart and Buy the Way are ubiquitous, all carrying simple foodstuffs such as sandwiches (₩1500 and up), instant noodles (from ₩800), crisps and chocolate bars; all have free hot water for making noodles, and chairs to sit on while you're eating. Noodles aside, these items are all good hiking fare, though Koreans like to bring along a roll or two of *gimbap* from one of the fast food chains. Smoke from **barbecues** blankets the banks of the Hangang on summer evenings; you'll likely be able to join a party of friendly locals without too much difficulty, but if you fancy doing it yourself disposable barbecue sets (and chopsticks) are available from convenience stores, and meat from your nearest supermarket.

Other than meat, Korean supermarkets (슈퍼; *syupeo*) are good for basics such as fruit, vegetables and salad ingredients, as are the many open-air markets (시장;

shijang); your accommodation will be able to point you to the nearest one. Also note that non-native **fruit** can be almost absurdly expensive in Korea: W20,000 is a bit steep for a mango.

Western goodies can be tricky to find, with cheese at the top of many an expat's wish list. For these, it's best to head to one of the major hypermarkets such as *Lotte*, *E-Mart* and *Carrefour*. Each has a number of huge branches, but these tend to be out in the suburbs, and few are conveniently placed for foreign travellers; one Lotte store can be found in the basement of the *Lotte Hotel*, which has been marked on the Business district map, p.61.

9

Drinking and nightlife

C lubs pumping out techno, trance and hip-hop to wiggling masses; loungey subterranean lairs filled with hookah smoke and philosophical conversation; noisy live jazz and rock joints; neon-tinged cocktail bars in the bowels of five-star hotels: after a lengthy gestation, Seoul's nightlife scene is finally reaching the latter stages of development. It wasn't so long ago that drinking in Seoul was pretty much a male-only affair, taking place in restaurants or at a "hof", the ubiquitous faux-Western bars that, though still winning the battle for street-space, are increasingly being replaced by more genuinely imported ideas. That said, there's a pleasingly wide range of local elements that can be factored into a night out: Korean friends are likely to drag you before long into a **noraebang** singing room to belt out your favourite songs amid a cacophony of tambourines and castanets, while couples can end the night cuddled up in a DVD room (see box, p.85).

Bars and clubs

Koreans love going out, whether it's with family, colleagues, social acquaintances or old study friends, making Seoul a truly 24-hour city – day and night, year-round, its streets are a thrilling merry-go-round of noise, which ramps up as evening approaches, and stays at a maximum until the early hours. Each area of Seoul has its own particular flavour, with **Hongdae** by far the busiest. Its streets are saturated with bars, clubs and restaurants, and full every day of the week from early evening on. Towards midnight the crowds are swelled further with Seoul's clubber population, who get on the last subway services of the day to Hongdae, party all night, then slink off home as dawn breaks. Almost as busy at the weekend is **Itaewon**, which has some of the best bars, clubs and restaurants in the capital. It has long been a popular watering hole for American soldiers from the nearby army base; this has resulted in a mass of "sexy bars" (expensive venues where the bar-girls wear bikinis, hot-pants and the like, and the customers pay for their company) and brothels, many lining the upward slope termed "Hooker Hill". The side-street leading from this ("Homo Hill") has become the most popular **gay** area in the whole country, with some excellent bars catering to Seoul's ever-growing pink community; see p.130 for details. Also worth mentioning are **Sinchon**, one subway stop from Hongdae and full of cheap yet interesting bars; student **Daehangno**, which is busy every evening (though most drift towards Hongdae as midnight approaches); as well as a few relaxing places to wine and dine in Samcheongdong. South of the river, **Gangnam** has a couple of good clubs, and there are trendy bars aplenty in nearby **Apgujeong**. Entry fees only apply at major clubs and live music bars:

The "proper" Korean night out has long followed the same format, one that entwines food, drink and entertainment. The venue for stage one (*il-cha*) is the **restaurant**, where a meal is chased down with copious shots of *soju*. This is followed by stage two (*i-cha*), a visit to a **bar**; here priorities switch from food to drink, and beers are followed with snacks (usually large dishes intended for groups). Those still able to walk then continue to stage three (*sam-cha*), the **entertainment** component of the night, which usually involves a trip to a *noraebang* room for a sing-along (see p.136), and yet more drinks. Stages four, five and beyond certainly exist, but few participants have ever remembered them clearly.

Though Koreans largely favour beer and imported drinks, the country has more than a few superb **local hooches**, many of which go down very well indeed with the few foreigners lucky enough to learn about them.

Baekseju (백세주) A nutty, whisky-coloured concoction, about the same strength as wine. Its name means "one-hundred-year alcohol", on account of healthy ingredients including ginseng and medicinal herbs. Surely the tastiest path towards becoming a centenarian, *baekseju* is available at all convenience stores (W3600) and many barbecue houses (W6000 or so), though bar-restaurant chain *Baekseju Maeul* (p.128) is the most entertaining place to get your first hit.

Bokbunjaju (복분자주) Made with black raspberries, this sweet, fruity drink is somewhat similar to sugary, low-grade port. Available at all convenience stores (W6500), though those off on a mountain hike in late summer may be lucky enough to try some freshly made fare: it's sold by farmers at makeshift stalls.

Dongdongju (동동주) Very similar to *makkeolli*, *dongdongju* is a little heavier taste-wise, and since it can only be served fresh you'll have to head to a specialist place for a try. The restaurants most likely to have *dongdongju* are those also serving savoury pancakes known as *pajeon*; these establishments are usually rustic affairs decked out with Korean bric-a-brac, and serving *dongdongju* in large wooden bowls (W8000), to be doled out into smaller versions of the same. A word of warning: many foreigners have "hit the wall" on their first dabble, suddenly finding themselves floored by this deceptively quaffable drink.

Maehwasu (매화수) Similar to *baekseju* in colour, strength and price, this is made with the blossom of the *maesil*, a type of Korean plum, and some bottles come with said fruit steeping inside.

Makkeolli (막걸리) Usually around 8 percent alcohol by volume, this milky rice-wine was seen as grandad fuel for years, but a recent shift back towards Korean tradition has made its popularity go through the roof. The stuff is now sold in upscale bars such as *Chin Chin* (see opposite), and preliminary attempts have been made towards its marketing abroad. Interestingly, although it's the most expensive of Korea's alcohols to make, it's actually the cheapest to buy, since its centuries-old heritage has afforded it tax-exempt status. W1500 in a convenience store, W3000 in a barbecue house.

Soju (소주) The national drink, for better or worse. Locals are fond of referring to it as "Korean vodka", but it's only half the strength – a good thing too, as it's usually fired down in staccato shots over barbecued meat. It's traditionally made with sweet potato, but these days most companies use cheap chemical concoctions: the resultant taste puts many foreigners off, but some find themselves near-addicted within days of arrival. W1500 from a convenience store, W3000 at a restaurant.

prices have been mentioned where appropriate. Both bars and clubs are, almost without exception, open until the wee hours. As for prices, you'll likely be paying W3000–10,000 for a beer, and cocktails start at W7000.

Hongdae

All the places listed below are marked on the Hongdae map (p.84), and are within staggering distance of two subway stations: Sangsu (exit 1) or Hongdae (exit 5).

BricXX This candlelit underground lair is a popular place to take a date, with reasonably priced cocktails and excellent food – try the falafel. The seating areas are draped with curtains; try to get there in time to nab a seat in the ultra-chilled area lined with oriental silk pillows.

Chin Chin (찬찬) What the country has been begging for for years: an upscale *makkeolli* bar. There are now a few of them around, but this remains the best, serving rice-wine varieties from across the land in funky vases and goblets: in fact, drinking here brings to mind the Korova Milk Bar scenes from *A Clockwork Orange*. The food's also pretty good, and despite being so close to the university, few of the customers are students.

Club Tool Some of the best electronica DJs in town descend on this extremely stylish dance club, though the size of the floor, coupled with the occasional frostiness of the door staff, means that it can feel rather empty at times: a place to go with a group rather than on your own. Entry W20,000.

FF Both Fs stand for "funky", though you're more likely to see some good ol' rock at this highly popular live music venue. A great many of the bands are foreign, bringing their pals and staying on for the DJ sets afterwards, so it's a great place to make new friends. Entry is around W11,000 while the bands are on, and free for the DJ sets.

Flower (꽃) Something like a speakeasy: there's no sign outside, so you'll have to put your ear to the door to see if anything's going on. Weekends, however, see the small floor crammed with music fans, here to see the owner – Seoul's funkiest *ajumma* – and friends performing live reggae.

M2 The area's top nightclub, and accordingly packed to the gills on weekends, *M2* manages to rope in the occasional top international DJ to spin out some house. On weekends, you may be spending upwards of an hour waiting in line to get in. Entry W15,000, Fri & Sat W25,000.

Nabi 나비 This pleasing underground bar has finally brought the word "bohemian" to Hongdae's nightlife. Marked only by a small sign on the outside, once you're through the door it may feel as if you've entered another world – candles float on a small pond, arty folk sit on cushions passing the hookah around, and nobody feels as if they're in Seoul any more. Despite the secluded location, the secret is out, and it can get very crowded at weekends – if there's no floorspace, you'll just have to wait.

Oi Trendy, out-of-the-way bar whose cave-like multi-level drinking areas make it look like a set from the Smurfs. Mood lighting encourages a discerning atmosphere rare in this student area.

QVo Even though the music is usually hip-hop instead of house, *QVo* tends to mop up the overflow on the regular occasions that *M2* can't squeeze any more in. Add this to the dedicated hip-hop fans already bouncing away inside, and you're in for a good night. Entry W15,000, Fri & Sat W20,000.

Samgeori Pocha (삼거리포차) Though it's technically a restaurant (see p.118), this is an integral part of Hongdae's nightlife – after a dance or a drink, Koreans love to eat (and drink a little more), so if you've made new friends you may well find yourself dragged along to this rustic-looking place, where raw fish and steaming broths are on the menu, and tables are littered with empty *soju* bottles.

Shain Independent music is hard to track down in Korea, particularly if it's local stuff you're after. However, this bar plays nothing but Korean indie, and is run by the lead singer of *Huckleberry Finn*, one of the country's first such bands. A fair proportion of the customers here are members of other ensembles, and rarely for a Seoul bar, *makkeolli* is available by the glass.

Tinpan A meat market, yes, but Hongdae's best. It's W10,000 on weekends to get into either of the two *Tinpans* that face each other across a nightclub-filled road; once inside, drinks are cheap and the dance floors are packed with a largely young crowd shaking to generic hip-hop.

Vinyl Get takeaway cocktails from the window of this small bar, where you can get Pina Coladas and Sex on the Beach in what appear, at first glance, to be colostomy bags. Such ingenuity brings the price down – W4000 for a cocktail, or just W2000 for a slightly larger bag of beer.

Itaewon

All the places listed below are marked on the Itaewon map, p.88, and are within walking distance of Itaewon subway station.

B1 Underground club with a decent sound system, and usually DJs that know how to make the most of it. With lounge areas and snazzy decoration, it's far classier than most dance venues in the area – at the beginning of the night, at least.

Bar Nana With its hanging fabrics, fake palm trees and relaxed vibe, this is the kind of bar you'd expect to find in Hongdae, and therefore a breath of fresh air in testosterone-fuelled Itaewon. Staff spin all kinds of music from ska to modern jazz, and there are regular live music nights.

Bungalow Bar There are drinking options aplenty in this loungey, multilevel bar – sup sangria on the swing-seats, drink martinis in the sand pit, have a romantic glass of wine on a candle-lit table or kick back with a beer on the outdoor terrace. The cocktails, however, are best avoided.

Embassy Lounge This cocktail bar isn't quite as stylish as it pretends to be – the arty wall-projections and quirky seating feel derivative, rather than innovative – though it ropes in the weekend crowds with some excellent DJ sets.

Function Taking up the rear of *Macaroni Market* restaurant (p.118), this is the most upscale drinking venue in Itaewon: no soldiers or microskirt-wearing teens, but plenty of sharply dressed young locals. Try one of the house cocktails.

Gecko's Terrace Unlike most Itaewon bars, *Gecko's* is busy every day of the week. A lively mix of Koreans and foreigners, it's popular with people who don't feel like dancing, and those filling up on cheap beer before a night on the tiles – local draught beer is just W2500, and pints of Guinness reasonable for Korea at W8000.

Hollywood Grill The name says it all – this is an American-style bar which shows Premier League football, Major League baseball or any other sport coverage in demand from Seoul's expat community. At quieter times, it's a pleasant place for a game of pool or darts, while during major sporting events you'll be lucky to find standing room.

Spy Bar Located on the basement level of a building that also houses the *Nashville Sports Bar*, weekends see this sometimes-house-sometimes-trance club heaving under the weight of a sexy, youthful crowd. American soldiers, expat teachers, scantily clad Korean girls and aspiring Eastern European models – a truer microcosm of Itaewon society would be hard to find. Fri & Sat entry W10,000.

The business and palace districts

Baekseju Maeul (백세주마을) **Jongno. Jonggak station; see map, p.55.** This bar-restaurant prides itself on *baekseju* (see box, p.126), and serves local food to go with it. Other branches are marked on the maps of Hangang (p.82) and Gangnam (p.92).

Dugahun (두가헌) **Sagandong. Anguk station; see map, p.44.** A charmingly characteristic venue to fall into for a glass of wine, set as it is in a revamped *hanok* building. Their selection runs the gamut from under W70,000 to well over W1,000,000 per bottle, augmented by fine European cuisine from the kitchens. Some of the views disappoint, so choose your table carefully.

Pierre's Bar **Jongno. Euljiro 1-ga station; see map, p.61.** Adjoining the superb *Pierre Gagnaire* restaurant (see p.115) at the top of the *Lotte Hotel*, this stylish bar is a firm favourite with international businessmen. Despite the modern yet opulent surroundings, and the sky-high food prices next door, drinks are surprisingly cheap – W15,000 or so for a cocktail, and less than that for a glass of beer.

Story of the Blue Star (푸른별주막) **Insadong. Anguk station; see map, p.55.** Though technically a restaurant serving earthy food from rural Gangwon province, this *hanok* venue really comes alive in the evening, serving a variety of superb *makkeolli*: the rice wine is flavoured with ingredients such as green tea, pine needles and mugwort. You'll need to order at least one dish.

Top Cloud **Jongno Tower. Jonggak station; see map, p.55.** Sup cocktails – W15,000 and up – while enjoying a commanding view of Seoul's twinkling lights: this 33-storey-high bar-restaurant (see p.116) sits perched nine levels above Jongno Tower on a pedestal of steel, and is an excellent place to impress dates or toast a business deal.

After hours

Seoul has many options for **alfresco alcohol consumption**, and visitors from countries where outdoor drinking is prohibited by law tend to find this something of a liberation. The capital's ubiquitous twenty-four-hour **convenience stores** – which in warmer months tend to be surrounded by plastic chairs and tables, kindly laid on for customer use – make for one of Seoul's cheapest possible nights out, and can be just as good for meeting locals as the city's bars. Indeed, the choice of local liquor is far better at convenience stores than almost any bar in town: see p.128 for some recommended drinks. *Geonbae!*

Other areas north of the Hangang

Comfort Zone Daehangno. Hyehwa station; see map, p.72. The best bar in the area by a country mile. Here you'll be able to chill out over cocktails in the curtain-filled upstairs lounge, pop downstairs for a beer and a game of darts, or have a quiet chat on the outdoor veranda. Turn left out of exit four of Hyewha subway and walk along the road until you come to *Burger King*; it's down the alley to the left.

Dan Vie Daehangno. Hyehwa station; see map, p.72. Tucked into a basement next door to *Comfort Zone*, this bar is a curious mix of decorative styles – some areas are cordoned off with dangling beads or shower curtains, others have space-station-style swivel chairs, and movies are projected onto the far wall.

Naos Nova Huamdong. Seoul station; see map, p.61. Seoul is slowly learning the ropes of the wine world, but this achingly cool bar-restaurant has already summited Grape Mountain. No fewer than three hundred varieties of wine can be imbibed here, all selected by a sommelier burdened by several international prizes. Good wine needs good food to go with it, and the menu here is largely Italian, with a few local elements sneaking in.

Woo Bar Gwanjang-dong. Gwangnaru station. Located in the entrance lobby of the futuristic *W Hotel*, this is almost a rite of passage for young Seoulites with a bit of cash to flash. Simply breathing ultra-trendiness, it's not for everyone, but if egg-shaped chairs, UV-lit sofas or space-helmet-like DJ booths sound appealing, this is the place to head. Drinks are expensive, but the staff are way too cool to make any fuss about those who spend all night sipping a single beer.

Gangnam & Apgujeong

Blush COEX. Samseong station; see map, p.92. Located in the *Grand InterContinental* (see p.109), this is one of Seoul's better hotel bars, though cheap enough to be a viable option for just about anyone. Draught beer goes for W9000, with cocktails around double that amount, and there's food on offer – try the chicken satay.

Club Eden Nonhyeondong, ⓦ www.eden-club .co.kr. Sinnonhyeon station; see map, p.92. Gangnam uber-club that has, for years, been *the* place to see and be seen, having transcended the boundaries of generic house and hip-hop by roping in a slew of top DJs. Entry is usually W30,000, and you'll have to be dressed up. It's in the basement of the *Ritz-Carlton* (see p.109).

Club Heaven Yeoksamdong. Yeoksam station; see map, p.92. A slightly less salubrious (and, some would say, less stuck-up) version of *Club Eden*, but also regularly finds itself host to top-notch DJs. Entry usually W25,000 and up.

Lound Cheongdamdong. Apgujeong station; see map, p.96. Under the same ownership as *Seventy Four* down the road (see p.120), this bar's pricey cocktails (W20,000) are regularly voted "best in Seoul" by the bloggers and magazine writers who get to cast such judgement. The ground level is for drinking and dining; heading upstairs will get you into a club-like space with cool iPhone drink menus, which enable you to place orders electronically.

Marcie Samseongdong. Seolleung station; see map, p.92. Few bars in the country offer rooftop views of dead kings, but here you can sip your beer while looking down on the green burial mounds of Samneung Park (see p.94), located a kilometre west of the COEX complex.

Platoon/Kunsthalle **Nonhyeondong. Apgujeong station; see map, p.96.** This quirky "creativity space" (see p.133) is also an atmospheric spot to have a drink. They have a small range of international beers and wines, and if you visit on an event night you're likely to get one or two drinks for free.

Gay & lesbian nightlife

Seoul's burgeoning queer nightlife scene has come on in leaps and bounds since the year 2000, when star actor **Hong Seok-cheon** came out of the closet – the first Korean celebrity to do so. Initially shunned by family and friends, he found himself out of work and living in a bedsit, before opening up an Italian restaurant named **Our Place** on **Itaewon's** famed "Hooker Hill". At the same time, the city government were shutting up many of the area's brothels; *Our Place* had, to Hong's own surprise, proved a hit with repressed locals as well as gay foreigners, and similar places opened up in some of the newly-vacant brothels. One side-street, now known as "Homo Hill", remains the centre of the country's gay community, and home to numerous bars. Though Itaewon tends to suffice for foreign visitors, Seoul *does* have other gay areas. The zone around Jongno 3-ga station has long been home to underground gay bars, and recent years have seen the scene becoming more and more open. Unfortunately, few venues are foreigner-friendly. Finally, the university district of **Sinchon** is popular with the local **lesbian** community, many of whom congregate of an evening in "Triangle Park", a patch of concrete near exit 1 of Sinchon subway station (take the first right).

Always Homme Itaewon station; see map, p.88. Homo Hill institution with charismatic bar staff and excellent drinks. Shares much of its clientele with *Queen*, just down the road.

Barcode Jongno 3-ga station; see map, p.55. The Jongno district has umpteen gay bars, but most of these are essentially off-limits to foreigners. This is perhaps the only exception, a fun place with English-speaking staff.

Labris Sinchon station; see map, p.82. A female-only bar and social space, within walking distance of the Hongdae nightlife district. Unlike some similar places in the area, foreigners are welcome here.

My Bed Itaewon station; see map, p.88. Loungey bar run by Hong Seok-cheon, Korea's first openly gay celebrity (see above). Hong has created something of a pink industry in Itaewon, with half-a-dozen establishments to his name. You'll often find him upstairs from *My Bed* at *My Thai*, a restaurant entirely staffed with, as Hong puts it, "handsome young men".

Queen Itaewon station; see map, p.88. The most popular gay bar on Homo Hill, with inviting staff and highly comfortable chairs. On warm weekend evenings, even these can't stop the crowd spilling out onto the street for a dance.

Starmoon Jongno 3-ga station; see map, p.55. Young gays and other liberally minded folks congregate throughout the day at this café, located at the bottom of the *Fraser Suites* (see p.110).

Trance Itaewon station; see map, p.88. A thriving transgender bar on the main Itaewon drag, hosting regular strip nights that most foreign visitors find hugely entertaining, whatever their sexual orientation.

Art and entertainment

T here's no real excuse for being bored in Seoul. The city has a jaw-dropping amount going on almost every single day of the year, anything from **traditional dance** performances to **classical music** or **live jazz**. Even more ubiquitous are the capital's **art galleries**, which reach astonishingly high levels of concentration around Insadong and Samcheongdong.

For **listings**, two good sources are the official city tourist site (Ⓦ www.visitseoul .net) and *10* magazine (see p.25), while the English-language dailies (p.25) have comprehensive weekend supplements.

Galleries

Information about current **exhibitions** can be found in the aforementioned magazines and newspapers. Those who can read at least a little Korean should track down the *Seoul Art Guide*, a monthly booklet available for free at most galleries; it has comprehensive maps and gallery **listings**, as well as features on the latest exhibitions.

Also of note to the artistically inclined are **Heyri**, a dedicated art zone just outside Seoul (see p.153), and the nearby architectural treasure-trove of **Paju Book City** (p.153).

Insadong

All of these galleries are on or around Insadonggil, and have been marked on the map on p.55. They can be reached via several subway stations: Jonggak (exit 3), Jongno 3-ga (exit 5) or Anguk (exit 6).

Artside Ⓦ www.artside.org. With a sister gallery in Beijing, Artside is one of two galleries in Seoul (the other is Arario in Samcheongdong) that regularly exhibits work from China's increasingly interesting contemporary art scene. Exhibitions change every month or so. Daily 10am–6.30pm; free unless there's a special exhibition.

Center for Peace Museum This unassuming but well-curated gallery west of Insadong has regular exhibitions of art and photography, all seeking to promote peace by highlighting the dangers of conflict. Mon–Sat 10am–5pm; free.

Insa Art Centre This interesting building's seven floors of exhibitions could keep you busy for some time – the acres of wallspace display a wide range of modern styles. Those spending a while in Seoul can return for further helpings, as the place is stripped every week to make room for new works. Usually open 10am–7pm; closes early Tues and opens late Wed to install new exhibitions; free unless there's a special exhibition.

Insa Gallery Ⓦ www.insagallery.net. This three-floored gallery's collection features some of the most interesting Korean artists of recent times. Its exploration of modern themes and styles is renowned in this competitive neighbourhood, and the twice-monthly changearounds keep things fresh. Daily 10am–6.30pm; free.

Kim Young Seob Photo Gallery Ⓦ www .gallerykim.com. A tiny photo gallery on the fourth level of a building that also features a café on the third floor, and a toy gallery-cum-shop on the second (see below). The international collection of photographs continues to grow, and most notably includes a few from the very influential Man Ray. Daily 10am–7pm; W3000.

Kyungin Museum of Fine Art Exhibitions are rarely poor at this long-time local favourite, whose tradition-with-a-twist style reflects a desire to fuse the conventional with the contemporary. Its four rooms are pleasant and spacious, and are centred around a leafy traditional courtyard that's also home to a decent tearoom (see p.122). Daily 10am–6pm; free.

Ssamziegil A little too modern for some, this gallery hides away in the basement of the spiralling Ssamzie building (see p.55). On the same floor you'll find *Gogung*, an excellent restaurant (see p.116), as well as dozens of paintings for sale from locals artists, usually youngish folk of moderate or imminent fame. Daily 10am–6pm; free.

Sun Art Center ⓦ www.sungallery.co.kr. Spoken about in hushed tones by curators at other Insadong galleries, this houses probably the most renowned collection in the area. It mainly consists of early twentieth-century paintings, and shows that modern art in Korea goes back way before the country's growth into an economic power – look for pieces by Kim Sou, who had a Rubens-like obsession with flesh, or the floral works of Kim Chong Hak. Daily 10am–6pm; free.

Toto Is it a gallery, a museum or a shop? Regardless, Toto is filled with toy planes, trains and automobiles, as well as action figures that wear their underpants on the outside. Some pieces are rare, but there are cheaper ones to take away as quirky souvenirs. Daily 10am–6pm; W1000.

Samcheongdong

Anguk subway station (exit 1) is best for the following galleries, which are all marked on the map on p.44.

Arario Seoul ⓦ www.ararioseoul.com. This large venue lends itself to sculpturework or large paintings, and the offerings are always from renowned artists. With a sister gallery in Beijing (as well as one in Cheonan; see p.163), Arario is often a great place to check out the latest offerings from the increasingly interesting art scene over the Yellow Sea. Tues–Sun 11am–7pm; free.

Daelim Contemporary Art Gallery ⓦ www.daelimmuseum.org. A string of fascinating exhibitions have put this gallery up with Seoul's most highly regarded. The focus is on photography but the curators branch off into other fields: clothes from Paul Smith and furniture from Jean Prouve have found their way into past exhibitions. 10am–6pm; closed Mon; tickets usually W5000.

Gallery Hyundai ⓦ www.galleryhyundai.com. This large gallery possesses the most esteemed collection in the area; in existence since the 1960s, it's Korea's longest-running commercial gallery. The focus has long been on artists born before 1930, but times are changing and there's an ever-increasing emphasis on newer trends. Tues–Sun 10am–6pm; free.

Kukje Gallery ⓦ www.kukjegallery.com. The Kukje is one of the most important players in the area, actively promoting Korean artists abroad, and hauling a wide, well-selected range of exhibits into its own space, near the palace side of Samcheongdonggil. It's surrounded by excellent cafés and restaurants – including one adjoining the gallery (*The Restaurant*; see p.117). Mon–Sat 10am–6pm, Sun till 5pm; free.

Sun Contemporary ⓦ www.sungallery.co.kr. The contemporary side of the excellent Sun Art Center in Insadong (see opposite), this gallery's collection is equally well put together, and occupies a few floors in a building near trendy Samcheongdonggil. To get to other floors, you'll have to go through what looks like a fire escape from the entry room. Daily 9am–6pm; free.

Toykino This is the place to head if you're into toys and figurines: over 30,000 pieces amassed since the 1980s, ranging from Batman and other western characters to Japanese collectors' pieces. Tues–Sun 9am–6pm; W5000.

Northern Seoul

Neither of these galleries is anywhere near a subway station; they're best accessed by shuttle bus (see p.71 for details). They're marked on the map on p.72.

Gana Art Centre Pyongchangdong, ⓦ www.ganaart.com. The largest art gallery in the land nestles in relative obscurity, way up on the Pyongchangdong slopes. Designed by French architect Jean-Michel Wilmotte, it's a fabulous treasure-trove of modern art, with a delightful sculpture garden out back. Daily 10am–7pm, W3000.

Whanki Gallery Buamdong, ⓦ www.whanki museum.org. This little-visited gallery is a shrine of sorts to the unfortunately monikered Kim Whanki, one of Korea's first modern artists. In the 1940s, Kim proved a conduit between east and west, mopping up ideas from the Paris avant-garde movement while disseminating Asian techniques to a curious Europe. 10am–6pm; closed Mon; W3000.

Around City Hall

These galleries are all a short walk from exit 1 of City Hall subway station, and have been marked on the map, p.61.

National Museum for Contemporary Art Inside the grounds of Deoksugung palace and set in a colonial-era structure, this museum hosts regular exhibitions of modern art. Most of the offerings are local in nature, and they're always of high quality. 9am–8pm, closed Mon; W10,000–10,000.

Museum of History The ground floor of Seoul's main historical museum (see p.62) has dedicated halls for exhibitions of local art, sculpture work or photography, and entrance is free (though ticketed). Tues–Fri 9am–9pm, Sat & Sun 9am–6pm; closed Mon.

SeMA ⓦseoulmoa.seoul.go.kr. Sizeable venue that hosts most of the city's big-name draws: Picasso, Monet, Van Gogh and Renoir have all found temporary homes here. Tickets to see these larger names will weigh in at around W15,000, though there are always free secondary exhibitions to peruse, most commonly the work of local (or at least Asian) artists. Tues–Fri 10am–9pm, Sat & Sun 10am–6pm.

South of the river

Hwa Su Mok Cheongdamdong. Cheongdamdong station; see map, p.96. Fronting an upscale bar in trendy Cheongdamdong, this one-room gallery has an interesting manifesto. Exhibitions usually combine the works of two artists, one from Korea and one from the west, and works (generally a combination of paintings and sculpture work) seep over into the adjoining bar. Daily 10am–late; free.

Platoon/Kunsthalle Nonhyeondong, ⓦwww.kunsthalle.com. Apgujeong station; see map, p.96. Part gallery, part design lab, part bar, part German restaurant and occasional live music venue, this jaw-dropping space is a magnet for Seoul's more creative sorts. The body of the structure is made from 28 shipping containers; these have been painted army green, and staff float around in faux military garb. The themed installations rotate every month or two, and tend to be sponsored by large corporations: there are usually a few free drinks to be had on exhibition opening days. Daily 11am–late; free.

Cinema

Wherever you find yourself in Seoul, you won't be too far from the nearest **cinema**. Koreans love to watch films, though the emphasis is firmly on Hollywood and Kollywood **blockbusters** – the popularity of major movies snowballs to such a degree that most of the country will have seen them just a week after release. *CVG* and *Megabox* are the two major cinema chains; foreign films are shown in their original language with Korean subtitles, though bar the two exceptions listed below, local films are Korean-only. There are also a few options for those looking for something a little more **arthouse**, with some establishments catering to foreigners; in all cases, tickets cost from W5000–10,000. Note that it's also possible to watch movies in a **DVD-bang** – see box, p.85 for details, and Contexts pp.184–186 for a few Korean film recommendations.

Cinematheque Jongno 3-ga station; see map, p.55. Also going under the names of "Hollywood" and "Seoul Art Cinema", this sits on top of the Nakwon Arcade, a building that local authorities have been planning to tear down for years. Now given a stay of execution, the cinema here has a rolling calendar of themed events, some of which are based around foreign films; pop by and pick up a pamphlet.

CGV Yongsan station; see map, p.82. The Yongsan branch of Korea's biggest cinema chain shows some Korean films with English subtitles, as well as all of the latest block-busters from abroad. Some films are shown in "4D", with wind machines, vibrating chairs and choreographed scents making you feel part of the show - not quite time travel, but quite an experience nonetheless. Tickets W7000; 4D W18,000.

Korea Film Archive ⓦwww.koreafilm.org. This institution regularly screens films from home and abroad, and has a large selection of Korean classics that can be rented for viewing on the premises. Access is a little tricky; see their website for details.

Korea Foundation Cultural Center ⓦlibrary .kf.or.kr. City Hall station; see map, p.61. Good news for those wanting to watch Korean films, this venue has a large selection of

DVDs which can be rented for viewing on the premises in tiny cubicles. You'll have to register, though, and they may ask for proof that you're resident in Seoul.

Megabox Samseong station; see map, p.92. The chain's huge COEX branch shows some of its Kollywood hits with added English subtitles. There are other branches all over the city.

Mirospace Seodaemun station; see map, p.61. Interesting hundred-seat venue showing arty films, usually from abroad. For once, there's no popcorn on offer, and after the movie customers can glide into the sleek adjoining bar.

Sangsangmadang Sangsu station; see map, p.84. The basement of this arts complex has some arty English-language screenings, of which around half are from abroad. Interestingly, they try to show films whose themes match what's on show in the second-floor gallery. Tickets W7000.

Theatre and performance arts

Stage buffs will have plenty to choose from in Seoul. Most popular with foreign travellers are **traditional performances** and **musicals**; the latter tend to be based in dedicated theatres.

Battle B-Boy Hongdae B-Boy Theater ⓦsjbboys .com. Hongdae station; see map, p.84. One way to get into the B-Boy breakdancing still enthralling the nation, this long-running play tells the story of a dance romance, and has some pretty incredible routines. Sat 2pm & 6pm, Sun 2pm, Wed–Fri 8pm; W50,000.

Chongdong Theatre Near City Hall ⓦwww .chongdong.com. City Hall station; see map, p.61. The 80min traditional shows of song and dance hosted by this theatre are extremely popular with foreign visitors. It's located on a quiet road near the western wall of Deoksugung. Performances (daily except Mon; April–Sept 8pm; Oct–March 4pm; from W20,000) are in Korean, though English subtitles appear next to the stage. Also on offer are classes in the *janggu*, a Korean drum.

Dongsoong Art Center Daehangno ⓦdsartcenter.co.kr. Hyehwa station; see map, p.72. This Daehangno arts complex has long been putting on some of Seoul's best experimental drama, though as perform-ances are in Korean only you'll need some language skills or an open mind. The on-site

cinema shows some interesting films and documentaries from home and abroad.

Jump Cinecore Theater ⓦwww.hijump.co.kr. Jongno 3-ga station; see map, p.44. Ever wondered what a family entirely made up of martial arts experts would be like? Experience all of the inevitable jumps and kicks in this musical, which takes place at the Cinecore Theater near Insadong. Performances Tues–Sat 4pm & 8pm, Sun 3pm & 6pm; W40,000.

Korea House Chungmuro ⓦwww.koreahouse .or.kr. Highly polished traditional performances from some of the top artistes in the country, combined with some of Seoul's best food (see p.114): this is one of the city's most popular nights out. The wonderful shows include fan dances, *pansori* opera and the long-ribboned hats of the "farmers' dance". Take exit three from Chungmuro subway station and walk up the side-street. Perform-ances daily 7pm and 8.50pm; W50,000.

Munye Theatre Daehangno. Hyehwa station; see map, p.72. One of the most popular theatres with those studying performance arts in the area, this shrine to modern

Pansori

Usually marketed to foreigners as "Korean opera", **pansori** performances are a modern-day derivative of the country's shamanic past. Songs and incantations chanted to fend off evil spirits or ensure a good harvest slowly mutated over the years into ritualized presentations. As might be expected, the themes also evolved, with tales of love and despair replacing requests to spirits unseen.

A good *pansori* may go on for hours, but each segment will be performed by a cast of just two – a female singer (the *sorikkun*) and a male percussionist (*gosu*). The *sorikkun* holds aloft a paper fan, which she folds, unfolds and waves about to emphasize lyrics or a change of scene. While the *gosu* drums out his minimalist finger taps on the *janggo*, he gives his singer words (or, more commonly, grunts) of encouragement known as *chuimsae*, to which the audience are expected to add their own. The most common are "*chalhanda!*" and "*olshi-gu!*", which are roughly equivalent to "you're doing good!" and "hm!", a grunt acknowledging appreciation, usually delivered with a refined nod. Just follow the Korean lead, and enjoy the show.

dance hosts regular shows, as well as a spring festival.

Namsan Gugakdang Chungmuro. Chungmuro station; see map, p.61. Those looking for a traditional Korean performance should make this their first port of call. Part of the Namsangol complex (see p.70), its shows revolve around *gugak*, an ancient style of Korean music, but the savvy curators bring a pleasant variety to the offerings with regular thematic events of song, music, dance or a combination of the three. Ticket prices vary but are usually in the region of W30,000.

Nanta Nanta Theatre ⓦ www.nanta.co.kr. City Hall station; see map, p.61. This madcap kitchen-based musical has gone down a storm since opening up in 1997 (making it Korea's longest-running show), with song, circus tricks and all sorts of utensil drumming mixed with a nice line in audience participation. Performances Mon–Sat 4pm & 8pm, Sun 3pm & 6pm; W40,000.

Music

Seoul isn't exactly renowned for the quality of its music. From pre-teen girls to bad-boy bike nuts, most of the country listens to sugary K-pop, generic hip-hop and little else. However, there are a few venues at which you can hear more highbrow offerings such as **jazz** or **classical music**, and an ever-increasing number of international **mainstream acts** are arriving in Korea (though most of these are past their sell-by dates in their home countries). In addition, a few of the bars in the Hongdae listings are good for **live rock** and similar music; see p.127 for details.

All That Jazz Itaewon, ⓦ www.allthatjazz.kr. Itaewon station; see map, p.88. An Itaewon institution, this has been roping in jazz lovers for donkey's years. The atmosphere is fun, rather than stuffy, and audience inter-action is commonplace – some spectators have ended up playing on stage with the band. Performances begin 7pm Sat & Sun, 8.30pm Mon–Fri; tickets usually W5000.

Club Evans Seogyodong. Sangsu station; see map, p.84. Hongdae's most popular jazz venue by a mile, this is small enough to generate some decent acoustics, but large enough to create a good atmosphere. The acts are usually of more than acceptable quality, and the experience surprisingly refined for this nightclub-filled street. 7pm–midnight; tickets usually W7000.

Once in a Blue Moon Sinsadong. Apgujeong station; see map, p.96. Perhaps the most renowned of Seoul's many jazz bars, and certainly the closest approximation to a western venue. The music spans the full gamut of styles, played while customers dine on French or Mexican cuisine, and a choice from the lengthy wine and cocktail lists. Performances start 7.30pm; admission free.

Seoul Arts Centre Ⓦ www.sac.or.kr. Nambu Bus Terminal station; see map, p.92. The home of Korea's national ballet and opera companies, as well as the symphony orchestra, there's always something interesting going on at this rambling complex. See website for details of upcoming events.

Sejong Centre Gwanghwamun Ⓦ www .sejongpac.or.kr. Gwanghwamun station; see map, p.44. Gigantic venue offering a truly diverse array of music: everything from traditional Korean *gugak* to concertos from world-famous pianists. There'll be something going on every night of the week; check the website for details.

Singing rooms

Karaoke may be a Japanese concept, but is actually even more common in Korea: you'll find a **noraebang** (literally "song room") on almost every street in Seoul. Rather than embarrassing yourself in front of strangers, the Asian norm is to bundle into a small room with a group of friends, arm yourselves with microphones and tambourines, then sing until you're hoarse. Most of the available songs are Korean, of course, but there are always some western favourites on the list; rooms usually go for W12,000 or so per hour. **Luxury Su**, a Hongdae venue next door to Sangsangmadang (see p.134), has achieved particular fame thanks to sumptuously decorated rooms, and even a few with floor-to-ceiling windows visible from the street: show-offs, this is your big chance.

Gambling

Gambling is technically illegal in Korea, but there are a couple of ways to lose your money. There are two foreigner-only **Seven Luck Casinos** (Ⓦ www.7luck.com) in the capital: one in COEX (p.95), and the other in the *Millennium Hilton* (p.106), while another casino can be found in the *Walkerhill* hotel (p.108). Casual attire is permitted in all of these establishments. Alternatively, you can bet on horses with the locals at **Seoul Racecourse Park** - near Seoul Grand Park (p.99), or on bicycle races at the **velodrome** in Olympic Park (weekends only).

Shopping

S hopaholics will find themselves quite at home in Seoul: the city has everything from trendy to traditional and markets to malls. High on the itinerary of many tourists are the colossal **markets** of Dongdaemun and Namdaemun (see p.68), but there's much more on offer – **clothing** running the gamut from traditional to designer via tailored suits, a range of artistic produce including excellent **pottery** and Joseon-era **antiques**, and all the **electrical goods** you could possibly desire.

Opening hours tend to be long (most commonly 10am until late evening), and very few stores take any days off. International credit cards were once a no-no but most stores now accept them. Haggling is almost unheard of, markets being the only exception to this unwritten rule.

Department stores, malls and duty-free outlets

Department stores can be found all over the city, each with a wide range of cosmetics on their ground floor, level after level of clothing above, and usually a food court on top. The bustling streets of **Myeongdong** host stores from the biggest nationwide chains – Migliore, Shinsegae, Lotte and Galleria – and there are also luxury examples in Apgujeong. Most department stores are much of a muchness, but the most interesting have been listed below.

Given the prevalence of department stores, it's perhaps not much of a surprise that **mall** culture has yet to truly permeate the Korean shopping scene. There are

---

10 top shopping picks

Seoul has an almost bewildering range of shopping possibilities, but since the city specializes in certain products, it may be best to put these on top of your list of priorities. Here are the best places to shop in each category:

Antique furniture Royal Antiques (p.140)

Contemporary *hanbok* Lee Young Hee (p.139)

Duty-free products Donghwa Duty Free (p.138)

Fake designer goods Dongdaemun market (p.68)

Hangeul-character ties Lee Geon Maan (p.139).

Ladies' shoes Suecomma Bonnie (p.140)

Oriental fabrics Mono Collection (p.140)

Pottery Kwang Ju Yo (p.140)

Tailored shirts Hamilton Shirts (p.139)

Tailored suits Hahn's Custom Tailoring (p.139)

only two such places of note in Seoul: the underground **COEX mall** (Ⓦwww .coex.co.kr) in Gangnam (see p.95), and **Times Square** (Ⓦwww.timessquare .co.kr), a more typically Western-style mall near Yeongdeungpo subway station, just south of Yeouido (see map, p.82). Both are open from 10.30am–10pm.

Lastly, Seoul has a few places in which you can do your **duty-free** shopping before getting to the airport. Two such places are in the *Shilla* (p.107) and *Walker-hill* (p.108) hotels, and there's the dedicated Donghwa Duty Free just outside exit 6 of Gwanghwamun subway station. Cosmetics, beauty and body products, alcohol and designer bags are the most popular purchases, though you'll need to bring along your passport and plane tickets.

Galleria Apgujeongno. Apgujeong station; see map, **p.96.** Almost universally agreed to be the country's most exclusive department store, this is arranged in two buildings facing each other across a major road. The artistically designed west wing features a range of local designers, while the even more expensive east wing is home to international mega-labels. 10.30am–8.30pm.

Hyundai Apgujeongno. Apgujeong station; see map, **p.96.** Nowhere near as exclusive as Galleria down the road, but this is a better hunting ground for clothing from local designers – particularly recommended are Solidhomme for the gents, Son Jung Wan for the ladies, and Andy & Debb for both. 10.30am–8.30pm.

Lotte Euljiro. Euljiro 1-ga station; see map, **p.61.** Popular with expats thanks to a well-stocked supermarket, located on the basement level. Also within the huge complex are *Lotte Hotel* (see p.106) and the Amore Spa (p.146). 10.30am–8pm.

Shinsegae Myeongdong. Myeongdong station; see map, **p.61.** Designed back in the 1930s as a branch of the Japanese Mitsukoshi chain, this was Korea's first department store. Goods from luxury clothing and jewellery brands can be found inside, while the exterior of the old wing is quite charming at night, and extremely striking around Christmastime. 11am–8.30pm.

Markets

Seoul has a quite phenomenal number of outdoor markets – there will be one within walking distance wherever you are, with the *gimchi* and fish products on offer making it almost literally possible to follow your nose. As well as a range of food, each market will also have a clothing section, with fake designer goods a particularly popular speciality. The largest and most central markets are Dongdaemun (p.68) and Namdaemun (p.65), though the fish market at Noryangjin (p.87) deserves a special mention, as does Gwangjang market (see opposite), an offshoot of the mammoth Dongdaemun complex. Though far smaller, there's also an interesting weekly flea market at Nolita Park in Hongdae (p.85).

Clothing

The city's **department stores** (see above) sell a wide range of (largely expensive) clothing, the brand names in question a mix of local and international. Beware, though; as soon as you dare to even look at something, a grinning attendant in uniform will race up to you, invading your comfort zone until you try something on or leave. **Apgujeong** has the country's grandest department stores, notably the twin Galleria malls (see above), while further up the road is a parade of brand-name flagship shops such as Gucci, Prada and Louis Vuitton; there is also a clutch of boutique stores around nearby Dosan Park. The Hongdae area is full of cheaper clothing boutiques, though almost all cater for women only; oddly, men will find richer pickings outside Ehwa Women's University, just down the road. Finally, the narrow lanes around Samcheongdonggil are also home to a number of small clothing shops, with these spanning the full range from budget to designer.

Itaewon has long been popular with foreign businessmen, so most shopkeepers can speak a little English; an increasing number actually hail from abroad. Here you can get all sorts of things, including leather shoes and jackets, **tailored suits** and fake watches. Outside Itaewon, foreigners should note that sizes tend to be on the small side, particularly around the hips for females. Most upper-body wear is sold as small, medium, large (with a couple of extras on each side), while for waistlines a confusing mishmash of systems is employed; the American system is most common. Footwear is a different matter, with sizes almost exclusively in millimetres.

Babo Shirts ⊛ www.baboshirts.com. Like Lee Geon Maan (see below), this foreign-run online store has made money selling Koreans their own alphabet: their occasionally ironic t-shirt slogans have proved popular with locals and expats alike.

Euljiro Tunnel 을지로지하상가 A trip back in time, this tunnel's shops have been serving the same people since the 1970s, and as such are a great place to head for a rare piece of retro Korea – see p.67 for more. The tunnel stretches for several kilometres between City Hall and Dongdaemun History & Culture Park station, and has entrances every 50m or so; many shops open at daybreak, and some stay open till midnight and beyond.

Gwangjang Market 광장시장 Jongno 5-ga station; see map, p.61. Though most famed for its culinary offerings, this sprawling market has a truly excellent secondhand section, with all manner of zany shirts, coats and jackets imported from abroad. It's a little hard to find: hunt down the staircase on the western side of the market, and head for the second floor.

Hahn's Custom Tailoring Itaewondong, ⓔ hanstailor@hotmail.com. Itaewon station; see map, p.88. Get a perfectly tailored suit for around US$500. Affable owner Hahn speaks excellent English, and will be pleased to discuss the particular style you're after; his tailors also make good shirts. 10am–9pm.

Hamilton Shirts Itaewondong, ⊛ www.hs76.com. Itaewon station; see map, p.88. Tailored shirts at prices less than you'd pay for factory-made fare on your local high street: most shirts go for around US$40. The quality is amazingly high for the price. 10am–9.30pm.

Jilkyungyee Gwanakdong, ⊛ www.jilkyungyee .co.kr. Anguk station; see map, p.55. Store selling cheap, slightly modernized takes on traditional Korean clothing, which make wonderful keepsakes of a visit to Seoul. 10am–7.30pm.

Lee Geon Maan Gwanhundong. Anguk station; see map, p.55. Well-located store selling ties for men and handbags for the ladies. Their unique selling point is an innovative use of *hangeul*, the Korean text conspicuous by its absence on Korean clothing. 10.30am–8pm.

Lee Young Hee Sinsadong, ⊛ www.leeyounghee .co.kr. Apgujeong station; see map, p.96. Korea's traditional clothing, *hanbok*, is alright to wear for a photo-shoot, but since it looks a little ridiculous on foreigners, few of them would actually go out and buy the stuff. This store sells contemporary takes on the style, and counts Hillary Clinton as a customer at their New York branch. 11am–6.30pm.

Nohke J Sinsadong, ⊛ www.nohke.com. Apgujeong station; see map, p.96. Small local boutique selling futuristic feminine designs; the coats here are particularly striking. Although still young, designer Misun Jung has already made clothing for several major Korean singers and models. 11am–7.30pm.

Space Mue Cheongdamdong. Apgujeong station; see map, p.96. This Apgujeong multishop (a Konglish term for a store selling various brands) sells clothing from upscale international brands, but even if you can't afford to spend US$100 on a t-shirt it's worth popping into for the gorgeous interior alone, its hexagonal motif making it look something like a futuristic beehive. 11am–8pm.

Stori Samcheongdong, ⊛ www.storisac.com. Anguk station; see map, p.44. Made with distinctively Korean materials and patterns, Stori's handbags have gone down a storm in London and other European cities in recent years. 10am–7pm.

Suecomma Bonnie Cheongdamdong, ⓦwww
.suecommabonnie.com. Apgujeong station; see
map, p.96. Superb ladies' footwear made by
local diva Bonnie Lee. If her designs were
good enough for *Sex and the City*, they're
good enough for you. There's a smaller
branch off Samcheongdonggil. 10am–7pm.

Arts, crafts and antiques

The best place to head for anything vaguely arty is **Insadonggil** and its side-streets. As well as numerous galleries (see pp.131–132 for some of the most interesting), there are **craft** shops selling paints, brushes, calligraphy ink and handmade paper. For **antiques**, Itaewon is best, with a road known as "Antiques Alley" stretching south from the subway station. There's quite a lot of authentic Joseon-era furniture out there; in a country of neophiliacs these were once absolute bargains (indeed, it's still occasionally possible to find antiques lying out on the streets), but demand from abroad has pushed supply down and prices up. Replica dynastic furniture is cheaper and more abundant. All antiques shops will be able to organize overseas shipping.

**Curious Curious Itaewondong. Noksapyeong
station; see map, p.88.** Gorgeous jewellery
items including bangles, necklaces and
earrings, all handmade at this charming
Itaewon boutique store. Prices are reasonable – think W40,000 for a pair of earrings.
10am–9pm.

🏃 **Hyojae 효재 Seongbukdong. Hansung
University station; see map, p.72.** Tiny
shop with a big reputation for producing
high-quality traditional fabrics, clothing and
pottery. Of most interest to foreign
customers will be silk wrapping cloths
known as *bojagi*; these make great small
souvenirs. 10am–6pm.

🏃 **Kwang Ju Yo Gahoedong ⓦwww
.kwangjuyo.com. Anguk station; see map,
p.44.** Korea has been at the forefront of
world pottery for centuries, and this
conveniently located store is one of the best
places to go shopping for it. Celadon bowls
and porcelain vases are among the items on
offer, while they also sell Andong *soju* (a
particularly potent form of the national drink,
at 41 percent alcohol by volume) in elaborate
jars: perfect souvenirs. 10am–9pm.

**Millimeter Milligram Angukdong ⓦwww
.mmmg.net. Anguk station; see map, p.55.**
Seoul-based design team making cutesy
cups, cutlery, stationery and the like. They
have a branch at Ssamziegil (p.132), though
more fun is the Anguk shop, which is set
into a lovely café. 9am–9pm.

**Mono Collection Buamdong ⓦwww
.monocollection.com; see map, p.72.** This tiny
store sells Korean-styled fabrics including
curtains, pillowcases and tablecloths. Given
the slightly out-of-the-way location, it may
be easier to pop into their booth in *Korea
House* (see p.114), or the one at Incheon
International Airport. 10am–6pm.

🏃 **Royal Antiques Itaewondong ⓦwww
.royal-antique.com. Itaewon station; see
map, p.88.** Not on "Antiques Alley" itself, but
this is the best place to head if you're
hunting for a genuine Joseon-era piece of
furniture. The owners are friendly sorts and
can speak English. 9.30am–8.30pm.

**Sangsangmadang Gahoedong. Sangsu station;
see map, p.84.** Unbelievable though it may
sound, Hongdae was once more famed for
its art than its bars. Times have changed,
but the university that the area is named
after is still artistically focused. This arty
complex features a gallery, café and
cinema, while the ground floor sells small
lifestyle goods designed by local students.
9am–9pm.

**Ssamziegil Gwanhundong. Anguk station; see
map, p.55.** A wonderfully designed building
whose spiral walkway plays host to
countless small shops, selling traditional
clothing, handmade paper, jewellery and the
like. There's also a rooftop market on
weekends, selling all manner of quirky arts
and crafts. 10.30am–9pm.

**Tongin Building Insadong. Anguk station; see
map, p.55.** Colonial structure with whole
floors full of antique cases, cupboards,
medicinal racks and other furniture, much of
it in a distinctively oriental style; at least one
of the proprietors will be able to speak
English, and the store can arrange shipping.
10am–8pm.

Books

Most of Seoul's larger **bookshops** have dedicated English-language sections stocked with novels, history books and language study-guides for those studying Korean or teaching English. There are a couple of smaller specialist foreign-language stockists in Itaewon.

Bandi & Luni Jongno. Jonggak station; see map, p.55. Large underground bookshop in the second basement level of Jongno Tower (see p.59), and the best place to go to pick up other *Rough Guides*. 9.30am–10pm.

Foreign Book Store Itaewondong. Itaewon station; see map, p.88. Rambling affair with a selection of mostly secondhand books; stick around a while and you're bound to find a gem or two, remnants of decades' worth of Itaewon expats. 10am–9pm.

Kyobo Books Jongno. Jonggak station; see map, p.44. Taking up the basement level of the huge Kyobo building, this is the country's largest bookshop, and the best by far for foreign-language books. There's also a branch in Gangnam, just south of Sonnonhyeong station. 9.30am–10pm.

Seoul Selection Sagandong. Anguk station; see map, p.44. Small, friendly shop run by the team behind *Seoul* magazine (see p.26), this is particularly good for English-language books pertaining to Korean culture. 9.30am–6.30pm; closed Sun.

What the Book Itaewondong. Noksapyeong station; see map, p.88. Dedicated foreign-language bookshop that's extremely popular with expats; everyone seems to end up here at some point. 10am–9pm.

Youngpoong Jongno. Jonggak station; see map, p.55. The runt of the litter around Jonggak station, at least in foreign-language terms, but the selection is still fairly good. 9.30am–10pm.

Music

The Korean **music** scene may be flooded with K-pop and local hip-hop, but there are a few shops dotted around Seoul that dare to venture underground. Mainstream fare can be found at one of the large bookstores above. If you want to play music rather than listen to it, head straight to the large Nakwon arcade in Insadong, where more than a hundred small shops sell **musical instruments**; with customers and shop owners alike testing the products in this pleasantly crusty building, it can be quite atmospheric.

Harvest Music Myeongdong station; see map, p.61. Only worth popping into if you're in the Myeongdong area, but has a few gems amid its secondhand vinyl collection; the same can be said for a number of tiny stores in the nearby underground arcades. 10am–8pm.

Pung Wol Dang Apgujeong station; see map, p.96. Next door to the superb *Rozen Kavalier* café (p.122), this classical music shop claims to be the largest such stockist in the world. Utter tripe, but you're likely to find what you want. 9.30am–8pm.

Purple Record Sangsu station; see map, p.84. The best selection of foreign independent music in Korea, and a thoroughly pleasant place to hang out and sift through records. 10am–11pm.

Record Forum Sangsu station; see map, p.84. You'll hear this store long before you enter – they've been enticing customers in with noisy outdoor speakers for years. Not quite as good as Purple Record down the road, but a good selection nonetheless. 10am–11pm.

Films

The global popularity of Korean films is increasing with each passing year, and as you'd expect, Seoul is a great place to go shopping for them; see pp.184–186 for

Grandmother techno

While modern K-pop has swept across continental Asia, there are a couple of local strains of music that you may well come across on your way around Seoul: "**bongjak**" songs, fast-paced electronic ditties set to odd synthesized rhythms, and best described as a kind of grandmother techno; and "**trot**", slower (but still fast-paced) ballads, crooned out in a semi-compulsory warbly voice. *Bongjak* has been around since the 1970s, and remains hugely popular with Korea's older set, as anyone who's seen a clutch of grannies getting down to the beats will testify. *Trot* has its roots in the 1930s, but ironically this style is not the sole preserve of the elderly, and is unlikely to go out of fashion for some time – you'll find university students belting hits out in *noraebang* (Korean karaoke dens) and kids listening to them on tape, while young artists such as Jang Yoon-jeong have scored big by crossing the genre with the ballads that younger Koreans tend to prefer. Ubiquitous cabaret shows mean that *trot* is rarely off the television, and you'll be able to buy CDs (or, more commonly, tapes) at music shops across Seoul.

some recommendations. The best-stocked places for both Korean and foreign films are the large bookstores listed on p.141. DVDs tend to cost around W20,000–40,000, but all of these shops sell old and unwanted stock for bargain prices of W2500–10,000; the large electronics markets noted below also have good bargain sections. Note that Korea is in region 3 for DVD compatibility; this is not an issue for the pirated copies sold from street stalls, abundant in the area between Jonggak subway station and the southern end of Insadonggil.

Cameras and electronic equipment

Korea may have found renown as one of the world's most innovative producers of electronic goods, but global market dynamics mean that both the prices of such goods and the range on offer here are little different to those in most western countries. The one exception is the field of cutting-edge mobile phones, though since you're usually required to sign a two-year contact, these do not exactly constitute a viable purchase for most visitors. However, you'll be able to take a peek at futuristic mobile phone designs at the fascinating Samsung D'light showroom in Gangnam (see p.93). Technophiles have two main shopping choices in Seoul – one is **Yongsan Electronics Mart**, a multi-level giant rising up alongside the Yongsan train and subway station, and the other is **Techno Mart**, an equally massive mall near Gangbyeon subway station on line 2. At the Yongsan market, essentially part of the huge train and subway station of the same name, many staff speak a little English, but Techno Mart tends to be a little cheaper. In either case, prices are generally about twenty percent less than elsewhere in the country; this can rise to fifty percent for imported goods. Note that Korean plugs have two round pins, similar to those in continental Europe.

For **used camera equipment**, the streets south of Chungmuro station are a happy hunting ground, and some shop owners speak enough English to help out. For new cameras, Techno Mart and Yongsan will be your best bet.

Sports and health

O n the face of things, Seoul may not seem the world's easiest place to keep in shape, but the city has a small but interesting range of ways to keep sport nuts entertained. Most of these will be familiar to Westerners, since Korean martial arts are primarily active rather than passive affairs, and the only local spectator sport – *ssireum*, a form of wrestling – has largely died a death, only really rearing its head during the Dano festival (see p.27). One tradition still going strong, however, are the **jjimjilbang**, Korea's wonderfully idiosyncratic take on the humble sauna. This is a must-do activity, providing a fascinating (and pleasurable) window into local society. Lastly, there's simple exercise equipment for public use on almost every mountainside, as well as in parks, and dotting the banks of the Hangang and other waterways.

Sports

Seoul offers sporty sorts a number of ways to get their kicks (perhaps even literally: how about an hour or two of **taekwondo** practice?), with baseball, football, golf and rugby among the range of activities on offer. In warmer months it's possible to have a dip in one of several outdoor **swimming pools** or rent a bike; the Han-side banks of Yeouido are the best places for both (see box, p.83). Additionally, you'll be able to find **pool tables** in many of Itaewon's foreigner bars, usually free to use. More common are pool halls that cater to **four-ball**, a pocketless version of the game so popular in Korea that live matches are regularly broadcast on television.

Baseball

Seoul has two main professional teams: **LG Twins** and the **Doosan Bears**, long-time rivals who both play in Jamsil Baseball Stadium – take subway line 2 to Sports Complex station, exit five or six. Games take place most days from April to October, and tickets can cost as little as W3000. Avid players can get some practice at a number of **batting nets** dotted around the city, particularly in student areas; these cost just W1000 for a minute's worth of balls. One is marked on the Insadong map, p.55.

Bowling

Bowling has not permeated Korean society as much as other American sports, but there are a few alleys around the city. Most popular is Pierrot Strike in Apgujeong (daily 6pm–3am, see map, p.96), which charges W5000 per person for a game – a cheap price to pay considering the snazzy futuristic interior. The venue also has dartboards, pool tables and a bar.

Football

Those wanting to watch some **K-League** action can catch FC Seoul at

the World Cup Stadium (Ⓦwww
.fcseoul.com; tickets from ₩10,000),
with games taking place on weekends
from March to October. Seongnam
and Suwon, the two most dominant
Korean teams of recent times, also play
near Seoul; the atmosphere at all
grounds is fun but they can be on the
empty side, unless you're lucky enough
to be around for a major international
game (Ⓦwww.fifa.com). Those who
prefer to play rather than watch can
try their luck with the highly competitive **foreigners' football league**
(Ⓦssflkorea.com); this has been in
operation for a number of years, and
most of the competing teams are based
in Seoul, though as the standard is quite
high you'll have to be a decent player to
get a regular game.

Golf

Korean **golf** courses are among the
most expensive in the world – would
you believe that many local golfers visit
Japan to *save* money? In addition, the
courses around Seoul usually require
membership – it's almost impossible to
organize this independently, so any
action is best arranged by your accommodation or a tourist office (see p.39).
However, it's possible to keep your
swing in shape at one of many small
driving ranges dotted around Seoul –
look for the buildings topped with
green nets. These are cheap at around
₩10,000 for fifty balls, and clubs can be
borrowed for free. It's also possible to
watch the professionals in action near
Seoul: an event on the men's OneAsia
Tour, the **Korea Open** is held each
September on the Woo Jeong Hills
course, near the satellite city of
Cheonan. This event has been growing
in size and importance, and recent years
have seen top golfers such as Vijay Singh
and Sergio Garcia lifting the trophy. See
Ⓦwww.koreaopen.com for more.

Ice-skating

Those visiting in winter will be able
to skate outdoors at various points in
the city: Seoul Plaza (see p.64) and
Gwanghwamun Plaza (p.58) turn into
a gigantic ice-rinks for the season
(usually mid-Dec to Feb; 10am–10pm;
₩1000), though skaters are turfed off
every 15 minutes or so for surfacing.
The ticket price includes skate and
helmet rental. There's also a year-
round rink in Lotte World (p.98),
which charges ₩13,000 for entry and
skate rental (10am–9.30pm); far
cheaper is the Olympic-size rink at
Korea National University (2–6pm;
₩5000); it's within walking distance
of Korea University subway station.

Rugby

Though it may be a minority sport in
Korea, rugby players can keep in shape
by training with **Seoul Survivors
RFC** (Ⓦwww.survivorsrfc.com), an
expat squad who practise most weeks.
They take part in a few competitions in
Korea, and make occasional international tours, including an annual
pilgrimage to a 10s tournament in the
Philippines. There's also **Seoul Sisters**
(Ⓦwww.ssrfc.com), a women's team
which has confounded the men by
surviving for more than a couple of
years; they also play in international
tournaments, and a few exhibition
games around Korea. You'll likely need
to be living in Seoul if you want to take
part in the matches themselves, but
both clubs welcome casual visitors to
their practice sessions.

Swimming

Unless you're staying at a higher-end
hotel or serviced apartment, you may
find it tricky to get a swim in Seoul.
There are **municipal pools** in most
parts of the city; enquire at a tourist
office (p.39) to track down the one
closest to you. In summer months, a
number of **outdoor pools** open up
around the Hangang; most convenient for visitors are those on the
western side of Yeouido park; see
p.83 for details.

Seoul food

Korean cuisine, a tantalizingly diverse mishmash of ingredients
served with lashings of eye-watering red-pepper paste,
remains little known in the West. It would be remiss of the
visitor to pass up the opportunity to plunge in and sample it:
safe pasta or steak dishes are available everywhere but with
just a small leap of faith, you could be barbecuing chunks
of beef at your table, wrestling with still-wriggling seafood,
or dining like a Joseon king. Perhaps most pleasingly of all,
almost every Korean meal comes surrounded by a troupe of
banchan – tapas-like side dishes, replenished at no extra cost

Barbecue dens

Seoul is a carnivore's dream come true. Its countless barbecue restaurants give diners a chance to play chef with a plate of **raw meat**, which is cooked at the table myriad ways but most typically over a red-hot **charcoal** briquette. As excess fat drips off the meat it releases the occasional tongue of flame, lending a genuine air of excitement to the meal, one heightened by tantalizingly aromatic wisps of smoke. A wide variety of meats are on offer, but **galbi** (갈비) – marinated pork or beef rib – is particularly popular with foreign visitors. The meat is usually served with a tray of leaves, which are essential for the full Korean experience: take one of these in your left hand, then with your chopsticks add a piece of meat, a smudge of soybean paste and a few morsels from the **banchan** (반찬); roll the leaf around to make a ball, and you're ready to go.

Galbi cooking at the table ▲

Gimchi at Korea House restaurant ▼

Dynastic and neo-Korean cuisine

A whole clutch of Insadong restaurants offer **banquet-style cuisine** once served to the aristocratic elite of the **Joseon dynasty**. Deceptively simple in nature, the multitude of dishes on the table in fact showcase a perfect balance of colour, taste and texture, Korean food at its most refined. A couple of places go one step further and serve actual **royal banquets**, where your table will be creaking under the burden of dishes such as braised pheasant, charcoal-roasted pork, julienned lotus root and sea bass with fried ginseng. Although these meals were sophisticated enough to appease the fussy Joseon kings and queens, they're available at prices that you'd expect at average restaurants in the West.

Forming a pleasing contrast with the dynastic banquets is **neo-Korean cuisine**. This curious term has been gaining currency among Seoul's culinary cognoscenti of late, and refers to traditional Korean dishes mixed with non-native ingredients, or prepared with Western techniques. Wonderfully varied in nature and almost impossible to describe, this vague term encompasses such mouth-watering "inventions" as lime jelly salads, soy tiramisu, and sherbet made with the five-flavoured *omija* berry.

▲ Neo-Korean cuisine at *Kongdu* restaurant

▲ *Deokbokki* stand in Myeongdon

▼ A platter of nine ingredients at a royal banquet

▼ Food stalls at Dongdaemun market

Wild and wonderful market treats

Seoul's markets are as characterful as they come, and for visitors prepared to jump in at the deep end they're one of the best places to eat. Dongdaemun market (see p.68) is the largest, with the food at its offshoot Gwangjang market deservedly popular.

▶▶ **Bindaedeok** (빈대떡) A slightly greasy mung-bean pancake, filled with beansprouts and green onion. You'll be given a saucer of soy sauce for dipping.

▶▶ **Makkeolli** (막걸리) A milky rice-wine, about 6 percent alcohol, this goes down particularly well if you're eating at the market. Those in the mood for something a little stronger should note that *soju* is also readily available.

▶▶ **Modeum jeon** (모둠전) This dish provides a varied mix of battered, refried comestibles known as *jeon*, which may include veggie or fish segments, *gimchi* pancakes or potato pancakes.

▶▶ **Sora** (소라) Boiled, snail-like sea creatures in conch shells – an acquired taste, though some people throw them back like there's no tomorrow.

▶▶ **Yukhoe** (육회) Essentially Korean steak tartare: raw beef ground and mixed with pepper, sesame seeds, garlic and onion, topped with raw egg yolk and served with julienned cucumber and pear.

Noryangjin fish market ▲

Bibimbap ▼

Seafood

Seoul is close enough to the coast to offer a mind-boggling array of excellent seafood. All manner of fish, slimy crustaceans and salty goodness-knows-what lurk in tanks in markets and outside restaurants – much of what's on offer is still alive before you buy it. Live baby octopus (*sannakji*, 산낙지) forms an initiation ceremony of sorts for many visitors, but safer recommendations include grilled eel (*jangeo-gui*, 장어구이) and barbecued shrimp (*sae-u*, 새우). To make things really easy, just ask for modeum-hoe (모듬회), and you'll get a mixed platter of sashimi.

Temple food

Salvation for vegetarians comes in the form of restaurants serving Buddhist temple cuisine. Given that Korea is historically a Buddhist nation, there are surprisingly few such places, but those able to track one down will soon be stuffing themselves with all manner of roots, shoots and leaves, as well as heartier chunks of vegetables and the occasional river fish. One of Korea's staple meals is bibimbap (비빔밥), a rice dish which is also Buddhist in origin, and can be found everywhere. *Bibimbap*'s ingredients were derived from the five principal colours of Korean Buddhism – red for the red-pepper paste, yellow for the yolk of the fried egg, white for the bed of rice, blue for the minced beef, and green for the vegetables.

5 top places to eat

▶▶ **Seafood** Noryangjin fish market, p.87
▶▶ **Barbecued meat** *Woo Rae Oak*, p.115
▶▶ **Buddhist temple food** *Baru*, p.115
▶▶ **Royal banquets** *Goongyeon*, p.117
▶▶ **Neo-Korean cuisine** *Wooriga*, p.120

Taekwondo

There are a number of ways in which foreign visitors can have a go at this Korean martial art. **Training sessions** take place every day bar Monday at Gyeonghuigung palace (see p.62; W15,000 per session). The 10.30am sessions are for basic moves, 1.30pm for self-defence and 3.30pm for "breaking techniques" (pine boards, not people). Reservations can be made through a tourist information office, who can also organize longer programs: figure on around W50,000 per day. In addition, the home of Korea's national sport is **Kukkiwon** (Mon–Fri 9am–5pm; free), a hall near Gangnam station; here there are occasional performances and tournaments, though it's empty at other times.

Tennis

The **Korean Open**, a WTA event, is held at Seoul Olympic Park every September. This is a fairly major event on the women's calendar, and past winners have included Venus Williams and Maria Sharapova. Check out Ⓦ www.hansolopen.com for more details. The few public courts around the city are members-only affairs, though it may be possible to get a game at some high school courts (after classes have finished, of course).

Jjimjilbang

For travellers willing to take the plunge and bare all in front of curious strangers, saunas known as **jjimjilbang** (찜질방) are one of the most unique of Seoul experiences. They're also the cheapest way to get a night's sleep. Overnighting in a sauna may sound a little curious, but Korea's take on the concept is almost entirely devoid of the seedy connotations that may dog similar facilities abroad: *jjimjilbang* are large, round-the-clock establishments primarily used by families escaping their homes for the night, businessmen who've worked or partied beyond their last trains, or teenage groups having a safe night out together. They can be found all over Seoul, or indeed any Korean city, typically costing W5000–10,000. Facilities consist of a shower and pool area, a sauna or steam room, and a large playschool-style quiet room or two for communal napping; most establishments also have snack bars and internet terminals, and some even have *noraebang* (singing rooms, see p.136). Upon entry, guests are given a locker key and matching t-shirts and shorts to change into – outside clothes are not allowed inside the complex, though it's okay to wear underwear. All must be sacrificed on entry to the pools,

Taekwondo

The martial art of **taekwondo** (태권도) is perhaps Korea's only well-known cultural export to the wider world. It has its roots in the Three Kingdoms period (57 BC–668 AD), when several different forms of unarmed combat existed across the peninsula. Local martial arts faded away during the philosophical Confucianist heyday of the Joseon kingdom (1392–1910), and came close to extinction during the subsequent period of Japanese occupation (1910–45), which saw attempts at a systematic annihilation of Korean culture. Taekwondo only truly came into existence in 1955, at the close of the Korean War – short on money and equipment, the local military used martial arts as a cheap way of keeping soldiers fit, and lassoed together what remained of the dynastic styles; it is still used as an integral part of military training to this day. Taekwondo has since become a staple martial art around the world, with official organisations in more than one hundred countries. It was introduced as a demonstration sport at the **Seoul Olympics** of 1988, and became a medal event in 2000.

which are segregated by gender. The common rooms are uniformly clean but vary in style; some have televisions and hi-tech recliner chairs, others invite you to roll out a mini-mattress, but all will have a floorful of snoring Koreans.

You're never far from a *jjimjilbang*, but the two most popular with foreigners are **Dragon Hill**, a huge facility just outside Yongsan station (see map, p.82), and **Itaewon Land**, a homelier place in Itaewon (see map, p.88).

Spas

Spa culture has well and truly hit Seoul, with an ever-increasing number of world-class facilities sprouting up around the city. Most of the top hotels have a resident spa, while others are affiliated to major cosmetics brands.

Amore Spa Namdaemunno ⓣ02/2118-6221. Euljiro 1-ga station; see map, p.61. No Korean cosmetics brand enjoys as much global fame as Amore Pacific, who use Eastern elements such as ginseng, green tea and bamboo sap in their products. They're best enjoyed at the company's renowned spa, located on the tenth floor of the huge Lotte complex (see map, p.61); figure on W100,000 and up for facials, and at least double that for full-body treatments.

Guerlain Spa Jangchungdong ⓣ02/2233-3131, ⓦwww.guerlainspa.com. Dongguk University station; see map, p.61. Have your tootsies pampered while enjoying a mountain view in this elegant spa, tucked away inside the *Shilla* hotel (see p.107). Treatments range from simple hour-long facials

(from W155,000) to full-day packages (W900,000 and up).

Whoo Spa Palace Cheongdamdong ⓣ080/022-0303. Cheongdamdong station; see map, p.92. Operated by History of Whoo, Korea's top cosmetics label, this is the fanciest spa in town, fusing Chinese herbal medicine with a range of Oriental hand-massage techniques. Treatments can be customized to focus on the body or face; prices start at W165,000 and race into the millions.

Will COEX ⓣ02/3466-8100. Samseong station see map, p.92. A small, friendly spa conveniently located in the COEX complex. Packages on offer range from familiar rubs to quirky treatments such as ginseng baths or "chocolate fondue" wraps. Prices are 20–50 percent lower than other establishments listed here.

Around Seoul

Around Seoul

Around Seoul

T here's no reason for your trip to begin and end with the city centre, since there's a wonderful array of sights within easy day-tripping range of the capital. Most popular is a visit to the **Demilitarized Zone** (DMZ) separating North and South Korea, a 4km-wide buffer zone often described as one of the most dangerous places on earth. It's even possible to step across the border here, in the infamous **Joint Security Area**. The DMZ forms the northern boundary of Gyeonggi, a province that encircles Seoul. This is one of the world's most densely populated areas – including the capital, almost 25 million people live here. Most cities here are commuter-filled non-entities, but a couple are worthy of a visit. **Incheon**, to the west of Seoul, was the first city in the country to be opened up to international trade, and remains Korea's most important link with the outside world thanks to its hub airport and ferry terminals. It sits on the shores of the West Sea, which contains myriad tranquil **islands**. Heading south of Seoul you come to **Suwon**, home to a renowned fortress, and useful as a springboard to several nearby sights. Further south again (and outside Seoul's greater urban area) are **Cheonan**, famed as the launchpad for Korea's largest museum, and the small city of **Gongju**, now a sleepy place but once capital of the famed Baekje dynasty. For the area covered by this chapter, see the **colour map** at the back of the book.

The Demilitarized Zone

As the tour bus crawls out of Seoul and heads slowly north through the traffic, the seemingly endless urban jungle slowly diminishes in size before disappearing altogether. You're now well on the way to a place where the mists of the Cold War still linger, and one that could well have been ground zero for the Third World War – the **DEMILITARIZED ZONE**. More commonly referred to as "the DMZ", this no man's land is a 4km-wide buffer zone that came into being at the end of the Korean War in 1953. It sketches an unbroken spiky line across the peninsula from coast to coast, separating the two Koreas and their diametrically opposed ideologies. Although it sounds forbidding, it's actually possible to enter this zone, and take a few tentative steps into North Korean territory – thousands of civilians do so every month, though only as part of a **tightly controlled tour**. Elsewhere are a few platforms from which the curious can stare across the border, and a **tunnel** built by the North, which you can enter.

The Axe Murder Incident and Operation Paul Bunyan

Relations between the two Koreas took a sharp nose-dive in 1976, when two American soldiers were killed by a pack of **axe-wielding North Koreans**. The cause of the trouble was a **poplar tree** which stood next to the Bridge of No Return: a UNC outpost stood next to the bridge, but its direct line of sight to the next Allied checkpoint was blocked by the leaves of the tree, so on August 18 a five-man American detail was dispatched to perform some trimming. Nobody is quite sure how this piece of military gardening descended into violence, since both sides claim to have reacted in self-defence; the American story is accepted in the west, though for some reason the key moments are missing from their video of the incident. Whoever made the first attack, KPA troops were soon attacking UNC personnel, in some cases using the axes the team had been using to prune the tree. The attack lasted less than a minute, but claimed the life of First Lieutenant Mark Barrett, as well as Captain Bonifas, who was apparently killed instantly with a single Karate chop to the neck (one of the only facts that both sides agree on).

Three days later, the US launched **Operation Paul Bunyan**, a show of force that must go down as the largest tree-trimming exercise in history. A convoy of two dozen UNC vehicles streamed towards the poplar tree, carrying more than eight hundred men, some trained in taekwondo, and all armed to the teeth. These were backed up by attack helicopters, fighter planes and B-52 bombers, while an aircraft carrier had also been stationed just off the Korean shore. This carefully managed operation drew no response from the KPA, and the tree was successfully cut down.

Some history

For the first year of the **Korean War** (1950–53), the tide of control yo-yoed back and forth across the peninsula. Then in June 1951, General Ridgeway of the United Nations Command got word that the Korean People's Army (KPA) would "not be averse to" armistice talks. These took place in the city of Kaesong, now a major North Korean city, but were soon shifted south to **Panmunjeom**, a tiny farming village that suddenly found itself the subject of international attention.

Ceasefire talks went on for two long years and often degenerated into venomous verbal battles littered with expletives. One of the most contentious issues was the repatriation of prisoners of war, and a breakthrough came in April 1953, when terms were agreed; exchanges took place on a bridge over the River Sachon, now referred to as the **Bridge of No Return**. "Operation Little Switch" came first, seeing the transfer of sick and injured prisoners (notably, six thousand returned to the North, while only a tenth of that number walked the other way); "Operation Big Switch" took place shortly afterwards, when the soldiers on both sides were asked to make a final choice on their preferred destination. Though no **peace treaty** was ever signed, representatives of the KPA, the United Nations Command (UNC) and the Chinese People's Liberation Army put their names to an **armistice** on July 27, 1953; South Korean delegates refused to do so. The hut where the signing took place was built specially for the occasion, and cobbled together at lightning speed by KPA personnel; it now forms part of most tours to North Korea.

An uneasy truce has prevailed since the end of the war – the longest military deadlock in history – but there have been regular spats along the way. In the early 1960s a small number of disaffected American soldiers **defected** to the North, after somehow managing to make it across the DMZ alive, while in 1968 the crew of the captured *USS Pueblo* walked south over the Bridge of No Return after protracted negotiations. The most serious confrontation took place in 1976, when two American soldiers were killed in the **Axe Murder Incident** (see box opposite), and in 1984, a young tour leader from the Soviet Union fled North Korea across the border, triggering a short gun battle that left three soldiers dead. For more on the Korean War, see p.175.

Panmunjeom and the Joint Security Area

There's nowhere in the world quite like the **Joint Security Area** ("the JSA"), a settlement squatting in the middle of the world's most heavily fortified frontier, and the only place in DMZ territory where visitors are permitted. Visits here will create a curious dichotomy of feelings: on one hand, you'll be in what was once memorably described by Bill Clinton as "the scariest place on earth", but as well as soldiers, barbed wire and brutalist buildings you'll see trees, hear birdsong and smell fresh air. The village of **Panmunjeom** (판문점) itself is actually in North Korean territory, and has dwindled to almost nothing since it became the venue for armistice talks in 1951. But such is the force of the name that you'll see it on promotional material for most **tours** that run to the area; these are, in fact, the only way to get in.

The JSA tour

"The visit to the Joint Security Area at Panmunjeom will entail entry into a hostile area, and possible injury or death as a direct result of enemy action"

disclaimer from form issued to visitors by United Nations Command.

Situated just over an hour from Seoul is **Camp Bonifas**, an American army base just outside the DMZ. Here you'll meet your guides (usually young, amiable recruits from the infantry), and be given a briefing session reminding you of the various dos and don'ts. Once inside the **JSA** itself, keep your fingers crossed that you'll be allowed to enter one of the three meeting rooms at the very centre of the complex, which offer some serious travel kudos – the chance to step into North Korea. The official Line of Control runs through the very centre of these cabins, the corners of which are guarded by South Korean soldiers, who are sometimes joined by their Northern counterparts, the enemies almost eyeball-to-eyeball. Note the microphones on the table inside the room – anything you say can be picked up by North Korean personnel. The rooms are closed to visitors when

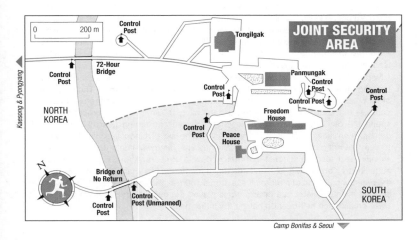

Camp Bonifas & Seoul ▽

151

⑬

meetings are scheduled, which is just as well since they have occasionally descended into farce. One such charade occurred when members of one side – it's not clear which – brought a bigger flag than usual to a meeting. The others followed suit with an even larger banner, and the childish process continued until the flags were simply too large to take into the room; at this point, both sides agreed on a standard flag size.

From an outdoor **lookout point** near the cabins you can soak up views of the North, including the huge flag and shell-like buildings of "**Propaganda Village**" (see box below). You may also be able to make out the jamming towers it uses to keep out unwanted imperialist signals – check the reception on your phone. Closer to the lookout point, and actually within JSA territory, is the **Bridge of No Return**, the venue for POW exchange at the end of the Korean War (and also for James Bond in *Die Another Day* – though for obvious reasons it was filmed elsewhere).

On arriving back at Camp Bonifas you'll usually have time to pop into a gift shop, stocked with "I did the DMZ" T-shirts and a nice line in North Korean blueberry wine. Also in the area is a **golf course** once named by *Sports Illustrated* as the most dangerous on Earth, but there's only one hole (a par-three) and you won't be allowed to use it.

Practicalities

Almost all **tours** to the DMZ start and finish in Seoul, and there are a great number of outfits competing for your money. Note that some are much cheaper than others – these probably won't be heading to **the JSA**, the most interesting place in the DMZ, so do check to see if it's on the schedule. Most people go with the ✈ USO (☎02/724-7781, ⓦ www.uso.org/korea; US$77); tours should be booked at least

---

Daeseongdong and "Propaganda Village"

The DMZ is actually home to two small settlements, one on each side of the Line of Control. With the southern village rich and tidy and its northern counterpart empty and sinister, both can be viewed as a microcosm of the countries they belong to.

The southern village – **Daeseongdong** (대성동) – is a small farming community, but one off-limits to all but those living or working here. These are among the richest farmers in Korea: they pay no rent or tax, and DMZ produce fetches big bucks at markets around the country. Technically, residents have to spend 240 days of the year at home, but most commute here from their condos in Seoul to "punch in", and get hired hands to do the dirty work; if they're staying, they must be back in town by nightfall, and have their doors and windows locked and bolted by midnight. Women are allowed to marry into this tight society, but men are not; those who choose to raise their children here also benefit from a school that at the last count had twelve teachers, and only eight students.

North of the line of control is **Kijongdong** (기정동), an odd collection of empty buildings referred to by American soldiers as "**Propaganda Village**". The purpose of its creation appears to have been to show citizens in the South the communist paradise that they're missing – a few dozen "villagers" arrive every morning by bus, spend the day taking part in wholesome activities and letting their children play games, then leave again in the evening. With the aid of binoculars, you'll be able to see that none of the buildings actually has any windows; lights turned on in the evening also seem to suggest that they're devoid of floors. Above the village flies a huge **North Korean flag**, one so large that it required a fifty-man detail to hoist, until the recent installation of a motor. It sits atop a 160m-high flagpole, the world's tallest, and the eventual victor in a bizarre game played out over a number of years by the two Koreas, each hell-bent on having the loftier flag.

four days in advance. You'll find pamphlets from other operators in your hotel lobby, and most operators speak enough English to accept a reservation by telephone; most notable are Young Il Tours (☏02/730-1090, ⓦiloveseoultour .com), which adds a session of pistol shooting to the regular rounds (W105,000), and Panmunjom Travel Center (☏02/771-5593, ⓦkoreadmztour.com), which offers a tour led by a North Korean defector (W77,000).

For all these tours you'll need to bring your **passport** along. Note that these excursions come with a number of **restrictions**, most imposed by the United Nations Command. Citizens of certain countries are not allowed into DMZ territory, including those from most nations in the Middle East, some in Africa, and communist territories such as Vietnam, Hong Kong and mainland China. A dress code also applies (no flip-flops, ripped jeans, "clothing deemed faddish" or "shorts that expose the buttocks"), but most things are OK. Also be warned that schedules can change in an instant, and that in certain areas **photography** is not allowed – you'll be told when to put your camera away. Lastly, remember that you'll be entering an extremely dangerous area – this is no place for fooling around or wandering off by yourself.

The Third Tunnel of Aggression

A short drive south of Panmunjeom is the **Third Tunnel of Aggression**. This is one of four tunnels found so far, all apparently dug by North Korean soldiers in preparation for an invasion of the south. Such contentions have, like other such reports, been refuted by Pyongyang, which claims that they were merely coal mines. All the tunnels were fairly narrow, but would have been able to accommodate the transportation of light machinery (even tanks, in a couple of cases) across the border; discovered in 1974, this was the third tunnel found, and the closest to Seoul, a city that would have been just a day's march away had the plan been carried out. It's regularly included in DMZ tour packages, though many emerge from the depths underwhelmed – it is, after all, just a tunnel, even if you get to walk under **DMZ territory** up to the line of control that marks the actual border. On busy days it can become uncomfortably crowded – not a place for the claustrophobic. Before entering the tunnel, visitors are usually ushered into a small theatre to be shown an explanatory movie. This is a ghastly but mercifully brief pro-unification shocker that gives no account at all of how the separation actually occurred, instead showing the ground literally splitting to force a young girl from her family: Kim Jong-Il himself would be proud of such nonsense.

Paju and around

The sprawling satellite town of **Paju** (파주) is home to some of the most interesting sights in the border area, and for once some do not revolve around North Korea. Easiest to reach is **Paju Book City** (파주출판문화재단; ⓦwww.pajubookcity .org), a publishing district filled with excellent **modern architecture** – quite a rarity in this land of sterile high-rise. There's no focus as such to the area, but strolling the quiet streets is rather pleasurable, and it's even possible to stay here at *Jijihyang* (☏031/955-0090; W110,000), an appropriately stylish streamside hotel. Similar architectural delights are on offer at **Heyri Art Valley** (헤이리문화예술마을), just 7km to the north; this artists' village is home to dozens of small galleries, and its countryside air is making it an increasingly popular day-trip for young, arty Seoulites. Sitting atop a hill just 1km west of Heyri is **Odusan observatory** (daily 9am–5pm; W3000), where you'll be able to peer across the border through binoculars, and buy alcoholic drinks from North Korea.

To get to Heyri or the Book City, take bus #2200 from exit 2 of Hapjeong subway station (50min; W1400); alternatively they're both within a W15,000 taxi ride of Daehwa subway station, the terminus of line 3. Buses to the observatory are irregular and tricky to find, so take a cab from either village; there won't be any taxis waiting when you exit, so check the return schedules at the observatory entrance and you'll be able to head back by bus.

Incheon and the West Sea islands

INCHEON (인천) is an important port and Korea's third most populous city. Despite its being home to the country's main international airport and ferry terminal, few foreign travellers see anything of the city itself, with the overwhelming majority of people preferring to race straight to Seoul. However, in view of its colourful recent history, it's worth at least a day-trip from the capital. This was where Korea's "Hermit Kingdom" finally crawled out of self-imposed isolation in the late nineteenth century and opened itself up to international trade, an event that was spurred on by the Japanese following similar events in their own country (the Meiji Restoration). The city was also the landing site for **Douglas MacArthur** and his troops in a manoeuvre that turned the tide of the Korean War (see box, p.156). Now a thoroughly modern place, the city has also been chosen as host of the **2014 Asian Games**, and is busily setting about smartening itself up in preparation for the event.

The most interesting part is **Jung-gu**, the country's only official Chinatown, a small but appealing area sitting below **Jayu Park**, where a statue of MacArthur gazes out over the sea. The only other area of note is **Songdo New Town**, an area being built on land reclaimed from the sea. At the time of writing this resembled a war zone (though with perfect roads, running buses and the odd hotel and apartment block), but by 2015 it should be more or less complete, and home to the 151 **Incheon Tower**, set to be the world's second-tallest structure (a whopping 601m high) on completion.

Arrival, orientation and information

There's no need to transit in Incheon to get to and from the **international airport**: there are dedicated airport bus connections from Seoul and all over the country. To get to Incheon from the airport, you can go via one of several limousine bus routes, or city bus #306 to Incheon subway station, the western terminus of Seoul's line 1. Note that the city is also a base for **ferries** from China (see p.22) and some Korean islands in the West Sea (pp.157–159).

The city itself spreads far and wide in an unruly sprawl of buildings and industry, with its western fringe dissolving into the sea in a mess of cranes, ships and containers. Incheon's main sights lie in Jung-gu, a western district of the city best accessed via Incheon or Dong-Incheon **subway** stations,

CHINATOWN

Incheon Station

Centennial Monument

Jayu Park

Statue of General MacArthur

Jung-gu District Office

STREET OF CULTURE & HISTORY

Former Japanese Banks

JEMULLYANGNO

N

Airport

ACCOMMODATION
Athene	B
Harbor Park	C
Paradise	A

0   200 m

INCHEON

RESTAURANTS
Gunghwajun	1
Harbor Park	C
Hyangmanseong	2
Tochon	3

Songdo New Town, Incheon Tower & Ferry Terminals ▼

the last two on Seoul's line 1 (1hr). From Seoul, be sure to board a train bound for Incheon, as line 1 splits south of the capital. Outside Incheon subway station is a helpful **tourist information** office (daily 9am–6pm; ☎032/773-2225); further offices can be found in the international ferry terminals.

Accommodation

Incheon's proximity to Seoul means that most people choose to visit on a day-trip, but with accommodation prices a little lower than in the capital it may be worth spending a night here.

Athene Motel Songhakdong ☎032/772-5233. This hard-to-find gem of a motel is tucked away in a quiet area behind the Jung-gu district office, near the *Tochon* restaurant (see p.157). Rooms and common areas have some nice floral touches, both real and pictorial; combined with the pleasant drowsiness of the area, it's easy to put big-city bustle out of mind. W30,000.
Harbor Park Hotel Hangdong ☎032/770-9500, ⓦwww.harborparkhotel.com. The newest and best option in Jung-gu, with excellent service standards and great sea views. Unfortunately, standard rooms can be

extremely small, so try to check a few if possible; suites, on the other hand, are generously sized. W240,000.
Paradise Hotel Hangdong ☎032/762-5181, ⓦincheon.paradisehotel.co.kr. Though service can be a little ropey at times, and the crane-filled views may not appeal to some, this old favourite is still going strong. It has benefited from recent refurbishments, and competition from the nearby *Harbor Park* has forced prices down – rooms here are usually half the price of those at its neighbour. W120,000.

The City

To get to **Jung-gu** (중구), Incheon's most absorbing district, head to Incheon subway station, which sits at the end of a line that runs all the way from Seoul. On exiting the gate, you'll immediately be confronted by the city's gentrified Chinatown, sitting across the main road and demarcated by the requisite oriental gate. Not so long ago, this area was dowdy and run-down, and lent an unintentional air of authenticity by displaying cracked roads, rubble and grime; it has since been given a makeover, and is now a pleasant and surprisingly quiet area to walk around with a belly full of Chinese food. Uphill roads heading northeast from Chinatown lead to **Jayu Park** (자유공원), also within easy walking distance of the subway station, and home to a statue of **General Douglas MacArthur**, staring proudly out over the seas that he conquered during the Korean War (see box, p.156). Also in the park is the Korean–American Centennial Monument, made up of eight black triangular shards that stretch up towards each other but never quite touch – feel free to make your own comparisons with the relationship between the two countries. Views from certain parts of the park expose Incheon's port, a colourful maze of cranes and container ships that provide a vivid reminder of the city's trade links with its neighbours across the seas.

The cultural district

From Chinatown, it's possible to take a pleasant, relatively traffic-free walk through Incheon's past on the way to Dong-Incheon station – pick up the *History through Modern Architecture* pamphlet from the tourist office, which will guide you directly to a road studded with distinctive **Japanese colonial buildings**. Surprisingly Western in appearance, three of these were originally banks, and two have been converted into small **museums**. The former 58th Bank of Japan (9am–5pm,

General MacArthur and the Incheon landings

"We drew up a list of every natural and geographic handicap... Incheon had 'em all."

Commander Arlie G. Capps

On the morning of September 15, 1950, the most daring move of the **Korean War** was made, an event that was to alter the course of the conflict entirely, and is now seen as one of the greatest military manoeuvres in history. At this point the Allied forces had been pushed by the North Korean People's Army into a small corner of the peninsula around Busan, but **General Douglas MacArthur** was convinced that a single decisive movement behind enemy lines could be enough to turn the tide.

MacArthur wanted to attempt an amphibious landing on the Incheon coast, but his plan was greeted with scepticism by many of his colleagues – both the South Korean and American armies were severely under-equipped (the latter only just recovering from the tolls of World War II), Incheon was heavily fortified, and its natural island-peppered defences and fast tides made it an even more dangerous choice.

However, the plan went ahead and the Allied forces performed **successful landings** at three Incheon beaches, during which time North Korean forces were shelled heavily to quell any counterattacks. The city was taken with relative ease, the People's Army having simply not anticipated an attack on this scale in this area, reasoning that if one were to happen, it would take place at a more sensible location further down the coast. MacArthur had correctly deduced that a poor movement of supplies was his enemy's Achilles heel – landing behind enemy lines gave Allied forces a chance to cut the supply line to KPA forces further south, and Seoul was duly retaken on 25 September.

Despite the Incheon victory and its consequences, MacArthur is not viewed by Koreans – or, indeed, the world in general – in an entirely positive light, feelings exacerbated by the continued American military presence in the country. While many in Korea venerate the General as a hero, repeated demonstrations have called for the **tearing down** of his statue in Jayu Park, denouncing him as a "war criminal who massacred civilians during the Korean War", and whose statue "greatly injures the dignity of the Korean people". Documents obtained after his eventual dismissal from the Army suggest that he would even have been willing to bring nuclear weapons into play – on December 24, 1950, he requested the shipment of 38 atomic bombs to Korea, intending to string them "across the neck of Manchuria". Douglas MacArthur remains a controversial character, even in death.

---

closed Mon; free) offers interesting photo and video displays of life in colonial times, while the former 1st Bank down the road (same times; free) has a less interesting display of documents, flags and the like. In a small outdoor display area between the two museums, you'll find some fascinating pictures taken here in the 1890s, on what was then a quiet, dusty road almost entirely devoid of traffic, peopled with white-robed gents in horsehair hats – images of a Korea long gone. However, one block to the north on a parallel road, the city has tried to evoke this bygone era on the slightly bizarre **Street of Culture and History**; the new wooden fronts added to the buildings are the only discernable things that constitute such a grand title, though they look decidedly pretty.

Eating

Rarely for a Korean city, and perhaps uniquely for a Korean port, Incheon isn't renowned for its food, though the presence of a large and thriving **Chinatown** is a boon to visitors. Don't expect the food to be terribly authentic, since Koreans have their own take on Chinese cuisine. Top choices here, and available at every single restaurant, are sweet-and-sour pork (탕수육; *tansuyuk*), fried rice topped with a fried egg and black-bean paste (볶음밥; *bokkeumbap*), spicy seafood broth (짬뽕; *jjambbong*), and the undisputed number one: *jjajangmyeon* (짜장면), noodles topped with black-bean paste.

Gunghwajun Bukseongdong. This is where Korea's *jjajangmyeon* fad started - it has been served here since the 1890s. W5000 will buy you a bowl, or you could try the sautéed shredded beef with green pepper (W20,000).
Harbor Park Hotel Hangdong. The buffet restaurant in this hotel (see p.155) is open to guests and non-guests alike, and dishes are superbly prepared; lunch is a steal at W18,000.
Hyangmanseong Bukseongdong. Various Chinese dishes are on offer at this small

Chinatown institution, in operation since the 1960s. They're proudest of the braised prawns in chilli sauce, but best value are the set deals, which start at around W20,000 per person (2 person minimum).
Tochon Songhakdong. A wonderfully rustic lair, whose ground floor is surrounded on three sides by interconnected fish tanks. Fishy set meals go for W25,000 or more, though cheaper dishes are available, such as delicious mountain *bibimbap* for W7000.

West Sea Islands

Incheon's perforated western coast topples into a body of water known as the **West Sea** to Koreans, and the Yellow Sea to the rest of the world. Land rises again across the waves in the form of dozens of **islands**, almost all of which have remained pleasantly green and unspoilt; some also have excellent **beaches**. Life here is predominantly fishing-based and dawdles by at a snail's pace – a world away from Seoul and its environs, despite a few being close enough to be visited on a day-trip. Easiest to reach are **Ganghwado**, a slightly over-busy dot of land studded with ancient dolmens, and its far quieter neighbour **Seongmodo**. These are best accessed directly from Seoul, but you'll have to head to Incheon for ferries to **Deokjeokdo** and **Baengnyeongdo**, both beautiful and sufficiently far away from the capital to provide perfect escapes for those in need of a break.

Ganghwado

One look at a map should make clear the strategic importance of **GANGHWADO** (강화도), an island which not only sits at the mouth of Seoul's main river, the Han, but whose northern flank is within a frisbee throw of the **North Korean border**. Before the Korean War, this unfortunate isle saw **battles** with Mongol, Manchu, French, American and Japanese forces, among others (see p.173). Unlike most West Sea islands, Ganghwado is close enough to the mainland to be connected by road – buses run regularly from Sinchon bus terminal in Seoul (200m up the road from exit 7 of Sinchon subway station), taking around ninety minutes to arrive in **Ganghwa-eup**, the ugly main settlement. Some continue on to the fishing village of **Oepo** (외포; pronounced "Way-paw") on the island's western coast, and by far its most appealing place to stay; the *Santa Lucia* (☎032/933 2141; W40,000), near the bus stop is one of the only buildings to take advantage of the village's sea views.

Despite its incendiary recent history, Ganghwado's foremost sights date from further back than even the earliest of these fisticuffs – a clutch of **dolmens** scattered around the northern part of the island, dating from the first century BC and now on UNESCO's World Heritage list. Misty remnants from bygone millennia, these dolmens are overground burial chambers consisting of flat capstones supported by three or more vertical megaliths. The Korean peninsula contains over thirty thousand of these ancient tombs – almost half of the world's total – and Ganghwado has one of the highest concentrations in the country. Most can only be reached by car or bike, though one is situated near a main road and accessible by bus. From Ganghwa-eup, take one of the buses bound for Changhu-ri, which depart every hour or so, and make sure that the driver knows where you want to go – ask to be dropped off at the **Goindol** (고인돌; 24hr; free), a granite tomb which sits unobtrusively in a field as it has for centuries: a stone skeleton long divested of its original earth covering, with a large five-by-seven-metre capstone. The surrounding countryside is extremely beautiful, and you can combine a visit to the dolmen with a delightful walk.

Seongmodo

Half-hourly ferries (10min; W2000) run from Oepo's tiny terminal to **Seongmodo** (석모도), an island just across the water from Ganghwado; ornithophobes should note that large flocks of seagulls tend to circumnavigate the vessel for the entire journey, waiting to catch thrown crisps. Buses meet the ferries and head to **Bomunsa** (보문사), a charming temple that constitutes the island's main sight. The complex is a five-minute uphill pant from the bus stop, with a small tearoom (9am–5pm) at its entrance; many visitors choose to give their legs an extra work-out by taking the mountain path behind the temple, which leads to a clutch of small grottoes that function as **Buddhist shrines**, and boast wonderful sea views. Ferries back to Ganghwado dry up at 8.30pm, but this is a wonderfully peaceful place to be stranded – there are restaurants and simple accommodation around both the temple and ferry terminal.

Deokjeokdo

Possibly the prettiest and most tranquil of the West Sea isles, **DEOKJEOKDO** (덕적도) feels a world away from Seoul, though it's quite possible to visit from the capital on a day-trip. There's little in the way of sightseeing, and not much to do, but that's just the point – the island has a couple of stunning beaches and some gorgeous mountain trails, and makes a refreshing break from the hustle and bustle of the mainland. Around the ferry berth are a few shops, restaurants and *minbak*, while a bus meets the ferries and makes its way round to **Seopori Beach** on the other, quieter side of the island – also home to a few *minbak*. Most who stay here for a day or two spend their time chatting to locals, lazing or throwing back beers on the beach, going fishing or taking the easy climb up to the island's main peak.

Three fast **ferries** (1hr; W21,900) run to Deokjeokdo from Incheon's Yeonan pier, departing at 9am, 9.30am & 2.30pm; slower ferries (2hr 30min; W12,100) depart at 8am from the same terminal.

Baengnyeongdo

Four hours' ferry-ride from Incheon is **BAENGNYEONGDO** (백령도), an island almost tickling the North Korean coastline and as such home to many military installations. In 2010, an incident occurred just off the island, which was to seriously damage relations between the two Koreas; see box, p.179 for details. Baengnyeongdo literally means "White Wing Island", receiving this name on account of its apparent resemblance to an ibis taking flight, and although the reality is somewhat different you'll find yourself gawping at Baengnyeongdo's spectacular **rock formations**, best seen from one of the tour boats that regularly depart the port. Some of the most popular are off Dumujin, to the west of the island, while at Sagot Beach the stone cliffs plunge diagonally into the sea.

The tranquil nature of these islands is sometimes diluted by swarms of summer visitors – it's best to visit on weekdays, or outside the warmest months. Thrice-daily **ferries** (W57,400) head to Baengnyeongdo from Incheon's Yeonan pier, departing at 8am, 8.50am & 1pm; return sailings are at 8am, 1pm & 1.50pm. There's also simple **accommodation** on Baengnyeongdo, though given the island's distance from Incheon it's best to organize this at a tourist information office before heading out.

Suwon and around

Heading south from Seoul by train, the capital's dense urban sprawl barely thins before you arrive in **SUWON** (수원), a city with an impressive history of its own, best embodied by the gigantic **fortress** at its centre. Suwon, in fact, came close to usurping Seoul as Korea's seat of power following the murder of prince Sado (see box, p.53), but though it failed to overtake the capital, the city grew in importance in a way that remains visible to this day. Its fortress walls, built in the late eighteenth century, once enclosed the whole of Suwon, but from the structure's upper reaches you'll see just how far the city has spread, the never-ending hotchpotch of buildings now forming one of Korea's largest urban centres. Making up for the dearth of sights in Suwon itself is an interesting and varied range of possibilities in a corridor stretching east of the city. Twenty kilometres away, the **Korean Folk Village** is a vaguely authentic portrayal of traditional Korean life; though too sugary for some, it redeems itself with some high-quality dance, music and gymnastic performances. Twenty-five kilometres further east is **Everland**, a huge amusement park.

An hour away from central Seoul, Suwon is certainly within easy **day-trip** territory of the capital, and the same can be said for its surrounding sights – few choose to stay the night here. The city is accessible from Seoul by **rail** (30min) and **subway** (1hr on line 1). A useful **information office** (daily 7am–10pm; ☏031/228-4672) can be found just outside Suwon station – take a left from the train exit, and look for a squat, traditional-style building; tours of the city start here at 10am and 2pm every day except Monday, lasting two or three hours and costing W8000. Buses to all places of interest can be picked up from the main road outside.

Accommodation

There are plenty of **motels** in the area bounded by the fortress wall, but you'd do well to disregard all images that staying inside a World Heritage site may bring to mind, as it's one of the seediest parts of the city.

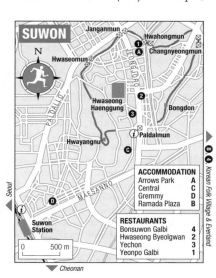

SUWON

N

Janganmun

Hwahongmun

Hwaseomun

Changnyeongmun

Hwaseong Haenggung

Bongdon

Paldalmun

Hwayangnu

Seoul

MAESANNO

Suwon Station

0   500 m

ACCOMMODATION	
Arrows Park	A
Central	C
Gremmy	D
Ramada Plaza	B

RESTAURANTS	
Bonsuwon Galbi	4
Hwaseong Byeolgwan	2
Yechon	3
Yeonpo Galbi	1

Korean Folk Village & Everland

Cheonan

Arrows Park Janganmun. Just inside the fortress gate, this motel's clean rooms make it a rare blessing in the central area. The *Ruby* opposite has slightly inferior rooms at marginally lower prices. W25,000.

Hotel Central Gyodong ☏ 031/246-0011. In an excellent location for the fortress, as the name suggests, and not too run down for a Korean tourist hotel. Rooms are reasonably good value and have cable TV; a mini-buffet breakfast is also thrown in for free, but staff are unlikely to speak English, and the bar-filled street outside can get noisy at night. W60,000.

Motel Gremmy Maesanno ☏ 031/254-7557. Most Korean motels are a little "love-oriented", but at least this one is honest about it – racy pictures in the corridors, laid-on contraception and "special interest" videos to choose from in the lobby. It's obviously not for everyone, but rooms are large and clean, with the more expensive ones housing cavernous bathrooms. W40,000.

Ramada Plaza Umandong ☏ 031/230-0001, ⓦ www.ramadaplazasuwon.com. Suwon's best hotel, though in an uninteresting corner of the city, attracts well-heeled visitors – primarily Europeans here on business – and offers all the comfort you'd expect of the chain. Some of the suites are truly stunning, though even standard rooms have been designed with care. W230,000.

Hwaseong fortress

Central Suwon has but one notable sight – **Hwaseong fortress** (화성; free), one of Korea's few entries on the UNESCO list of world heritage, and the most accessible outside Seoul. Completed in 1796, the complex was built on the orders of **King Jeongjo**, one of the Joseon dynasty's most famous rulers, in order to house the remains of his father, Prince Sado. Sado never became king, and met an early end in Seoul's Changgyeonggung Palace at the hands of his own father, King Yeongjo (see box, p.53); it may have been the gravity of the situation that spurred Jeongjo's attempts to move the capital away from Seoul.

Towering almost ten metres high for the bulk of its course, the **fortress wall** rises and falls in a 5.7km-long stretch, most of which is walkable, the various peaks and troughs marked by sentry posts and ornate entrance gates. From the higher vantage points you'll be able to soak up **superb views** of the city, but while there's also plenty to see along the wall itself, the interior is disappointing: other fortresses around the country, including Gongsanseong in Gongju (p.164), have green, tranquil grounds with little inside save for trees, squirrels, pagodas and meandering paths, but Hwaseong's has had concrete poured into it, and is now a cityscape filled with restaurants, honking traffic and ropy motels. Even on the wall itself, it's hard to escape the noise, which is often punctuated by screaming aircraft from the nearby military base. Most visitors start their wall walk at **Paldalmun** (팔달문), a gate at the lower end of the fortress, exuding a well-preserved magnificence now diluted by its position in the middle of a traffic-filled roundabout. From here there's a short but steep uphill path to Seonammun, the western gate.

In the centre of the area bounded by the fortress walls is **Hwaseong Haenggung** (화성 행궁), once a government office, then a palace, and now a fine place to amble around; its pink walls are punctuated by the green lattice frames of windows and doors, which overlook dirt courtyards from where you can admire the fortress wall that looms above. There's a martial arts display (Tues–Sun 11am), and traditional dance and music performances take place at 2pm on Saturdays and Sundays from April to November.

Paldalmun is a 20-minute walk from the train station (take the charming narrow road, west of the main one), though several **buses** ply this route, including #11, #13, #36 and #39; the #300 heads there from the bus terminal.

Mister Toilet

Bar its fortress, central Suwon carries precious little sightseeing potential, though one interesting facet is what may be the world's greatest concentration of **public toilets** – they all have names, and some are even marked on tourist maps. This concept was the brainchild of Sim Jae-deok, a man referred to, especially by himself, as "Mister Toilet". Apparently afflicted by something of a cloacal obsession (best evidenced by his house, custom-built to resemble a giant loo), Sim claims to have been born in a public restroom, but transcended these humble beginnings to become mayor of Suwon, and a member of the National Assembly. He then went on to create, and declare himself head of, the World Toilet Organization (the *other* WTO). Undoubtedly spurred on by his team's debatable finding that the average human being spends three years of their life on the toilet, Sim desired to improve his home city's facilities for the World Cup in 2002, commissioning dozens of individually designed public toilets. They're still around today: features may include skylights, mountain views or piped classical music, though such refinement is sadly sullied, as it is all over Korea, by the baskets of used toilet paper discarded throne-side.

Eating

Suwon is famous for a local variety of *galbi*, whereby the regular meat dish is given a salty seasoning. You will more than likely find something appealing on **Rodeo Street**, where the city's youth flocks to in the evening to take advantage of the copious cheap restaurants.

Bonsuwon Galbi Umandong. Around the back of *Hotel Central*, and therefore a little out of the way for those not staying there, is what may well be the best *galbi* restaurant in the city. The succulent meat doesn't come cheap (W20,000 per portion), but the chance to try Suwon's local take on Korea's most pyromaniacal eating experiences shouldn't be missed.

Hwaseong Byeolgwan Paldallo. Not far from the entrance to Haenggung, this presentable restaurant – though devoid of English-language menus – serves extremely cheap *bibimbap* and pork cutlet, as well as more expensive meat specials. The beef stew-like *ddukbaegi bulgogi* (뚝배기불고기)

is great value at W7000. Look for the sign saying "Korean Royal Palace Cuisine".

Yechon Paldallo. Low-key, traditionally-styled establishment serving savoury pancakes known as *jeon* (전) in many different styles (W7000–15,000), as well as superb *makkeolli* from Jeonju, a city in the southwest of the country.

Yeonpo Galbi Buksudong. Just inside the fortress wall lies the best restaurant in this quiet area. The *galbi* meat is rather expensive, but cheaper noodle dishes are available, and those who arrive before 3pm can get a huge *jeongsik* (set meal) for W15,000, which includes several small fish and vegetable dishes.

Korean Folk Village

This re-creation of a traditional **Korean Folk Village** (한국민속촌; March–Oct 9am–6.30pm; Nov–Feb to 5pm; W12,000) has become one of the most popular day-trips for foreign visitors to Seoul, its thatch-roofed houses and dirt paths evoking the sights, sounds and some of the more pleasant smells of a bygone time, when farming was the mainstay of the country. Its proximity to the capital makes this village by far the most-visited of the many such facilities dotted around the country, which tends to diminish the authenticity of the experience. Nevertheless, the riverbank setting and its old-fashioned buildings are impressive, though the emphasis is squarely on performance – shows of tightrope-walking and horse-riding take place regularly throughout the day. Traditional wedding ceremonies provide a glimpse into Confucian society, with painstaking attention to detail including gifts of live chickens wrapped up in cloth like Egyptian mummies. Don't miss the **farmers' dance** (11am & 2.30pm; sometimes also 1.40pm), in which costumed performers prance around in highly distinctive ribbon-topped hats amid a cacophony of drums and crashes – quintessential Korea.

Free **shuttle buses** to the folk village leave from outside Suwon's tourist information office every half-hour from 10.30am to 2.30pm (30min; free with entry ticket), though the last one back to Suwon departs the village frustratingly early – usually 5pm. Regular city buses are available for those who want to stay a little longer. There are a few good **restaurants** on site, as well as an excellent tearoom.

Everland

Everland (daily, usually 9.30am–10pm; W30,000, discounts after 5pm; Ⓦeng .everland.com) is a colossal theme park that ranks as one of the most popular domestic tourist attractions in the country – male or female, young or old, it's hard to find a *hangukin* (Korean person) who hasn't taken this modern-day rite of passage. Most are here for the fairground rides, and the park has all that a roller-coaster connoisseur could possibly wish for. Other attractions include a **zoo** (which features a safari zone that can be toured by bus, jeep or even at night), a speedway track, a golf course, and the surprisingly good **Hoam Museum**, which contains a few excellent examples of Buddhist art, and some interesting French sculpture in an outdoor garden. The most popular part of the park, however, is **Caribbean Bay** (usually 9.30am–5pm, closes 7pm Sat & Sun; W30,000–65,000 depending upon season), with an indoor zone that's open year-round containing several pools, a sauna and a short river that you can float down on a tube, as well as massage machines and relaxation capsules. The **outdoor section** (same times June–Aug; W40,000–60,000) with its man-made beach is what really draws the summer crowds. Off the beach, facilities include a water bobsleigh, which drops you the height of a ten-floor building in just ten seconds, and an artificial surfing facility.

Most locals drive to Everland, creating long queues on busy days, whereas foreign visitors tend to take the **bus**. These leave on the half-hour from outside the train station in Suwon, and take around an hour. Several routes head here from Seoul; one of the most frequent and useful runs from the Dong-Seoul bus terminal via Jamsil subway station (50min; W2,200), and a second from just north of Gangnam subway station exit six, via Yangjae (40min; W1,600).

Cheonan and around

After years in the shadows, **Cheonan** (천안) is a city on the up: now connected to Seoul by the steel veins of subway and high-speed train, it's awash with money from those deserting the capital, and improving at a rate of knots. However, despite the flashy new department stores and housing complexes, there's not much here to detain the traveller – visitors mainly use Cheonan as a jumping-off point for the largest museum in the country, the fascinating **Independence Hall of Korea**.

Arario Gallery

One notable exception to Cheonan's dearth of sights is the excellent **Arario Gallery** (11am–7pm, closed Mon; W5000) right next to the bus terminal, the main base of the eponymous gallery in Seoul (see p.132), which makes a good pit stop en route to the independence hall. Outside the main entrance sits one of Damien Hirst's body-with-bits-exposed sculptures, alongside a tall tower of car axles that pokes fun at the city's ever-declining reputation as a mere transit hub; inside are two exhibition floors, both small but almost always brimming with high-quality modern art. The gallery's bosses have excellent connections in China (there's another Arario in Beijing's *798* gallery-cum-factory district), which means that it's often possible to catch glimpses of the burgeoning art scene across the West Sea.

Independence Hall of Korea

Set in a wooded area east of Cheonan, Korea's largest museum, the **Independence Hall of Korea** (독립기념관; 9.30am–5pm, Nov–Feb until 4pm; closed Mon; W2000; ⓦwww.independence.or.kr), is a concrete testament to the country's continued struggle for independence during its most troubled time from 1910 to 1945, when it suffered the indignity of being **occupied by Japan**. Though this was a relatively short period, the effects were devastating (see box, p.75), and despite the Korean government's initial appeal for their citizens not to be "filled with bitterness or resentment", the popularity of the place and the size of its seven large exhibition halls – all of which would probably function quite well as individual museums – show that the wounds are still sore. Scarcely an opportunity is missed to insert a derogatory adjective against the Japanese people and policies of the time; it's this combination of vitriol and history that makes the place such an absorbing visit.

Each of the halls highlights different aspects of the occupation, with the most important displays labelled in English. However, many locals head straight for those detailing **Japanese brutality** during the colonial period – "Torture done by Japan", a life-size display featuring some unfortunate mannequins, is one of the most popular exhibits, but there are also numerous photographs on show. Should you tire of the unrelenting indignation, the "Hall of National Heritage" is filled with less bombastic displays detailing traditional Korean life.

A number of city **buses** run to the museum from the bus and train stations in central Cheonan (all have three-digit numbers beginning with 4); the journey takes around half an hour. Ask for *Dongnip Ginyeom-gwan*, if you can get your tongue around it, and the driver will drop you off outside.

Practicalities

Cheonan's **train** and **bus** stations are fairly close to each other in the city centre; outside the former is a small **tourist information** booth (daily 9am–5pm; ☎041/550-2445). Note that high-speed KTX services terminate at a dedicated station a few subway stations to the west on line 1. Good **accommodation** is a little thin on the ground, but the *Hotel Metro* (☎041/622-8211 to 4, ⓦwww.hotelmetro.co.kr; W130,000), visible to the left of the train station exit, is a reliable option, and also offers an airport shuttle service. The carpeted rooms are decent with vault-like doors, though bathroom goings-on can be sometimes too visible through the frosted glass that separates them from the bedrooms. The best area for **budget-seekers** is diagonally opposite the crossroads from Arario; here, the *Western Hotel* (☎041/551-0606; W35,000) is excellent value and offers free internet access, soft drinks, snacks and international calls. On the same road, the *Hotel California* (T041/566-3311 or 2; W30,000) also deserves a mention; rooms are furnished with black tiles and dark wood, and you'll find a free can of beer waiting in the fridge.

For **eating and drinking**, it's best to head to the Arario building, whose complex houses a Japanese restaurant, a colossal café, and an excellent barbecue joint. The nuked meat at the latter is largely western, rather than Korean, in nature, but for real *galbi* head across the road to a branch of *Bulgogi Brothers* (see p.114), which sits almost directly opposite the bus station.

Gongju

Presided over by the large fortress of Gongsanseong, the small, sleepy city of **GONGJU** (공주) is one of the best places to see relics from the **Baekje dynasty** that it ruled as capital in the fifth and sixth centuries. Don't be fooled by its apparent distance from Seoul – good roads and regular buses mean that Gongju is just 90 minutes from the capital, making it a perfectly feasible day-trip.

Once known as Ungjin, **Gongju** became the second capital of the realm in 475, but held the seat of power for only 63 years before it was passed to **Buyeo**, a day's march to the southwest. **King Muryeong**, Gongju's most famous inhabitant, lay here undisturbed for over 1400 years, after which his tomb yielded thousands of pieces of superlative jewellery that provided a hitherto unattainable insight into the splendid craft of the Baekje people. This jewellery attained an international reputation and went on to exert an influence on the Japanese craft of the time; some well-preserved examples in both cities can be found at Gongju's **museum**, which is one of Korea's best.

The city is divided by the Geumgang River, with its dilapidated **intercity bus terminal** standing defiantly on the north bank; express buses from Seoul will arrive at an adjoining terminal to the north. Gongju's small size means that it's possible to walk between the centre and the main sights, but **taxi** rides are cheap. The main **tourist information** centre (T041/856-7700; daily 9am–6pm; winter to 5pm) is located under Gongsanseong, and usually has English-speaking staff.

Gongsanseong

For centuries, Gongju's focal point has been the hilltop fortress of **Gongsanseong** (공산성; daily 9am–6pm; winter until 5pm; W2000), whose 2.6km-long **perimeter wall** was built from local mud in Baekje times, before receiving a stone upgrade in the seventeenth century. It's possible to walk the entire circumference of the wall, an up-and-down course that occasionally affords splendid views of Gongju and its surrounding area. The grounds inside are worth a look too, inhabited by stripy squirrels and riddled with paths leading to a number of carefully painted **pavilions**. Of these, Ssangsujeong has the most interesting history – where this now stands, a Joseon dynasty king named Injo (r.1623–49) once hid under a couple of trees during a peasant-led rebellion against his rule; when this was quashed, the trees were made government officials, though sadly are no longer around to lend their leafy views to civil proceedings. Airy, green Imnyugak has been painted with meticulous care and is the most beautiful pavilion; press on further west down a small path for great views of eastern Gongju. Down by the river there's a small temple, a refuge to monks who fought the Japanese in 1592, and on summer weekends visitors have the opportunity to dress up as a Baekje warrior and shoot off a few arrows. An hourly Baekje **changing of the guard** takes place at 2pm (April–June, Sept & early Oct).

Muryeong's tomb and the National Museum

Heading west over the creek from Gongsanseong, you'll eventually come to the **Tomb of King Muryeong** (무령왕릉; daily 9am–6pm; W1500), one of many regal burial groups dotted around the country from the Three Kingdoms period (see p.170), but the only Baekje mound whose occupant is known for sure. Muryeong, who ruled for the first quarter of the sixth century, was credited with strengthening his kingdom by improving relations with those in China and Japan; some accounts suggest that the design of Japanese jewellery was influenced by gifts that he sent across the sea. His gentle green burial mound was discovered by accident in 1971 during a civic construction project – after fifteen full centuries, Muryeong's tomb was the only one that hadn't been looted. All have now been sealed off for preservation, but the sound of summer cicadas whirring in the trees, and the views of the rolling tomb mounds themselves, make for a pleasant stroll. A small exhibition hall contains replicas of Muryeong's tomb and the artefacts found within.

To see the actual riches scavenged from Muryeong's tomb head west to **Gongju National Museum** (공주국립박물관; 9am–6pm, until 7pm weekends and holidays; closed Mon; W1000), set in a quiet wooded area by the bend in the river. Much of the museum is devoted to jewellery, and an impressive collection of Baekje bling reveals the dynasty's pre-Olympic penchant for gold, silver and bronze. Artefacts such as elaborate golden earrings show an impressive attention to detail, but clever use of shape and texture lends them an almost humble air. The highlight of the exhibition is the king's flame-like **golden headwear**, once worn like rabbit ears on the royal scalp, and now one of the most important symbols not just of Gongju, but of the Baekje dynasty itself.

Practicalities

Gongju's **accommodation** is centred around two areas; north of the river to the west of the bus terminal is a bunch of new establishments, while a group of older cheapies lie south of the river, across the road from Gongsanseong – a quainter and more atmospheric area, and slightly closer to the sights. North of the river, the 🍴 *Hotel Kumgang* (☎041/852-1071 to 3; W40,000) has friendly staff, spacious bathrooms, free internet access in most rooms and a moderately priced restaurant on the second floor. The best option south of the river is the red-brick *Gangseo-jang* by the creek (☎041/853-8323; W25,000), which has decent enough rooms.

Gongju is great for food, and its best **restaurant** is handily located directly opposite Gongsanseong: 🍴 *Gomanaru*, whose leafy interior is a good place to fill up with *ssambap-jeonsik*, a tableful of mostly vegetable dishes that are usually eaten rolled up in leaves. This costs W10,000 per person, but for an extra W5000 you can have the whole meal blanketed with edible flowers – a truly amazing experience. Just around the corner is 🍴 *Nongga*, an unassuming restaurant that makes use of chestnuts (*bam*, 밤), a Gongju speciality. W5000 will buy you a huge chestnut seafood pancake (*bam haemul pajeon*, 밤해물파전), a tray of chestnut dumplings (*bam mandu*, 밤만두) or even a bottle of chestnut *makkeolli* (*bam makkeolli*, 밤막걸리).

Contexts

Contexts

History

M odern Seoul has functioned continuously as a **capital city** since 1394, when the nascent Joseon dynasty selected it as the most auspicious place from which to rule their new kingdom, though **Neolithic** remains prove the area had already been a major centre of population for several thousand years prior to this. Seoul most likely first served as a place of power at around the same time that Augustus was inaugurating the Roman Empire: the **Baekje dynasty** proclaimed their first capital in 18 BC, on a site likely to have been within the present-day city limits. They soon moved the throne southwest to Ungjin (now known as Gongju), and Seoul was passed this way and that between the **Three Kingdoms** until the **Joseon dynasty** came to power in 1392, and favoured Seoul's position at the centre of the peninsula. Over a period of more than five centuries a full 27 kings came and went, alliances were made and broken with the Chinese and Japanese dynasties of the time and in the seventeenth century Korea retreated into its shell, becoming a **"Hermit Kingdom"**, effectively shut off to the rest of the world. In 1910, at a time of global turmoil, Joseon rule was snuffed out by the Japanese, bringing to an end Korea's monarchy. World War II ended **Japanese annexation**, after which Korea was split in two in the face of the looming Cold War. There then followed the brutal **Korean War**, and in 1953 the communist North and the capitalist South went their separate ways; Seoul remained a capital city, but only of the south of the peninsula, while Pyongyang became the northern centre of control. With its position almost exactly on the line of control, Seoul inevitably suffered **widespread destruction**, making it all the more remarkable when, within just one generation, the city rose from the ashes to become an **industrial powerhouse**.

The beginnings

Rivers tend to provide a road-map of civilization, and with its fertile valley, the wide **Hangang** likely proved a tempting base for hunter-gatherers during Paleolithic times. However, the first tangible evidence of habitation in Seoul itself is a clutch of **Neolithic** remains found in what is now the east of the city; dating from 7000 to 3000 BC, these artefacts detail the area's transition

Korea's major historical eras	
Gojoseon	c.2333 BC to c.109 BC
Three Kingdoms	c.57 BC to 668 AD
Silla	c.57 BC to 668 AD
Goguryeo	c.37 BC to 668 AD
Baekje	c.18 BC to 660 AD
Unified Silla	668–935
Goryeo	918–1392
Joseon	1392–1910
Japanese colonial period	1910–1945
Republic of Korea (South)	1945 to present day
Democratic People's Republic of Korea (North)	1945 to present day

from the Stone to the Bronze Age. In addition to the use of metal tools, from 7000 BC **pottery** was being produced with distinctive comb-toothed patterns (*jeulmun*) similar to those found in Mongolia and Manchuria. Fired earth also came to play a part in death rituals, a fact made evident by small, shell-like "jars" into which the broken bodies were placed together with personal belongings; these were then lowered into a pit and covered with earth. An even more distinctive style of burial was to develop in the first millennium BC, with some tombs covered with **dolmens**. Korea is home to over thirty thousand such burial mounds; these are spread across the country, but are most prevalent in **Ganghwado**, an island west of Seoul whose collection is recognized by UNESCO as a World Heritage site.

Today the peninsula's first kingdom is usually referred to as **Gojoseon** ("Old Joseon") in an effort to distinguish it from the later Joseon period (1392–1910). Its origins are obscure to say the least, but most experts agree that it got going in 2333 BC under the leadership of **Dangun**, who has since become the subject of one of Korea's most cherished myths – apparently, he was the son of a tiger turned human. Gojoseon initially functioned as a loose federation of fiefdoms covering not only parts of the Korean peninsula but large swathes of Manchuria too. By 500 BC it had become a single, highly organized dominion, even drawing praise from Confucius and other Chinese sages. Accounts of the fall of Gojoseon are also rather vague, but Seoul seems to have been at the forefront: the kingdom was apparently conquered by the nascent Chinese Han dynasty in 109 BC, who were in turn forced out over the following few decades by natives of the Hangang area at the start of what's now known as the "Three Kingdoms" period. Joseon's historical name lives on: North Korea continues to refer to itself as such (and South Korea as Namjoseon, or "South Joseon"), while many South Korean tourist brochures use "The Land of Morning Calm" – a literal translation of the term – as a national motto.

The Three Kingdoms period

By 109 BC, after the fall of Gojoseon, the peninsula had split into half-a-dozen fiefdoms, the most powerful of which – **Silla**, **Goguryeo** and **Baekje** – became known as the Three Kingdoms. Around this time, close ties with China brought **Buddhism** to Korea, while **Confucianism** (another Chinese import) provided the social building blocks, with a number of educational academies supplying the *yangban*, scholars at the head of the aristocracy. Great advances were made in the arts, particularly with regard to jewellery and pottery, and thousands of wonderful relics have been discovered in the grassy hill-tombs of dead kings and other formerly sacred sites.

Fertile and with good transportation routes, the Hangang valleys were in demand, and Seoul was to fall under the banner of all three kingdoms at different times. First in were the **Baekje**, a kingdom created in 18 BC as the result of great movements of people on the western side of the Korean peninsula. The dynasty was inaugurated by King Onjo, a man jealous of his brother's inheritance of the rival Goguryeo kingdom, itself started by their father Dongmyeong. **Wiryeseong**, which almost certainly lay within Seoul's present-day borders, became the first Baekje capital.

Goguryeo got their own back several generations down the line when the great king Gwanggaeto seized control of the Hangang area in 329 AD. Baekje retreated southwest, establishing new capitals at what are now Gongju and Buyeo,

Seoul's historical names	
Wiryeseong under Baekje rule, partly as capital	c.18 BC to 475 AD
Hanseong under Goguryeo rule	475 to 668
Hanyang under Unified Silla rule	668 to 918
Namgyeong under Goryeo rule	918 to 1392
Seoul as capital of the Joseon dynasty	1392 to 1910
Gyeongseong (Keijo) during Japanese occupation	1910 to 1945
Seoul again as capital of the Republic of Korea	1945 to present

and cultivating an artistic reputation. Baekje became friendly with the **Japanese kingdom of Wa**, and evidence of this close relationship can still be seen today – the lacquered boxes, folding screens, immaculate earthenware and intricate jewellery of Japan are said to derive from the influence of Baekje artisans. This relationship allowed Baekje to grow in power, and they were to retake Seoul, only to see it snatched back by Goguryeo's King Jangsu in 475, after which the city was renamed **Hanseong**.

Baekje were not done with Seoul, and formed an alliance with **Silla**, the peninsula's third kingdom. Together, they pushed Goguryeo north and out of Seoul in 551, though Silla was to become the senior party in the relationship, since the Japanese Wa did not provide Baekje such protection as the **Chinese Tang** dynasty gave Silla. After taking control of Seoul, Silla enlisted Tang help in 660 to eliminate the Baekje kingdom, whose last pockets of resistance literally toppled from a cliff in Buyeo's riverside fortress. This left only Goguryeo as peninsular rivals, and with a vice-like position between Silla to the south and the Tang to the north, it was only a matter of time (eight years, to be precise) before they too were vanquished, setting the scene for a first-ever **unified rule** on the peninsula.

Unified Silla

Following the quickfire defeats of its two competitor kingdoms in the 660s, the **Silla dynasty** instigated the Korean peninsula's first-ever unification. They kept the southeastern city of Gyeongju as their seat of power, renaming Seoul "Hanyang" but relegating it to a provincial power base. Silla set about cultivating a peninsular **sense of identity**, and the pooling of ideas and talent in the eighth century created a high-water mark of artistic development, particularly in metalwork and earthenware. However, rulers stuck to a rigidly Confucian "bone rank" system, which placed strict limits on what an individual could achieve in life, based almost entirely on their genetic background. Though it largely succeeded in keeping the proletariat quiet, this highly centralized system was to lead to Silla's demise: the late eighth century and most of the ninth were characterized by **corruption and in-fighting** at the highest levels of Silla society, and a near-permanent state of civil war. With the Silla king reduced to little more than a figurehead, the former kingdoms of Baekje and Goguryeo were resurrected (now known as "**Hubaekje**" and "**Taebong**" respectively). Silla shrunk back to within its Three Kingdoms-era borders, and after a power struggle Taebong took control of the peninsula; in 935, King Gyeongsun ceded control of his empire in a peaceful transfer of power to Taebong leader **Wang Geon**, who went on to become Taejo, the first king of the Goryeo dynasty.

The Goryeo dynasty

Having grown from a mini-kingdom known as Taebong, one of the many battling for power following the collapse of Silla control, it was the Goryeo dynasty that eventually gave its name to the English term "Korea". It began life in 918 under the rule of **Taejo**, a powerful leader who needed less than two decades to bring the whole peninsula under his control. One of his daughters married Gyeongsun, the last king of Silla, and Taejo himself wed a Silla queen, two telling examples of the new king's desire to cultivate a sense of national unity – he even gave positions of authority to known enemies. Relations with China and Japan were good, and the kingdom became ever more prosperous.

Following the fall of Silla, Taejo moved the national capital to his hometown, Kaesong, a city in present-day North Korea, while Seoul became **Namgyeong**, the "Southern Capital". Taejo and successive leaders also changed some of the bureaucratic systems that had contributed to Silla's downfall: power was centralized in the king but devolved to the furthest reaches of his domain, and even those without aristocratic backgrounds could, in theory, reach lofty governmental positions via a system of state-run examinations. Despite the Confucian social system, **Buddhism** continued to function as the state religion, and repeated refinements in the pottery industry saw Korean produce attain a level of quality only bettered in China. In fact, despite great efforts, some **pottery techniques** perfected in Goryeo times remain a mystery today, perhaps never to be replicated.

In 1248, Goryeo was attacked by Mongol hordes, and became a vassal state of the Great Khaans. Annexation came at a great human cost, one echoed in a gradual worsening of Goryeo's economy and social structure. This lasted almost a century, before **King Gongmin** took advantage of a weakening Chinese–Mongol Yuan dynasty (founded by Kublai Khaan) to regain independence. He made an attempt at reform, purging the top ranks of those he felt to be pro-Mongol, but this instilled fear of yet more change into the *yangban* elite, and he was eventually murdered. After a series of short-lived kings, powerful Joseon General **Yi Seong-gye** decided to take the mantle himself, and in 1392 declared himself King Taejo, the first leader of the Joseon dynasty.

The Joseon dynasty

The **Joseon era** started off much the same as the Goryeo dynasty had almost five centuries before, with a militaristic king named **Taejo** on the throne, a name that translates as "The Grand Ancestor". Joseon was to last even longer, with a full 27 kings ruling from 1392 until the Japanese annexation in 1910. Taejo moved the capital from Kaesong to **Seoul** (the first time the city had used its present name), and immediately set about entrenching his power with a series of mammoth projects. The first few years of his reign saw the wonderful palace of Gyeongbokgung, the ancestral shrines of Jongmyo and a gate-studded city wall go up. His vision was quite astonishing – the chosen capital and its palace and shrine remain to this day, together with sections of the wall. More grand palaces would rise in due course, while another four would at various times house the royal throne. From the start of the dynasty, Buddhism declined in influence as **Confucianism** permeated society ever more in its stead. Joseon's social system became more hierarchical in nature, with the king and other royalty at the top, and the hereditary **yangban** class of scholars and aristocrats just beneath, followed by various levels of employment with the servants and slaves at the bottom of the pile. All of these social strata were governed by heredity, but the *yangban* became increasingly powerful as the dynasty progressed, gradually starting to undermine the power of the king. They were viewed as a world apart by the commoners, and they placed great emphasis on study and the arts. However, only the *yangban* had access to education and literacy as Chinese characters were used. In the 1440s **King Sejong** (reigned 1418–50) devised **hangeul**, a new and simple local script that all classes could read and write (see p.191); the *yangban* were not fond of this, and it was banned at the beginning of the sixteenth century, lying largely dormant until it was resurrected by waves of nationalist sentiment that greeted the end of Japanese annexation in 1945.

The "Hermit Kingdom"

In 1592, under the command of feared warlord **Hideyoshi**, Japan set out to conquer the Ming dynasty, with China a stepping stone towards possible domination of the whole Asian continent. The Korean peninsula had the misfortune to be both in the way and loyal to the Ming. After King Seonjo refused to allow Japanese troops safe passage, Hideyoshi mustered all his military's power and unloaded the lot at Korea, with another major wave of attacks coming in 1597. Korea was then also affected by the internal strife of its closest ally, China. Following the dynastic transfer from Ming to Qing in the 1640s Joseon became a vassal state, forced to spend substantial sums paying tribute to the emperors in Beijing. After all this, it was no surprise that Korea turned inwards: it became known as the **"Hermit Kingdom"**, one of which outsiders knew little, and saw even less. One exception was a Dutch ship that crashed off Jeju Island in 1653 en route to Japan; the survivors were brought to Seoul, but their appeal for release was turned down by King Hyojong. They were essentially kept prisoner in Korea for thirteen years but finally managed to escape, and the accounts of one survivor, **Hendrick Hamel**, provided the western world with one of its first windows into isolationist Korea.

The Dutch prisoners had entered a land in which corruption and factionalism were rife, one that achieved little social or economic stability until the rule of **King Yeongjo** (1724–76), who authorized a purge of crooked officials, but also murdered his son (see box, p.53). Yeongjo's grandson **Jeongjo**, who came to the throne in 1776, became one of the most revered of Korea's kings, instigating top-to-bottom reform to wrench power from the *yangban* elite, and allowing for the creation of a small middle class. The lot of the poor also gradually improved.

The end of isolation

Following Japan's **opening up** to foreign trade in the 1860s (the Meiji Restoration), Korea found itself under pressure to do likewise, not just from the Japanese but from the United States and the more powerful European countries – warships were sent from around the globe to ensure agreement. Much of the activity occurred on and around the island of Ganghwado, just west of Seoul. The French occupied the isle but failed to advance on the mainland in 1866, their battle fought partly as retaliation for the murder of several French missionaries. Five years later, and in the same location, the Americans also attempted – and failed – to prise the country open to trade. The third bout of gunboat diplomacy – this time by the Japanese in 1876 – resulted in the Treaty of Ganghwa, which dragged Korea into the global marketplace on unfair terms. From this point until well after the Korean War, Korea would be a ship largely steered by foreign powers.

Through means both political and economic, the Japanese gradually strengthened their position in Korea. Local resentment boiled over into occasional riots and protests, and peaked in 1895 after the Japanese-orchestrated **murder of Empress Myeongseong** – "Queen Min" to the Japanese – in Gyeongbokgung palace. After this event, **King Gojong** (r.1863–1910) fled to the Russian embassy for protection; in 1897, when things had quietened down sufficiently, he moved into the nearby palace of Deoksugung where he set up the short-lived **Empire of Korea**, a toothless administration under almost full Japanese control. In 1902 Japan forged an alliance with the British Empire, recognizing British interests in China in return for British acknowledgment of Japanese interests in Korea. Sensing shifts in power, Russia began expanding into Korea, though they ran into the Japanese on the way. To avoid confrontation, Japan suggested that the two countries carve Korea up along the **38th parallel**, a line roughly bisecting the peninsula. Russia refused to accept, and the two fought the Russo-Japanese War across Manchuria and the Yellow Sea in 1904–05; after its surprise victory, Japan was in a position to occupy the peninsula outright. They were given tacit permission to do so in 1905 by US Secretary of State and future president William Taft, who agreed in a secret meeting to accept Japanese domination of Korea if Japan would accept the American occupation of the Philippines. Korea became a Japanese protectorate that year, and Japan gradually ratcheted up its power on the peninsula before a final **outright annexation** in 1910. Joseon's kings had next to no say in the running of the country during its last quarter-century of dynastic succession. Sunjong, the peninsula's final monarch, retreated into early retirement in Changdeokgung, and the book softly closed on Korea's near two thousand years of unbroken regal rule.

The Japanese occupation

After the signing of the Annexation Treaty in 1910, Japan wasted no time in filling all the top posts in politics, banking, law and industry with its own personnel; despite the fact that they never represented more than four percent of the peninsular population, they came to control almost every sphere of the country. Korea was but part of the Empire of Japan's dream of **continental hegemony**, and being the nearest stepping stone from the motherland, it was also the most heavily trampled on. While the Japanese went on to occupy most of Southeast Asia and large swathes of China, only in Korea did they have the time and leverage necessary to attempt a total annihilation of **national identity**. Some of the most powerful insults to national pride were hammered home early. The royal palace of **Gyeongbokgung** had all the Confucian principles observed in its construction shattered by the placing of a modern Japanese structure in its first holy courtyard, while Changgyeonggung suddenly found itself home to a decidedly un-royal theme park and zoo. Korean currency, clothing and even the language itself were placed under ever stricter control, locals were required to take Japanese names, and thousands of local **"comfort women"** were forced into sexual slavery. Korean productivity grew, but much of this was also for Japan's benefit – within ten years, more than half of the country's rice was heading across the sea.

The local populace, unsurprisingly, objected to this enforced servitude. In 1919, the **March 1st Movement** saw millions of Koreans take to the streets in a series of non-violent nationwide protests. A declaration of independence was read out in Seoul's Tapgol Park, followed by processions through the streets and the singing of the Korean national anthem. The Japanese police attempted to suppress the revolt through force; around seven thousand died in the months of resistance demonstrations that followed. A government-in-exile was established across the sea in Shanghai, but in Korea itself the main result of the resistance movement was a marked change of Japanese policy towards Korea, with Saito Makoto (the admiral in charge of quelling the chaos) agreeing to lift the bans on Korean radio, printed material and the creation of organizations, a policing that aimed to promote harmony rather than pushing the militarist line. The pendulum swung back towards oppression on the approach to World War II – in the late 1930s, Japan began forcing Koreans to worship at Shinto shrines, speak Japanese and even adopt a Japanese name (a practice known as *soshi-kaimei*), all helped by local **collaborators** (*chinilpa*).

The end of annexation

Throughout the occupation period, the Korean government-in-exile had been forced ever further west from China's eastern seaboard, eventually landing near the Tibetan plateau in the Sichuanese city of Chongqing. Modern Korean museums and history books extol the achievements of what was, in reality, a largely toothless group. In doing this they gloss over the fundamental reason for Korea's independence: the American A-bombs that fell on Hiroshima and Nagasaki, thereby ending both World War II and the Empire of Japan itself. With Tokyo busy elsewhere, Seoul was little affected by the war: the main change in city life was the conscription of tens of thousands of Korean men, many of whom never returned.

An even greater number of Koreans had moved to Japan prior to the war. Some, of course, were collaborators fearful of reprisals should they head home, but the majority were simply squeezed out of their impoverished homeland by Japanese land confiscations. Many of these Korean families remain in Japan today, and are referred to there as "Zainichi Koreans".

The Korean War

Known to many as the "**Forgotten War**", sandwiched as it was between World War II and the war in Vietnam, the Korean conflict was one of the twentieth century's greatest tragedies, laying waste to the city of Seoul, which stood more or less in the middle of the two warring parties. The impoverished Korean peninsula had already been pushed to the back of the global mind during World War II; the land was under Japanese control, but the Allied forces had developed no plans for its future should the war be won. In fact, at the close of the war US Secretary of State Edward Stettinius had to be told in a meeting where Korea actually was. It was only when the **Soviet Union** sent troops into Korea in 1945 that consideration was given to Korea's postwar life. During an emergency meeting on August 10, 1945, American officials and high-rankers (including eventual Secretary of State Dean Rusk) sat with a National Geographic map and a pencil, and scratched a line across the 38th parallel, just north of Seoul – a simple solution, but one that was to have grave repercussions for Korea.

The build-up to war

With World War II rapidly developing into the **Cold War**, Soviet forces occupied the northern half of the peninsula, Americans the south. Both countries imposed their own social, political and economic norms on the Koreans under their control, thereby creating two de facto states diametrically opposed in ideology that refused to recognize each other. The **Republic of Korea** (now more commonly referred to as "South Korea") declared independence in Seoul on August 15, 1948, exactly three years after liberation from the Japanese, and the **Democratic People's Republic of Korea** followed suit just over three weeks later. The US installed a leader favourable to them, selecting **Syngman Rhee** (ironically born in what is now North Korea), who had degrees from American universities. Stalin chose the much younger **Kim Il-sung**, who like Rhee had been in exile for much of the Japanese occupation. The foreign forces withdrew, and the two Koreas were left to their own devices, each hellbent on unifying the peninsula by absorbing the opposing half; inevitably, locals were forced into this polarization of opinions, one that split friends and even families apart. Kim wanted to wade into war immediately, and Stalin turned down two requests for approval of such an action. The third time, for reasons that remain open to conjecture, he apparently gave the nod.

War breaks out

Nobody knows for sure exactly how the **Korean War** started. Or, rather, everyone does: the other side attacked first. The South Korean line is that on June 25, 1950, troops from the northern **Korean People's Army** (KPA) burst across the 38th parallel, then little more than a roll of tape. The DPRK itself claims that it was the south that started the war, and indeed both sides had started smaller conflicts along the line on several occasions; declassified Soviet information seems to show that the main battle was kicked off by the north. With the southern forces substantially ill-equipped in comparison, Seoul fell just three days later, but they were soon aided by a sixteen-nation coalition fighting under the **United Nations** banner – the vast majority of troops were from the United States, but additional forces arrived from Britain, Canada, Australia, the Philippines, Turkey, the Netherlands, France, New Zealand, Thailand, Ethiopia, Greece, Colombia, Belgium, South Africa and Luxembourg; other countries provided non-combative support.

Within three months, the KPA had hemmed the United Nations Command (UNC) into the far southeast of the country, behind a short line of control that became known as the **Pusan Perimeter**, a boundary surrounding the (now re-romanized) city of Busan. Though the KPA held most of the peninsula, American general Douglas MacArthur identified a weak logistical spine and poor supply lines as their Achilles heel, and ordered amphibious landings behind enemy lines at **Incheon**, just west of Seoul, in an attempt to cut off their enemy. The ambitious plan worked to perfection, and UNC forces pushed north way beyond the 38th parallel, reaching sections of the Chinese border within six weeks. At this stage, with the battle seemingly won, the **Chinese** entered the fight and ordered almost a million troops into North Korea; with their help, the KPA were able to push back past the 38th parallel. The UNC made one more thrust north in early 1951, and after six months the two sides ended up pretty much where they started. The lines of the conflict settled around the 38th parallel, near what was to become the **Demilitarized Zone**. The fighting did not end for well over two years, until the signing of an **armistice agreement** on July 27, 1953. North Korea, China and the United Nations Command signed the document, but South Korea refused to do likewise, meaning that the war is still technically being fought today.

In effect, both sides lost. Seoul had **fallen four times** – twice to each side – and Korea's population was decimated, with over two million civilians killed, wounded or missing over the course of the war; to this can be added a combined total of around two million troops killed or injured in action. Had the war been "contained" and brought to an end when the line of control stabilized in early 1951, these figures would have been far lower. The war split thousands of families as the front line yo-yoed up and down the land, and as people were forced to switch sides to avoid starvation or torture, or to stay in contact with other family members. Though the course of the war was easy enough to understand, propaganda clouded many of the more basic details, and the conflict was largely forgotten by the West. For all the coverage of Vietnam, few know that a far greater amount of **napalm** fell on North Korea, a much more "suitable" target for the material thanks to its greater number of large urban areas. Also kept quiet was how close they came to using **nuclear weapons**. Since the end of the war there have been innumerable accounts of atrocities committed on both sides, many detailing beatings, torture and the unlawful murder of prisoners of war, others documenting the slaughter of entire villages. Korea lay in ruins, yet two countries were slowly able to emerge from the ashes.

To the present day

Considering its state after the war, Seoul's transformation is nothing short of astonishing. A rapid phase of industrialization, one often referred to as the "**Economic Miracle**" in the West, saw South Korea become one of Asia's most ferocious financial tigers, and Seoul morph from battle-scarred wasteland into one of the world's largest and most dynamic cities. The country's GDP-per-head shot up from under US$100 in 1963 to almost US$30,000 in 2010. Thanks in large part to the bullishness of large conglomerates (known as *jaebeol*) such as Samsung, Hyundai and LG, it now sits proudly on the cusp of the world's ten most powerful economies. And, since flinging off its autocratic straightjacket in the 1980s, it developed sufficiently to be selected as host of two of the world's most high-profile sporting events – the **Olympics** in 1988, and football's **World Cup** in 2002.

Problematic beginnings

Today's visitor to Seoul will scarcely be able to imagine the state that the city was in after the double-whammy of Japanese occupation and the Korean War. Korea was, essentially, a third-world country, with shantytowns widespread even in central Seoul. Indeed, over half of the city's population was left homeless and the construction of new housing was hampered by the fact that Japan had stripped the peninsula's trees for its own use. Neither were Korea's problems merely structural or economic in nature – every single person in the land carried memories of wartime atrocities in their minds, and countless families had been torn apart. In addition, accusations and recriminations were rife, and everyone knew that hostilities with the North could resume at any moment. American-educated **Syngman Rhee**, who had been selected as president before the war, ruled in an increasingly autocratic manner, making constitutional amendments to stay in power and purging parliament of those against his policies. In 1960 disgruntled students led the **April 19 Movement** against his rule, and after being toppled in a coup he was forced into exile, choosing Hawaii as his new home. One dictator was swiftly replaced with another: Yun Bo-seon came to office as a puppet of military general **Park Chung-hee**, who then swiftly engineered a coup and took the presidency himself in 1962. To an even greater degree than Rhee before him, Park's name became synonymous with corruption, dictatorship and the flouting of human rights – thousands were jailed merely for daring to criticize his rule. To his credit, Park introduced the economic reforms that allowed his country to push forward – until the mid-1970s, the South Korean economy actually lagged behind that of North Korea – and the country made great advances in automotive, electronic, heavy and chemical industries. This was, however, achieved at a cost, since Korean tradition largely went out of the window in favour of bare economic progress. These policies were a major factor behind the **loss of Korea's traditional buildings**: Seoul has almost none left. Park's authoritarian rule continued to ruffle feathers around the country, and the danger from the North had far from subsided – Park was the subject, and Seoul the scene, of two failed **assassination** attempts by North Korean agents. It was, however, members of his own intelligence service who gunned him down in 1979, claiming that he was "an insurmountable obstacle to democratic reform". Those responsible were hanged the following year. Park's eventual successor, **Chun Doo-hwan**, was also from the southeast of the country, and the resultant Seoul–Gyeongsang tangent of power saw those parts of the country developing rapidly, while others languished far behind. The arrest of liberal southwestern politician **Kim Dae-jung**, as well as the botched trials following the assassination of Park Chung-hee, were catalysts for mass uprisings across the land, though mainly concentrated in Jeju Island and the southwestern provinces. These culminated in the **Gwangju Massacre** of May 1980, where over two hundred civilians died after their protest was crushed by the military.

The Olympic legacy

Rather incredibly, just one year after the massacre, Seoul was given the rights to host the **1988 Summer Olympics**. Some estimates say the Gwangju Massacre resulted in a similar death count to the Tiananmen Square massacre, though it's hard to imagine Beijing being granted a similar honour the year after those events. Originally the brainchild of Park Chung-hee, the Olympic plan was followed through by Chun Doo-hwan in an apparent attempt to seek international recognition of his authoritarian rule. Though he may have regarded the winning of the 1981 Olympic vote as a tacit global nod of acceptance, the strategy backfired somewhat when the country was thrust into the spotlight. Partly as a result of this increased attention, Korea's first-ever free elections were held in 1987, with **Roh Tae-woo** taking the helm. During the same period Korean conglomerates, known as the *jaebeol*, were spreading their financial arms around the world. Korea's aggressive, debt-funded expansion worsened the effect of the Asian Currency Crisis on the country in 1997, and for several years after it struck the bare shells of over a hundred partially finished buildings stood around Seoul.

In 1998, once-condemned liberal activist **Kim Dae-jung** completed a remarkable turnaround by being appointed president himself. The first South Korean leader to favour a peaceable reunification of the peninsula, he wasted no time in kicking off his **"Sunshine Policy"** of reconciliation with the north; some minor industrial projects were outsourced across the border, and new Seoul-funded factories were built around the city of Kaesong, just north of the DMZ. In 2000, after an historic Pyongyang summit with North Korean leader Kim Jong-II, he was awarded the **Nobel Peace Prize**.

Into the twenty-first century

South Korea's international reputation was further enhanced by the hugely successful co-hosting of the **2002 World Cup** with Japan. However, that same year a series of incidents gave rise to something of an anti-American (and, by extension, anti-Western) sentiment. Most significant was the accidental killing

The sinking of the Cheonan, and the Yeonpyeongdo attacks

On March 26, 2010, the *Cheonan*, a South Korean naval vessel, sank in the waters off Baengnyeongdo, killing 46 of its crew of just over one hundred, and claiming the life of one rescue worker. With the incident taking place in waters so close to the North Korean border, there was immediate worldwide suspicion that Pyongyang was behind the attack; Seoul refused to be drawn into such a conclusion, choosing instead to wait for the results of a full investigation. South Korean **conspiracy theorists** initially pointed fingers at an American submarine which had "gone missing", though such rumours were hurriedly put to bed when the sub resurfaced a few days later on the other side of the world. One rumour that refused to go away was that the attack may have been an internal show of force from **Kim Jong-un**, who was at the time being groomed for leadership in North Korea. It was suggested that Kim may have used the incident to prove himself to the country's military leadership, who were known to be unhappy with a dynastic transfer of power from his father, Kim Jong-Il. Two months after the incident, an international team found that the *Cheonan* was sunk by a torpedo, most likely fired by a North Korean vessel.

Pyongyang continues to deny responsibility for the sinking of the *Cheonan*, but the attacks of November 23, 2010, were more directly attributable to North Korea. Almost two hundred shells and rockets were fired from North Korea's southern coast at the South Korean island of **Yeonpyeongdo** in response to Seoul's refusal to halt a military training exercise in nearby waters. The northern shelling appeared to be indiscriminate, killing two civilians and two soldiers from the South, which responded in kind with howitzers of its own. This was one of the most serious cross-border incidents since the Korean War, and many southerners formerly sympathetic to the North were suddenly favouring a powerful military response to any future attacks. At the time of writing, the situation remained tense.

of two local schoolgirls by an American armoured vehicle, which led to large protests against the US military presence (one that has declined, bit by bit, ever since). Late that year, **Roh Moo-hyun** was elected president on a slightly anti-American ticket; however, the fact that he sent Korean troops to Iraq so soon after taking office in early 2003 made him instantly unpopular, and he committed suicide in 2009, following a bribery scandal. Roh's presidency coincided with **Lee Myung-bak**'s tenure as mayor of Seoul. In 2003, Lee announced plans to gentrify the **Cheonggyecheon** creek which though, beloved by the public now was an expensive and therefore deeply unpopular project at the time. Lee was elected president in 2008, but as with Roh before him, there were almost immediate protests against his rule, this time thanks to a beef trade agreement made with the USA. Fears that mad cow disease would be imported to this beef-loving land resulted in mass protests around the city, and **rioting** around **Gwanghwamun Plaza**; one man died after setting fire to himself in protest (see box, p.56). The plaza itself was renovated shortly afterwards, and other major projects underway at the time of writing were construction of **Dongdaemun Design Plaza**, the new **City Hall** and some futuristic **floating islands** in the Hangang. Like Incheon Airport, these designs all run along a curvy, chrome-and-glass style architecture, intended to portray Seoul as a city of the future, surely one factor behind its selection as host of the **G-20 Summit** in 2010.

Religion

K orea has a long and fascinating religious history, one that continues to inform local life. **Buddhism** is the religion most closely identified with Korea, though **Christianity** now has a greater number of followers. The rise of the latter is particularly interesting when laid over Korea's largely **Confucian** mindset, which is often diametrically opposed to Christian ideals and beliefs – priests and pastors preach equality at Sunday service, but outside church relative age still governs many forms of social interaction, and women remain socially inferior to men.

Buddhism

Buddhism is a religion deriving from the teachings of the Buddha, also known as the Siddhartha Gautama or Sakyamuni, who lived in India sometime between the fourth and sixth centuries BC. Although there are two main schools of thought and several smaller ones, Buddhist philosophy revolves around the precept that karma, rebirth and suffering are intrinsic elements of existence, but that the cycle of birth and death can be escaped on what is known as the "Noble Eightfold Path" to nirvana.

An import from China (which had in turn imported it from the Indian subcontinent), Buddhism arrived in Korea at the beginning of the Three Kingdoms period. **Goguryeo** and **Baekje** both adopted it at around the same time, in the last decades of the fourth century – Goguryeo king Sosurim accepted Buddhism almost as soon as the first Chinese monks arrived in 372, while Baekje king Chimnyu adopted it after taking the throne in 384. The **Silla** kings were less impressed by the creed, but a major change in regal thought occurred in 527 after an interesting episode involving an official who had decided to switch to Buddhism. He was to be beheaded for his beliefs, and with his final few gasps swore to the king that his blood would not be red, but a milky white; his prediction was true, and the king soon chose Buddhism as his state religion.

Even in China, Buddhism was at this point in something of an embryonic phase, and Korean monks took the opportunity to develop the **Mahayana** style by ironing out what they saw to be inconsistencies in the doctrine. Disagreements followed, leading to the creation of several **sects**, of which the **Jogye** order is by far the largest, including about ninety percent of Korea's Buddhists; other notable sects include **Seon**, largely known in the west as Zen, the Japanese translation, and **Cheontae**, which is likewise better known under its Chinese name of Tiantai.

Ornate **temples** sprang up all over the peninsula during the **Unified Silla** period but, though Buddhism remained the state religion throughout the **Goryeo** era, the rise of Confucianism squeezed it during **Joseon** times. Monks were treated with scant respect and temples were largely removed from the main cities (one reason why there are relatively few in Seoul, the Joseon capital), but though the religion was repressed, it never came close to extinction. Further troubles came during the **Japanese occupation period**, during the latter years of which many Koreans were forced to worship at Shinto shrines. Mercifully, although many of the temples that weren't closed by the Japanese were burnt down in the Korean War that followed the Japanese occupation, reconstruction programmes have been so comprehensive that in most Korean cities you will seldom be more than a walk away from the nearest temple, each one still an active place of worship. Seoul has fared less well in this regard, but there are some temples in the city centre, and more on the slopes of the city's surrounding mountains.

Temples

Korea's many **temples** are some of the most visually appealing places in the country, though there are precious few good examples in Seoul. Most run along a similar design scheme: on entry to the temple complex you'll pass through the *ilchumun* (일주문), or "first gate", then the *jeonwangmun* (전왕문). The latter almost always contains **four large guardians**, two menacing figures towering on each side of the dividing walkway; these control the four heavens and provide guidance to those with a righteous heart. The central building of a Korean temple is the **main hall**, or *daeungjeon* (대웅전). Initially, it was only Sakyamuni – the historical Buddha – who was enshrined here, but this was soon flanked on left and right by bodhisattvas (a term for those who have reached nirvana). Most of these halls have doors at the front, which are usually only for elder monks; novices (and visiting foreigners) use side-entrances. Among the many other halls that you may find on the complex are the *daecheokgwangjeon* (대척광전), the hall of the Vairocana Buddha; *gwaneumjeon* (관음전), a hall for the Bodhisattva of Compassion; *geungnakjeon* (극락전), the Nirvana Hall and home to the celestial Amitabha Buddha; *mireukjeon* (미륵전), the hall of the future Maitreya Buddha; and *nahanjeon* (나한전), the hall of disciples. Some also feature the *palsangjeon* (팔상전), a hall featuring **eight paintings** detailing the life of the Sakyamuni Buddha, though these are more often found on the outside of another hall.

Somewhere on the complex you'll find the *beomjonggak* (범종각), a "**bell pavilion**" containing instruments to awaken the four sentient beings – a drum for land animals, a wooden fish for the water-borne, a bronze gong for creatures of the air, and a large bell for monks who have slept in. The bell itself can sometimes weigh upwards of twenty tonnes, and the best will have an information board telling you how far away it can be heard if you were to strike it lightly with your fist. Needless to say, you shouldn't test these contentions.

Confucianism

Like Buddhism, **Confucian thought** made its way across the sea from China – the exact date remains a mystery, but it seems that it first spread to Korea at the beginning of the Three Kingdoms era. Although Confucianism can't be classified as a religion – there's no central figure of worship, or concept of an afterlife – it is used as a means of self-cultivation, and a guide to "proper" conduct, particularly the showing of respect for those higher up the social hierarchy. For centuries it co-existed with the state religion, informing not only political thought but also national ethics, and in many ways it still governs the Korean way of life today. Central to the concept are the **Five Moral Disciplines** of human-to-human conduct, namely ruler to subject, father to son, husband to wife, elder to younger and friend to friend.

During the Three Kingdoms period, the concepts of filial piety began to permeate Korean life, with adherence to the rules gradually taking the form of ceremonial rites. In the Silla kingdom there developed a "bone rank" system used to segregate social strata, one that was to increase in rigidity until the Joseon era. This was essentially a **caste** system, one that governed almost every sphere of local life – each "level" of society would have strict limits placed on what they could achieve, the size of their dwelling, who they could marry and even what colours they were allowed to wear.

At the dawn of the Joseon dynasty in 1392, King Taejo had the **Jongmyo shrines** built in central Seoul, and for centuries afterwards, ruling kings would venerate their ancestors here in regular ceremonies. At this time, Confucianism truly took hold, with numerous academies (*hyanggyo*) built around the country at which students from the elite *yangban* classes would wade through wave after wave of punishing examinations on their way to senior governmental posts. Buddhism had been on the decline for some time with Confucian scholars arguing that making appeals to gods unseen had a detrimental effect on the national psyche, and that building ornate temples absorbed funds too readily. Some, in fact, began to clamour for the burning of those temples, as well as the murder of monks. As with other beliefs, some followers violated the core principles for their own ends and, despite the birth of great neo-Confucian philosophers such as **Yi-Yi** and **Toegye**, enforced slavery and servitude meant that the lot of those at the lower caste levels changed little over the centuries.

Confucianism today

It's often said that Korea remains the **most Confucian** of all the world's societies. In addition to several remaining academies and shrines – there's one of the latter at Inwangsan, just west of Gyeongbokgung – colourful ancestral ceremonies take place each year at Jongmyo in Seoul. Its impact on everyday life is also evident: on getting to know a local, you'll generally be asked a series of questions both direct and indirect (particularly with regard to age, marriage, education and employment), the answers to which will be used to file you into mental pigeonholes. Though foreigners are treated somewhat differently, this is the main reason why locals see nothing wrong in barging strangers out of the way on the street or showing no mercy on the road – no introduction has been made, and without knowledge of the "proper" behaviour in such a situation no moves are made towards showing respect. Among those who do know each other, it's easy to find **Confucian traits**: women are still seen as inferior to men (their salary continues to lag far behind, and they're usually expected to quit their job on having a child, never to return to the workplace); the boss or highest earner will usually pay after a group meal; family values remain high, and paper qualifications from reputable universities carry more weight than actual intelligence. Also notable is **bungsu**, a concept that involves the moving of ancestral grave sites. Perhaps the most high-profile examples of corpse-shifting have been before general elections. After Kim Dae-jung lost the elections in 1987 and 1992, he decided to move the graves of his ancestors to more auspicious locations, and he duly won the next election in 1998. However, Confucian ideas are slowly being eroded as Westernization continues to encroach, particularly as the number of Christians continues to grow.

Christianity

Making up well over a quarter of the country by population, **Christianity** is now Korea's leading religion by number of worshippers, having surpassed Buddhism at the start of the twenty-first century. Surprisingly, the religion has been on the peninsula since the end of the eighteenth century, having been brought across the waters by missionaries from various European empires. At the time, the Confucian *yangban* in charge were fearful of change, hardly surprising considering how far apart the fundamental beliefs of the two creeds are. Christianity's refusal to perform ancestral rites eventually led to its repression, and hundreds of Christians were **martyred** in the 1870s and 1880s. A number of French missionaries were also murdered in this period, before Korea was forcefully opened up for trade. The numbers have been growing ever since, the majority now belonging to the Presbyterian, Catholic or Methodist churches.

Churches tend to be monstrous concrete edifices (many visitors note that most sport rather Satanic-looking red neon crosses), and some are huge, with room for thousands of worshippers. In fact, the island of Yeouido, near Seoul, officially has the largest church in the world, with 170 pastors and over 100,000 registered deacons.

Film

F
or all of its efforts in finance, electronics and promoting its food and tradition, it's Korea's film industry that has had the most success in pushing the country as a global brand. While Korean horror flicks have developed an international cult following, and a number of esteemed directors have set international film festivals abuzz, special mention must be made of the locally produced television **dramas** that have caught on like wildfire across Asia. Like many of the movies, these are highly melodramatic offerings that don't seek to play on the heartstrings so much as power-chord the merry hell out of them – foremost among these is *Winter Sonata*, a series whose following became almost religious in Japan. All of these form part of the **Hallyeo movement**, a "New Wave" of Korean production that has been in motion since cinematic restrictions were lifted in the 1980s.

Following the Korean War, leaders on both sides saw movies as a hugely useful **propaganda tool**, and made immediate efforts to revive local cinema. In the south, President Syngman Rhee conferred tax-exempt status on moviemakers, who got busy with works looking back at the misery of wartime and the occupation period, and forward to a rosy future for non-communist Korea. By the end of the 1950s, annual movie output had reached triple figures, the most popular being watched by millions of people. The accession of **Park Chung-hee** to president in 1961 brought an end to what passed for cinematic freedom – in addition to the censorship and hard-fisted restrictions over local productions, foreign films were vetted and placed under a strict quota system, elements of which remained in place until 2006.

The South Korean government continued to provide funding for films until the 1999 release of *Swiri,* the country's first fully independent film. Since then the industry has moved forward in leaps and bounds, reaching an ever-wider international audience. Evidence of cinematic immaturity still remains – almost every film will feature at least one overlong shot of a pretty girl's face, during which time the viewer is expected to assess her beauty and nothing more – but a number of Korean directors such as *enfants terribls* **Kim Ki-duk** and **Park Chan-wook** are now globally acclaimed.

Kim Ki-duk

3-Iron (2004) Korean movies about eccentric loners are ten a penny. Here, the protagonist is a delivery boy who breaks into and then polishes up the houses that he knows to be empty. When he happens across one that's still home to a lonely girl, the couple begin a strange kind of silent relationship. Superbly acted, and an interesting take on the traditional love story.

Bad Guy (2001) A sadomasochistic thread runs through Kim Ki-duk's films, evident in *Bad Guy*, where a mute thug falls in love with a young beauty and tricks her into becoming a prostitute. This disturbing study of small-time gangsters and sexual slavery tells painful truths about Korean society, and though clichéd is thoroughly absorbing in more than a voyeuristic sense.

Samaritan Girl (2004) A storyline that's less explicit and far deeper than its premise may suggest. Two teenage girls looking to save up for a trip to Europe enter the murky world of prostitution, one sleeping with the clients, the other managing the affairs while keeping an eye out for the cops. Inevitably, things don't quite go according to plan.

Park Chan-wook

Sympathy for Mr Vengeance (2002) Acclaimed director Park Chan-wook kicked off a trio of films about revenge with this tale of a deaf-mute man who hatches a plot to find a kidney for his ailing sister, inadvertently starting a series of revenge-fuelled murders.

Oldboy (2003) The first Korean film to win big at Cannes, this is a dark and violent tale of a businessman mysteriously arrested after a night out, imprisoned for years then suddenly given three days to discover why he was put away and to hunt down those responsible. Riveting.

Sympathy for Lady Vengeance (2005) A teenage girl gets framed and sent down for killing a young boy, and spends her time in jail plotting revenge. On her release she's offered a plate of metaphorically cleansing white tofu by a Christian group; the tofu ends up on the floor as our heroine sets about getting back at the man to blame for her imprisonment.

War and history

Chihwaseon (2002) Sometimes going under the title *Painted Fire*, this beautifully shot tale of Jang Seung-eop – a nineteenth-century Seoulite painter best known by his pen name Owon – won the Best Director award at Cannes for Im Kwon-taek, a maverick who had been around for decades but was previously ignored on the international stage.

Joint Security Area (2000) Any Korean film about the DMZ is worth a look, as is anything by acclaimed director Park Chan-wook. Here two North Korean soldiers are killed in the DMZ; like *Memento* (which, incidentally, came out the following year), the story plays backwards, revealing the lead-up piece by piece.

Shiri (1999) Also known as *Swiri*, this was a landmark film in Korean cinema, marking the dawn of a Hollywood style long suppressed by the government. The mix of explosions and loud music is not of as much interest to foreigners as it is to Koreans, but the plot – South Korean cops hunt down a North Korean sniper girl – is interesting enough. The girl was played by Yunjin Kim, who later found fame on the American TV series *Lost*.

The King and the Clown (2005) A period drama with homosexual undercurrents, this was an unexpected smash hit at the box office. Set during the reign of King Yeonsan – whose short rule began in 1494 – it tells of a pair of street entertainers who find themselves in Seoul's royal court. One of them fosters an ever-closer relationship with the king.

Drama and horror

A Tale of Two Sisters (2003) In a manner similar to *The Shining*, this chiller seeks to petrify viewers not with lashings of ultra-violence but with that which cannot be seen. This adaptation of a Joseon-era folk story keeps its audience guessing, and some will find it Korea's best take on the horror genre.

The Host (2006) The tranquil lives of a riverside merchant are blown to smithereens when the formaldehyde disposed into the river by the American military creates a ferocious underwater creature. This comic thriller smashed box office records in Korea, but even though its international reception was nowhere near as fervent, it's worth watching.

Secret Sunshine (2007) It's somewhat rare for government ministers to go into the movie-making business, but so successful was Lee Chang-dong's effort that his film even won an award at Cannes. Focused on a woman entering middle age, it's a well-delivered interpretation of human suffering.

Comedy

My Sassy Girl (2001) A mega hit from Tokyo to Taipei, this tale doesn't add too much to the rom-com genre, but one scene was almost entirely responsible for a spate of high-school-themed club nights. It's worth watching, as is *My Tutor Friend*, a follow-up that hits most of the same buttons.

Save the Green Planet! (2003) A social recluse and his tightrope-walker girlfriend endeavour to save the earth by hunting down the aliens that they believe to have infiltrated mankind; once captured, the extraterrestrials

Thirst (2009) Winner of the Jury Prize at Cannes, this was director Park Chan-wook's follow-up to his hugely successful "vengeance trilogy". It's a romantic horror in which a priest, in love with his friend's wife, turns into a vampire – an odd concept that shouldn't work, but somehow Park pulls it off.

can only be destroyed by applying menthol rub to their groin and feet. Enough said.

The President's Last Bang (2005) Korea has long been crying out for some satire, particularly something able to inject a little fun into its turgid political reportage, and this hits the nail squarely on the head (as demonstrated by the lawsuit that followed). It's based on a true story, namely the assassination of president Park Chung-hee in 1979; the portrayal of Park as something of a Japanese-sympathetic playboy certainly ruffled a few feathers.

Books

Despite Korea's long and interesting history, the East Asian sections in most bookshops largely focus on China and Japan. The majority of books that are devoted to Korea cover **North Korea** or the **Korean War**; far less biased than most newspaper or television reports, these are the best form of reportage about the world's most curious state and how it was created.

History and Society

Michael Breen *The Koreans: Who they Are, What they Want, Where their Future Lies*. Although the four main sections of this book – society, history, economy and politics – may seem awfully dry, the accounts are relayed with warmth and a pleasing depth of knowledge.

Bruce Cumings *Korea's Place in the Sun: A Modern History*. The Korean peninsula went through myriad changes in the twentieth century, and this weighty tome analyzes the effects of such disquiet on its population, showing that the South's seemingly smooth trajectory towards democracy and capitalism masked a great suffering of the national psyche.

Kim Dong-uk *Palaces of Korea*. A photo-filled hardcover detailing not only the minutiae of Seoul's wonderful palaces, but how they vary in style and form from those found elsewhere in Asia.

Keith Pratt *Everlasting Flower: A History of Korea*. This thoroughly readable book provides a chronicle of Korean goings-on from the very first kingdoms to the modern day, its text broken up with interesting illustrated features on the arts and customs prevalent at the time.

Rhee Won-sok *Korea Unmasked: In Search of the Country, the Society and the People*. The peculiarities of Korean society are relayed here in an easy-to-read comic strip. While it could be said that it makes light of some serious problems, it's an entertaining primer on the local psyche for those looking to spend some time in the country.

Local literature

Cho Se-hui *The Dwarf*. Even miracles have a downside: Seoul's economy underwent a truly remarkable transformation in the 1970s, but at what cost to its people and culture? This weighty, tersely delivered novel uncovers the spiritual decline of Seoul's nouveaux riches, via twelve interconnected stories; "A Dwarf Launches a Little Bell" is one particularly recommended chapter, and has been reprinted hundreds of times in Korea.

Park Wan-Suh *Who Ate Up All the Shinga?* A semi-autobiographical mother-daughter story from one of Korea's most highly acclaimed writers, set during the Korean War. Fans of Park should also check out *Sketch of the Fading Sun*, a collection of short stories.

Yi Munyeol *Our Twisted Hero*. This tale of psychological warfare at a Korean elementary school has a deceptively twee plotline, managing to explore the use and misuse of power while providing metaphorical parallels to the Korean politics of the 1970s.

Young Ha Kim *Your Republic is Calling You* and *I Have the Right to Destroy Myself*. Two books from a man whose international reputation is growing by the year, his popularity and his existentialist tendencies marking him out as a possible Korean Murakami. The first book revolves around a North Korean spy torn between his homeland and the South, while the second, set in Seoul, is the dark tale of a refined thinker with suicidal tendencies.

North Korea and the Korean War

Bruce Cumings *North Korea: Another Country*. The US–North Korean dispute is far more complex than Western media would have you imagine, and this book provides a revealing – if slightly hard to digest – glance at the flipside. Cumings' meticulous research is without parallel, and the accounts of American atrocities and cover-ups both in the "Forgotten War" and during the nuclear crisis offer plenty of food for thought.

Max Hastings *The Korean War*. A conflict is not quite a war until it has been given the treatment by acclaimed historian Max Hastings. With his book on the Korean War, he has provided more than his usual mix of fascinating, balanced and well-researched material. The account of the stand of the Gloucesters on the Imjin is particularly absorbing.

Kang Chol-Hwan *The Aquariums of Pyongyang*. Having fled his homeland after spending time in a North Korean gulag, Kang's harrowing accounts of squalor, starvation and brutality represent one of the only windows into the world's most fenced-off social systems. He's not a natural author, however, and the confused sermonizing at the end of the book rather dilutes its appeal.

Don Oberdorfer *The Two Koreas: A Contemporary History*. Lengthy, but engaging and surprisingly easy to read, this book traces the various events in post war Korea, as well as examining how they were affected by the actions and policies of China, Russia, Japan and the US. You'd be hard pressed to find a book about North Korea more neutral in tone.

Recipe books

Cecilia Hae-Jin Lee *Eating Korean: From Barbecue to Kimchi, Recipes from My Home*. Easy-to-follow instructions to over a hundred Korean dishes. The more predictable rice and noodle dishes are supplemented with side dishes, soups, teas and desserts.

Young Jin Song *Korean Cooking: Traditions, Ingredients, Flavours, Techniques, Recipes*. As the sweeping subtitle suggests, this is not so much a recipe book as an all-encompassing guide to Korean cuisine.

Language

Language

Korean

T he sole official tongue of both North and South Korea, the **Korean** language is used by almost eighty million people, making it one of the world's twenty most-spoken tongues. It's a highly tricky language to pick up – much to the chagrin of linguists, it remains stubbornly "unclassified" on the global language tree, its very origins something of a mystery. Some lump it in with the **Altaic** group (itself rather vague), which would put it on the same branch as Turkish and Mongolian, though many view it as a **language isolate**. Korean is therefore in the same boat as Japanese, its closest linguistic brother; both share a **subject–object–verb** syntax and similar grammar, though well over half of the Korean words themselves actually originate from China. Korea also used Chinese text for centuries, even after creating its own characters (known as **hangeul**) in the 1440s, but now almost exclusively uses the local system for everyday functions.

Native speakers of European languages will encounter some pretty significant **grammatical differences** when attempting to get a handle on the Korean tongue. Korean **nouns** remain unaffected whether they refer to singular or plural objects, very little use is made of **articles**, and **verbs** do not change case according to who or what they're referring to – *gayo* can mean "I go", "he/she/it goes" or "we/they go", the meaning made clear by the context. Verbs do, however, alter depending on which **level of politeness** the speaker desires to use, and the relationship between speaker and listener; the conversation will sound quite different depending on whether it's between a child and a mother, a boss and an employee, or even good friends of slightly different age. In general, it's pretty safe to stick to verbs with the polite **–yo** ending; the verb forms given here are in a formal style which should suffice for most travellers. Unfortunately, there are few good books from which to learn Korean; those from the *Teach Yourself* and *Colloquial* series fall short of the two companies' usually high standards, but are about as good as you'll find.

Korean characters

Though it consists of a highly distinctive scrawl of circles and Tetris shapes, many foreigners find Korean text surprisingly **easy to learn**. Koreans tend to assume that foreigners don't have the inclination or mental capability to decipher *hangeul*, so your efforts will not go unappreciated. Koreans are immensely proud of *hangeul*, which they see as the world's most logical written system. While this is no great exaggeration, the efficiency also has a downside – user-friendly it may well be, but in reality *hangeul* is a very narrow system that cannot cope with sounds not found in the Korean language, a fact that partially explains the Korean people's occasionally curious pronunciation of foreign words.

Hangeul

Note that some consonants are pronounced differently depending upon whether they start or finish a syllable. In these cases, the terminal readings have been given in parentheses.

ㄱ	g (k)	ㅎ	h	ㅔ	e
ㄴ	n	ㅇ	ng	ㅐ	ae
ㄷ	d (t)	ㅏ	a	ㅖ	ye
ㄹ	r/l	ㅑ	ya	ㅒ	yae
ㅁ	m	ㅓ	eo	ㅟ	wi
ㅂ	b (p)	ㅕ	yeo	ㅞ	we
ㅅ	s (t)	ㅗ	o	ㅙ	wae
ㅈ	j (t)	ㅛ	yo	ㅘ	wa
ㅊ	ch (t)	ㅜ	u	ㅚ	oe
ㅋ	k	ㅠ	yu	ㅢ	ui
ㅌ	t	ㅡ	eu	ㅝ	wo
ㅍ	p	ㅣ	i		

Though it may seem surprising, *hangeul* was actually a royal creation, having been the brainchild of **King Sejong** in the 1440s. Up until then, his Joseon kingdom and the dynasties that went before had been using Chinese characters, but seeing that most of his citizens were illiterate and denied education, the king devised a system that would be easier for the common man to learn. He was forced to do much of his work in secret, as the change did not go down well with the Confucian *yangban* scholars, some of whom were almost king-like in their power at the time; as the only members of society to receive an education strong enough to make reading Chinese characters a possibility, they argued against the change in an effort to maintain their privileged access to historical texts and suchlike. *Hangeul* experienced periodic bursts of popularity, but was kept down first by the *yangban*, and then almost erased entirely by the Japanese during their occupation of the peninsula (1910–45), but it's now the **official writing system** of both North and South Korea, as well as a small autonomous Korean pocket in the Chinese province of Jilin. Students in Korea study at least two thousand Chinese characters at school, and some of the simpler ones are still used in daily life.

Korean characters are grouped into **syllabic boxes** of more-or-less equal size, and generally arranged left-to-right – if you see a line of text made up of eighteen of these character-chunks, it will have eighteen syllables when spoken. The way in which the **characters** fall into the boxes is rather unique and takes a bit of figuring out – some have two characters in the top half and one at the bottom (the top two are read left-to-right, followed by the bottom one, so 한 makes *han*), while others have two or three characters arranged vertically (these are read downwards, so 국 makes *guk*). Thus put together, we have 한국 – *hanguk*, meaning "Korea". The basic building blocks are listed in the box above, though note that some of these symbols **change sounds** depending on whether they're at the beginning or end of a syllable or word (syllable-ending sounds are bracketed in the boxed text), and that "ng" is used as an initial null consonant for syllables that start with a vowel. Guides to pronouncing the **vowel clusters** are given in the next section; there also exist consonantal clusters, though these are beyond the scope of this book.

Pronunciation

Pronouncing Korean words is a tough task – some sounds simply do not have English-language equivalents. You'll see from the *hangeul* box that there's only one character for "l" and "r", with its actual sound some way in between the two – try saying both phonemes at the same time. The letters "k", "d", "b" and "j" are often written "k", "t", "p" and "ch", and are pronounced approximately halfway towards those Roman equivalents; unfortunately, the second set also have their place in the official system, and are usually referred to as **aspirated consonants**, accompanied as they are by a puff of air. Consonants are fairly easy to master – note that some are doubled up, and spoken more forcefully – but pronunciation guides to some of the tricky **vowels** and **dipthongs** are as follows (British English readings offer the closest equivalents):

a	as in "**car**"	u	as in "**Jew**"
ya	as in "**yap**"	yu	pronounced "**you**"
eo	as in "**hot**"	eu	no English equivalent; widen your mouth and try an "**euggh**" sound of disgust
yeo	as in "**yob**"		
o	pronounced "**ore**"		
yo	pronounced as the British "**your**"	i	as in "**pea**"

Transliteratary troubles

Rendering the Korean language in Roman text is, simply, a battle that can never be won – a classic problem of square pegs and round holes. Numerous systems have been employed down the years, perhaps best exemplified in the Korean family name now usually romanized as "Lee": this has also been written as Rhee, Li, Ri, Lih, Rhi, Ree, Yi, Rii and more besides. Under the current system it would be "I", but the actual pronunciation is simply "ee" – it's amazing how much trouble a simple vowel can cause (especially when almost a fifth of the country has this name).

A Korean's age, schooling, family and even lifestyle influence the way that they'll romanize a given word, but official standards have long been in place. The **Yale** and **McCune–Reischauer** systems became widely accepted in the 1940s, and the latter is still much in evidence today; under its rules, aspirated consonants are marked with apostrophes, and certain vowels with breves. One problem – other than looking ugly – was that these punctuation markings are often neglected, even in language study books; though it remains the official system in North Korea, the South formulated its own system of **Revised Romanization** in the year 2000. While this is far from perfect, it's the official standard, and has been used throughout this book; exceptions include names of the many hotels, restaurants, universities and individuals who cling to the old ways. One other issue is the Korean syllable *shi*; this is now romanized as *si*, a rather ridiculous change since it takes Koreans years of language classes before they can pronounce the syllable without palatalizing it – "six" and "sister" will be pronounced "shix" and "shister". We've written it as *shi* in the language listings to help you achieve the correct pronunciation, but obeyed the official system in the rest of the book – Sinchon is pronounced "Shinchon", and so on.

Koreans themselves find it hard to render **foreign words** in *hangeul* as there are many sounds that don't fit into the system – the difficulties with "l" and "r" sharing the same character being an obvious example – but even when parallels exist they are sometimes distorted. The letter "a" is usually written as an "e" or "ae" in an unsuccessful effort to Americanize the pronunciation – "hat", for example, will be pronounced "het" by the majority of the population.

e	as in "b**e**d"		wa	as in "**wa**g"
ae	as in "**air**"		oe	as in the beginning of "**wa**y"
ye	as in "**ye**t"			
yae	as in "**yea**h"		ui	no English equivalent; add an "ee" sound to *eu* above
wi	as in "**wi**ndow"			
we	as in "**we**dding"			
wae	as the beginning of "**whe**re"		wo	as in "**wa**d"

Useful words and phrases

Basics

Yes	*ye/ne*	예/네
No	*aniyo*	아니요
Please (asking for something)	*…juseyo*	…주세요
Excuse me	*shillye hamnida*	실례합니다
I'm sorry	*mian hamnida*	미안합니다
Thank you	*gamsa hamnida*	감사합니다
You're welcome	*gwaenchan-ayo*	괜찮아요
What?	*muot?*	무엇?
When?	*eonje?*	언제?
Where?	*eodi?*	어디?
Who?	*nugu?*	누구?
How?	*eotteokke?*	어떻게?
How much?	*eolma-eyo?*	얼마에요?
How many?	*myeokke-eyo?*	몇 개에요?
I want…	*…hago-shipeoyo*	…하고 싶어요
Please help me	*dowa-juseyo*	도와주세요

Communicating

I can't speak Korean	*jeo-neun hangugeo-reul mot haeyo*	저는 한국어를 못 해요
I can't read Korean	*jeo-neun hangugeo-reul mok ilgeoyo*	저는 한국어를 못 읽어요
Do you speak English?	*yeongeo halsu-isseoyo?*	영어 할 수 있어요?
Is there someone who can speak English?	*yeongeo-reul haljul a-neun bun isseoyo?*	영어를 할 줄 아는 분 있어요?
Can you please speak slowly?	*jom cheoncheonhi mal haejuseyo?*	좀 천천히 말 해주세요?
Please say that again	*dashi han-beon mal haejuseyo*	다시 한번말 해주세요
I understand/I see	*alasseoyo*	알았어요
I (really) don't understand	*(jal) mollayo*	(잘) 몰라요
What does this mean?	*i-geot museun ddeushi-eyo?*	이것 무슨 뜻이에요?

How do you say (x) in Korean?	(x) eul/reul hanguk-eoro eotteoke mal haeyo?	(x) 을/를 한국어로 어떻게 말해요
Please write in English	yeongeo-ro jegeo jushillaeyo	영어로 적어 주실래요
Please wait (a moment)	(jamggan) gidariseyo	(잠깐) 기다리세요
Just a minute	jamggan manyo	잠깐 만요

Meetings and greetings

Hello; Good morning/afternoon/evening	annyeong haseyo	안녕 하세요
Hello (polite)	annyeong hashimnikka	안녕 하십니까
How are you?	jal jinaesseoyo?	잘 지냈어요?
I'm fine	jal jinaesseoyo/jo-ayo	잘 지냈어요 / 좋아요
Nice to meet you	bangapseumnida	반갑습니다
Goodbye (when staying)	annyeong-hi gaseyo	안녕히 가세요
Goodbye (when leaving)	annyeong-hi gyeseyo	안녕히 계세요
What's your name?	ireum-i eotteokke doeshimnikka?	이름이 어떻게 되십니까?
My name is...	ireum-i ... imnida	이름이... 입니다.
Where are you from?	eodi-eso wasseoyo?	어디에서 왔어요?
I'm from...	...eso wasseoyo	에서 왔어요
Korea	han-guk	한국
Britain	yeong-guk	영국
Ireland	aillaendeu	아일랜드
America	mi-guk	미국
Australia	oseuteureillia/hoju	오스트레일리아 / 호주
Canada	kae-nada	캐나다
New Zealand	nyu jillaendeu	뉴질랜드
South Africa	nam apeurika	남 아프리카
How old are you?	myeot-sal ieyo?	몇 살이에요?
I am (age)	(age)-sal ieyo	(age)살이에요
Do you like...?	...o-a haeyo?	...좋아 해요?
I like...	jo-a haeyo	좋아 해요
I don't like...	an jo-a haeyo	안 좋아해요
Do you have (free) time?	shigan-i isseoyo?	시간이 있어요?

Numbers

Rather confusingly, the Korean language has two separate number systems operating in parallel – a **native Korean** system, and a **Sino–Korean** system of Chinese origin – and you'll have to learn according to the situation which one to use. To tell the time, you'll actually need both – amazingly, minutes and hours run on different systems. The native Korean system only goes up to 99, and has been placed on the right-hand side of the readings. Dates and months use the Sino–Korean system alone, with *il* (sun) used as a suffix for days, and *wol* (moon) for months: June 7 is simply *yuk–wol chil-il*.

Zero	yeong/gong	영/공	Two	i (pronounced "ee")/dul	이/둘
One	il/hana	일/하나			

195

Three	sam/set	삼/셋		Thirty	sam-shib/ seoreun	삼십/서른
Four	sa/net	사/넷		One hundred	baek	백
Five	o/daseot	오/다섯		Two hundred	i-baek	이백
Six	yuk/yeoseot	육/여섯		Thousand	cheon	천
Seven	chil/ilgop	칠/일곱		Ten thousand	man	만
Eight	pal/yeodeol	팔/여덟		One hundred thousand	sim-man	십만
Nine	gu/ahop	구/아홉		One million	baeng-man	백만
Ten	ship/yeol	십/열		One hundred million	eok	억
Eleven	shib-il/ yeol-hana	십일/열하 나				
Twelve	shib-l/yeol-dul	십이/열 둘				
Twenty	i-shib/seumul	이십/스물				

Time and dates

Now	jigeum	지금		Wednesday	suyo-il	수요일
Today	o-neul	오늘		Thursday	mogyo-il	목요일
Morning	achim	아침		Friday	geumyo-il	금요일
Afternoon	ohu	오후		Saturday	toyo-il	토요일
Evening	jeonyok	저녁		Sunday	ilyo-il	일요일
Night	bam	밤				
Tomorrow	nae-il	내일		What time is it?	myo-shi-eyo?	몇시에요?
Yesterday	eoje	어제		It's 10 o'clock	yeol-shi-eyo	열시에요
Week	ju	주		10.20	yeol-shi i-ship-bun	열시 이십분
Month	wol/dal	월/달				
Year	nyeon	년		10.30	yeol-shi sam-ship-bun	열시 반이 삼십분
Monday	wolyo-il	월요일		10.50	yeol-shi o-ship-bun	분를 따르십시오
Tuesday	hwayo-il	화요일				

Transport and travel

Aeroplane	bihaenggi	비행기		Train station	yeok	역
Airport	gonghang	공항		Subway	jihacheol	지하철
Bus	beoseu	버스		Ferry	yeogaek-seon	여객선
Express bus (terminal)	gosok beoseu (teominal)	익스프레스 (터미널)		Ferry terminal	yeogaek teominal	여객 터미 널
Intercity bus (terminal)	shi-oe beoseu (teominal)	시외 버스 (터미널)		Left-luggage office	jimbogwanso	짐보관
City bus	shinae beoseu	시내 버스		Ticket office	maepyoso	매표소
Airport bus	gonghang beoseu	공항 버스		Ticket	pyo	표
				Platform	seunggangjang	승강장
City bus stop	jeong-ryu-jang	정류장		Bicycle	jajeon-geo	자전거
Train	gicha	기차		Taxi	taek-shi	택시

Directions and general places

Where is (x)?	*-i/ga eodi-eyo?*	-이/가 어디에 요?	Exit	*chul-gu*	출구
			Art gallery	*misulgwan*	미술관
			Bank	*eunhaeng*	은행
Straight ahead	*jikjin*	직진	Beach	*haebyeon*	해변
Left	*oen-jjok (pronounced "wen-chok")*	왼쪽	Department store	*baekhwajeom*	백화점
			Embassy	*daesagwan*	대사관
Right	*oreun-jjok*	오른쪽	Hot spring spa	*oncheon*	온천
Behind	*dwi-e*	뒤에	Museum	*bangmulgwan*	박물관
In front of	*ap-e*	앞에	Park	*gongwon*	공원
North	*buk*	북	Sea	*haean/bada*	해안/ 바다
South	*nam*	남			
East	*dong*	동	Temple	*Jeol/sachal*	절/사찰
West	*seo*	서쪽	Toilet	*hwajang-shil*	화장실
Map	*maep/jido*	맵/지도	Tourist office	*gwan-gwang annaeso*	관광 안내소
Entrance	*ip-gu*	입구			

Accommodation

Hotel	*hotel*	호텔	Key	*ki*	키
Motel	*motel*	모텔	Passport	*yeogwon*	여권
Guesthouse	*yeogwan*	여관	Do you have any vacancies?	*bang isseoyo?*	방 있 어요?
Budget guesthouse	*yeoinsuk*	여인숙	I have a reservation	*jeo-neun yeyak haesseoyo*	저는 예약 했어요
Rented room	*minbak*	민박			
Youth hostel	*yuseu hoseutel*	유스 호스텔	I don't have a reservation	*jeo-neun yeyak anhaesseoyo*	저는 예약 안했어요
Korean-style room	*ondol-bang*	온돌방			
Western-style room	*chimdae-bang*	침대방	How much is the room?	*bang-i eolma -eyo?*	방이 얼마에요?
Single room	*shinggeul chimdae*	싱글 침대	Does that include breakfast?	*gagyeok-e achim-shiksa poham-dwae isseoyo?*	가격에 아침식사 포함돼 있어요?
Double room	*deobeul chimdae*	더블 침대			
Twin room	*chimdae dugae*	침대 두 개	One/two/ three nights	*haruppam/ i-bak/ sam-bak*	하룻밤/ 이박/삼박
En-suite room	*yokshil-ddallin bang*	욕실 딸린방	One week	*il-ju-il*	일주일
Shower	*syaweo*	샤워	May I see the room?	*bang jom bolsu-isseoyo?*	방 좀 볼수 있어요?
Bath	*yokjo*	욕조			

Shopping, money and banks

Bank	eunhaeng	은행
Foreign exchange	woe-hwan	외환
Won	won	원
Pounds	pa-un-deu	파운드
Dollars	dalleo	달러
Cash	don	돈
Travellers' cheque	yeohaengja supyo	여행자 수표
How much is it?	eolma-eyo?	얼마에요?
It's too expensive	neomu bissayo	너무 비싸요
Please make it a little cheaper	jom kkakka-juseyo	좀 깎아주세요
Do you accept credit cards?	keurediteu kadeu gyesan dwaeyo?	크레디트 카드 계산 돼요?

Post and telephones

Post office	uche-guk	우체국	Telephone card	jeonhwa kadeu	전화카드
Envelope	bongtu	봉투	Internet café	PC-bang PC	방
Letter	pyeonji	편지	I would like to call...	...hante jeonhwa hago-shipeoyo	좀바꿔 주세요
Postcard	yeopseo	엽서			
Stamp	u-pyo	우표			
Airmail	hanggong u-pyeon	항공 우편			
Surface mail	seonbak u-pyeon	선박 우편	May I speak to...	...jom baggwo juseyo	저는 아파요
Telephone	jeon-hwa	전화	Hello?	yeoboseyo?	여보세요?
Fax	paekseu	팩스			

Health

Hospital	byeongwon	병원	Penicillin	penishillin	페니실린
Pharmacy	yak-guk	약국	Tampons	tampon	탐폰
Medicine	yak	약	I'm ill	jeo-neun apayo	저는 아파 요
Doctor	uisa	의사			
Dentist	chigwa-uisa	치과의사	I have a cold	gamgi geoll-yeossseoyo	감기 걸렸어요
Diarrhoea	seolsa	설사			
Nausea	meseukkeo-um	메스꺼움			
Fever	yeol	ø	I'm allergic to...	...allereugi-ga isseoyo	...알레르 기가 있어요
Food poisoning	shikjungdok	식중독	It hurts here	yeogi-ga apayo	여기가 아파요
Antibiotics	hangsaengje	항생제	Please call a doctor	uisa-reul bulleo juseyo	의사를 불러 주세요
Antiseptic	sodok-yak	독약			
Condom	kondom	콘돔			

Food and drink

Places

Restaurant	*sikdang*	식당
Korean barbecue restaurant	*galbi-jip*	갈비집
Korean staples (fast food) restaurant	*gimbap-cheonguk*	김밥천국
Seafood restaurant	*hoet-jip*	횟집
Western-style restaurant	*reseutorang*	레스토랑
Italian restaurant	*itallian reseutorang*	이탈리안 레스토랑
Chinese restaurant	*jungguk-jip*	중국집
Japanese restaurant	*ilshik-jip*	일식집
Burger bar	*paeseuteu-pudeu-jeom*	패스트푸드점
Convenience store	*pyeonui-jeom*	편의점
Market	*shijang*	시장
Café	*kape*	카페
Bar	*ba/suljip*	바/술집
Club	*naiteu-keulleob*	나이트클럽
Expat bar	*woeguk-in ba (pronounced "way-guk-in ba")*	외국인 바
Makkeolli bar	*makkeolli-jip*	막걸리집
Soju tent	*pojangmacha*	포장마차
Where's (a) ... ?	*...eodi isseoyo?*	...어디 있어요?

Ordering

Waiter/Waitress (lit. "Here!")	*yeogiyo!*	여기요!
How much is that?	*eolma-eyo?*	얼마에요?
I would like...	*...hago shipeoyo*	...하고 싶어요
May I have the bill?	*gyesanseo juseyo?*	계산해 주세요
I'm a vegetarian	*jeo-neun chaeshikju uija-eyo*	저는 채식주의자에요
Can I have this without meat?	*gogi bbaego haejushilsu isseoyo?*	고기 빼고 해주실수 있어요?
I can't eat spicy food	*maeun-geot mot meogeoyo*	매운 것 못 먹어요
Delicious!	*mashisseoyo!*	맛있어요!
Chopsticks	*jeot-garak*	젓가락
Fork	*po-keu*	포크
Knife	*nai-peu/kal*	나이프/칼
Spoon	*sut-garak*	숟가락
Menu	*menyu*	메뉴

Staple ingredients

L

Beef	*so-gogi*	쇠고기	Red-pepper paste	*gochu-jang*	고추장
Chicken	*dak-gogi*	닭고기			
Duck meat	*oti-gogi*	오리고기	Rice	*bap*	밥
Gimchi	*gimchi*	김치	Rice-cake	*ddeok*	떡
Fish	*saengsun/ hoe (raw fish)*	생선/회	Seaweed laver	*gim*	김
			Shrimp	*sae-u*	새우
Ham	*haem*	햄	Squid	*ojing-eo*	오징어
Meat	*gogi*	고기	Tuna	*chamchi*	참치
Noodles	*myeon*	면	Vegetables	*yachae*	야채
Pork	*dwaeji-gogi*	돼지고기			

Rice dishes

Bibimbap	*bibimbap*	비빔밥
Fried rice (usually with egg and vegetables)	*bokkeumbap*	볶음밥
Marinaded beef on rice	*bulgogi (deop-bap)*	불고기 (덮밥)
Rice rolls	*gimbap*	김밥

Meat dishes

Barbecued ribs	*galbi*	갈비
Boiled beef rolls	*syabu-syabu*	샤부샤부
Dog-meat soup	*boshintang/yeongyangtang*	보신탕/영양탕
Marinaded beef	*bulgogi*	불고기
Pork belly slices	*samgyeopsal*	삼겹살
Spicy squid on rice	*ojingeo deop-bap*	오징어 덮밥
Steamed ribs	*galbi-jjim*	갈비찜

Stews and soups

Beef and noodle soup	*seolleong-tang*	설렁탕
Beef rib soup	*galbi-tang*	갈비탕
Cold buckwheat noodle soup	*naengmyeon*	냉면
Dumpling soup	*mandu-guk*	만두국
Gimchi broth	*gimchi jjigae*	김치 찌개
Ginseng-stuffed chicken soup	*samgye-tang*	삼계탕
Noodles with vegetables and meat	*makguksu*	막국수
Soybean broth (miso)	*doenjang jjigae*	된장 찌개
Spicy fish soup	*maeun-tang*	매운탕
Spicy noodle soup	*ramyeon*	라면
Spicy tofu soup	*sundubu*	순두부
Tuna broth	*chamchi jjigae*	참치 찌개

LANGUAGE | Food and drink

Snacks and Korean fast food

Battered flash-fried snacks (tempura)	*twigim*	튀김
Breaded pork cutlet	*donkkaseu*	돈까스
Dumplings	*mandu*	만두
Fried dumplings	*gun-mandu*	군만두
Rice wrapped in omelette	*omeuraiseu*	오므라이스
Rice-cake in red-pepper paste	*ddeokbokki*	떡볶이
Savoury pancake with vegetables	*pajeon*	파전
Steamed dumplings	*jjin-mandu*	찐만두
Stuffed sausage	*sundae*	순대

Seafood

Broiled fish	*saengseon-gu-i*	생선구이	Raw fish platter	*modeum-hoe*	모듬회
Fried baby octopus	*nakji bokkeum*	낙지 볶음	Sliced raw fish	*saengseon-hoe*	생선회

Western food

Bread	*bbang*	빵	Fruit	*gwa-il*	과일
Cereal	*shiri-eol*	시리얼	Pizza	*pija*	피자
Cheese	*chi-jeu*	치즈	Spaghetti	*seupageti*	스파게티
Chocolate	*chokollit*	초콜릿	Steak	*seuteikeu*	스테이크
Eggs	*gyeran*	계란			

Tea

Black tea (lit. "red tea")	*hong-cha*	홍차	Green tea	*nok-cha*	녹차
Chrysanthemum tea	*gukhwa-cha*	국화차	Honey ginseng tea	*gyulsam-cha*	귤삼차
Cinnamon tea	*gyepi-cha*	계피차	"Job's Tears" tea	*yulmu-cha*	율무차
Citron tea	*yuja-cha*	유자차	Jujube tea	*daechu-cha*	대추차
"Five flavours" tea	*omija-cha*	오미자차	Medicinal herb tea	*yak-cha*	약차
Ginger tea	*saenggang-cha*	생강차	Plum tea	*maeshil-cha*	매실차
Ginseng tea	*insam-cha*	인삼차	Wild herb tea	*ma-cha*	마차

Alcoholic drinks

Baekseju	*baekseju*	백세주	Draught beer	*saeng maekju*	생맥주
Beer	*maekju*	맥주	Ginseng wine	*insamju*	인삼주
Blackberry wine	*bokbunja*	복분자	Makkeolli	*makkeolli*	막걸리
Bottled beer	*byeong maekju*	병 맥주	Plum brandy	*maeshilju*	매실주
			Soju	*soju*	소주
Cocktail	*kakteil*	칵테일	Wine	*wain*	와인
Dongdongju	*dongdongju*	동동주	Whisky	*wiseuki*	위스키

Other drinks

Coffee	*keopi*	커피	Milk	*uyu*	우유
Orange juice	*orenji jyuseu*	오렌지 쥬스	Mineral water	*saengsu*	생수
			Water	*mul*	물
Fruit juice	*gwa-il jyuseu*	과일 쥬스			

Glossary

ajeossi an older or married man.

ajumma an older or married woman.

-am hermitage.

anju bar snacks.

-bang room.

-bawi boulder or large rock.

-bong mountain peak. The highest peak in a park is often referred to as *ilchulbong* ("Number One Peak").

buk- north.

buncheong a Korean style of pottery that became popular in Joseon times. The end product is often bluish-green in colour.

celadon a Korean style of pottery (also common in China and Japan), used since the Three Kingdoms period but largely overtaken by *buncheong* in Joseon times. The end product is often pale green in colour, with a cracked glaze.

cha tea.

-cheon stream or river of less than 100km in length.

Chuseok Korean Thanksgiving.

dae- big, large, great.

Dangun mythical founder of Korea.

DMZ the Demilitarized Zone that separates North and South Korea.

-do island.

-do province.

-dong city neighbourhood; part of a *-gu*.

dong- east.

dongdongju a milky rice wine much favoured by Korean students; very similar to *makkeolli*.

DPRK Democratic People's Republic of Korea.

-eup town.

-ga section of a major street.

-gang river of over 100km in length.

-gil street.

gisaeng Female entertainers popular in dynastic times; see box, p.77.

-gu district of a city, subdivided into *-dong* neighbourhoods.

-gul cave.

-gun county.

-gung palace.

gwageo civil service examinations in the Joseon era.

Gyopo Koreans, or people of Korean descent, living overseas.

hae sea. Korea's East, West and South seas are referred to as *Donghae*, *Seohae* and *Namhae* respectively, though the international nomenclature of the first two (more readily referred to as the "Sea of Japan" and the "Yellow Sea" abroad) is a touchy subject with Koreans.

hagwon private academy for after-school study. Many expats in Korea are working at an English academy (*yeongeo hagwon*).

hallyu the "Korean New Wave" of pop culture, most specifically cinematic produce.

hanbok traditional Korean clothing.

-hang harbour.

hangeul the Korean alphabet.

hanja Chinese characters, which are still sometimes used in Korea.

hanji traditional handmade paper.

hanok a style of traditional, tile-roofed wooden housing.

-ho lake; also used for those artificially created after the construction of a dam.

hof a Korean-style bar.

hompy personal homepage.

insam ginseng.

jaebeol major Korean corporation.

-jeon temple hall.

jjimjilbang Korean spa-cum-sauna facilities, often used by families, youth groups and the occasional budget traveller (see p.145).

KNTO Korea National Tourism Organization.

KTX the fastest class of Korean train.

makkeolli a milky rice wine much favoured by Korean students; very similar to *dongdongju*.

minbak rented rooms in a private house or building, most commonly found near beaches and national park entrances.

mudang practitioner of shamanism; usually female.

mugunghwa Korea's third-highest level of train, one below a *saemaeul*. Named after Korea's national flower, a variety of hibiscus, also known as the "Rose of Sharon", which flowers punctually each July.

-mun city or fortress gate.

-myo Confucian shrine.

nam- couth.

-ni village; sometimes pronounced – *ri*.

-no large street; sometimes pronounced – *ro*.

nocheonnyeo an "over-the-hill" female – Korean women have long been expected to marry by the age of thirty, though this is slowly changing.

noraebang a "singing room" often the venue of choice for the end of a night out.

oncheon hot spring bath or spa.

ondol traditional underfloor system of heating, made by wood fires underneath traditional buildings, but replaced with gas-fired systems in Korean apartments and modern houses.

pansori Korean opera derived from shamanistic songs, sung by female vocalists to minimalist musical accompaniment.

-pokpo waterfalls.

pyeong Korean unit of measurement equivalent to approximately 3.3 square metres; still commonly used to measure the floorspace of housing or offices.

Red Devils a nickname for the South Korean national football team, or their noisy supporters.

-ri village; sometimes pronounced – *ni*.

-ro large street; sometimes pronounced – *no*.

ROK Republic of Korea.

-sa temple.

Saemaeul Korea's second-highest level of train, one faster than a *mugunghwa* but slower than a KTX. Also the name of the "New Community Movement" inaugurated by Korean president Park Chung-hee in the 1970s.

-san mountain; often used to describe an entire range.

sanseong mountain fortress.

seo- west.

Seon Korean Buddhist sect proximate to Zen in Japan.

seonsaengnim title for a teacher, which goes before the family name, or after the given name in the case of most expat teachers in Korea. Hence, a teacher named Martin will be referred to as "Martin *seonsaengnim*". It's also used as a version of "Mister".

seowon Confucian academy, most prevalent in Joseon times.

-si city, subdivided into *-gu* districts.

sijang market.

soju clear alcoholic drink (around 25 percent alcohol by volume) which is often compared to vodka, and usually cheaper than water at convenience stores up and down the land.

ssireum a Korean wrestling style inevitably compared to sumo, but far closer in form to Mongolian or Greco–Roman styles.

STO Seoul Tourism Organization.

taekwondo Korean martial art; now practised around the world.

tap pagoda.

tongil unification, a highly important concept on the divided Korean peninsula.

trot a highly distinctive style of Korean music much favoured by older generations.

woeguk-in foreigner; pronounced "way-goog-in". *Woeguk-saram* is also used.

yangban the scholarly "upper class" in Joseon-era Korea.

yeogwan Korean form of accommodation, similar to a motel but privately run and almost always older.

yeoinsuk Korean form of accommodation, similar to a *yeogwan* but with communal toilets and showers.

Small print and

Index

A Rough Guide to Rough Guides

Published in 1982, the first Rough Guide – to Greece – was a student scheme that became a publishing phenomenon. Mark Ellingham, a recent graduate in English from Bristol University, had been travelling in Greece the previous summer and couldn't find the right guidebook. With a small group of friends he wrote his own guide, combining a highly contemporary, journalistic style with a thoroughly practical approach to travellers' needs.

The immediate success of the book spawned a series that rapidly covered dozens of destinations. And, in addition to impecunious backpackers, Rough Guides soon acquired a much broader and older readership that relished the guides' wit and inquisitiveness as much as their enthusiastic, critical approach and value-for-money ethos.

These days, Rough Guides include recommendations from shoestring to luxury and cover more than 200 destinations around the globe, including almost every country in the Americas and Europe, more than half of Africa and most of Asia and Australasia. Our ever-growing team of authors and photographers is spread all over the world, particularly in Europe, the US and Australia.

In the early 1990s, Rough Guides branched out of travel, with the publication of Rough Guides to World Music, Classical Music and the Internet. All three have become benchmark titles in their fields, spearheading the publication of a wide range of books under the Rough Guide name.

Including the travel series, Rough Guides now number more than 350 titles, covering: phrasebooks, waterproof maps, music guides from Opera to Heavy Metal, reference works as diverse as Conspiracy Theories and Shakespeare, and popular culture books from iPods to Poker. Rough Guides also produce a series of more than 120 World Music CDs in partnership with World Music Network.

Visit www.roughguides.com to see our latest publications.

Rough Guide credits

Text editor: Róisín Cameron
Additional editing: Alice Park, James Smart,
Harry Wilson
Layout: Sachin Gupta
Cartography: Rajesh Chhibber
Picture editor: Nicole Newman
Production: Rebecca Short
Proofreaders: Stewart Wild, Daniel Choi
Cover design: Nicole Newman, Dan May
Photographer: Martin Richardson
Editorial: **London** Andy Turner, Keith Drew,
Edward Aves, Alice Park, Lucy White, Jo Kirby,
James Smart, Natasha Foges, James Rice,
Emma Beatson, Emma Gibbs, Kathryn Lane,
Monica Woods, Mani Ramaswamy, Harry Wilson,
Lucy Cowie, Alison Roberts, Lara Kavanagh,
Eleanor Aldridge, Ian Blenkinsop, Charlotte
Melville, Joe Staines, Matthew Milton, Tracy
Hopkins; **Delhi** Madhavi Singh, Jalpreen Kaur
Chhatwal, Jubbi Francis

Design & Pictures: **London** Scott Stickland, Dan
May, Diana Jarvis, Mark Thomas, Sarah Cummins;
Delhi Umesh Aggarwal, Ajay Verma, Jessica
Subramanian, Ankur Guha, Pradeep Thapliyal,
Sachin Tanwar, Anita Singh, Nikhil Agarwal
Production: Liz Cherry, Louise Minihane,
Erika Pepe
Cartography: London Ed Wright, Katie Lloyd-
Jones; **Delhi** Ashutosh Bharti, Rajesh Mishra,
Animesh Pathak, Jasbir Sandhu, Swati Handoo,
Deshpal Dabas, Lokamata Sahu
Marketing, Publicity & roughguides.com:
Liz Statham
Digital Travel Publisher: Peter Buckley
Reference Director: Andrew Lockett
Operations Coordinator: Becky Doyle
Operations Assistant: Johanna Wurm
Publishing Director (Travel): Clare Currie
Commercial Manager: Gino Magnotta
Managing Director: John Duhigg

Publishing information

This first edition published June 2011 by
Rough Guides Ltd,
80 Strand, London WC2R 0RL
11, Community Centre, Panchsheel Park,
New Delhi 110017, India

Distributed by the Penguin Group

Penguin Books Ltd,
80 Strand, London WC2R 0RL

Penguin Group (USA)
375 Hudson Street, NY 10014, USA

Penguin Group (Australia)
250 Camberwell Road, Camberwell,
Victoria 3124, Australia

Penguin Group (NZ)
67 Apollo Drive, Mairangi Bay, Auckland 1310,
New Zealand

Rough Guides is represented in Canada by
Tourmaline Editions Inc. 662 King Street West,
Suite 304, Toronto, Ontario M5V 1M7

Cover concept by Peter Dyer.

Typeset in Bembo and Helvetica to an original
design by Henry Iles.

Printed in Singapore

© Martin Zatko 2011

Maps © Rough Guides

216pp includes index

A catalogue record for this book is available from
the British Library

ISBN: 978-1-40538-000-3

This book was produced with the assistance of
the Seoul Tourism Organization.

1   3   5   7   9   8   6   4   2

SOUL OF ASIA

MIX
Paper from
responsible sources
FSC® C018179

Help us update

We've gone to a lot of effort to ensure that the first edition of **The Rough Guide to Seoul** is accurate and up-to-date. However, things change – places get "discovered", opening hours are notoriously fickle, restaurants and rooms raise prices or lower standards. If you feel we've got it wrong or left something out, we'd like to know, and if you can remember the address, the price, the hours, the phone number, so much the better.

Please send your comments with the subject line "**Rough Guide Seoul Update**" to ⓔmail @uk.roughguides.com. We'll credit all contributions and send a copy of the next edition (or any other Rough Guide if you prefer) for the very best emails.

Find more travel information, connect with fellow travellers and book your trip on ⓦwww .roughguides.com

Acknowledgements

Martin Zatko would like to thank the Seoul Tourism Organization for their generous commitment to and input into this project. Also fully deserving of appreciation and gratitude are Michael Spavor, Jason Strother and sister Nicole, who made restaurant and bar reviews far more enjoyable than a job should ever be. Thanks also to local buddies Juhee Jang and Misun Jung for their wonderful company.

Index

Map entries are in colour.

INDEX

So now we've told you about the things not to miss, the best places to stay, the top restaurants, the liveliest bars and the most spectacular sights, it only seems fair to tell you about the best travel insurance around

WorldNomads.com
keep travelling safely

Recommended by Rough Guides

Map symbols

maps are listed in the full index using coloured text

----·-	International boundary	♦	Place of interest
——··—	Regional boundary	ⓘ	Information office
———	Chapter division boundary	⊠	Post office
═══	Highway	♦	Museum
═══	Major road	🏛	Monument
═══	Minor road	🏛	Palace
- - - -	Tunnel	⟟	Border crossing
━━━	Railway line	⊙	Statue
- - - - -	Path	⊠	Gate
— —	Ferry route	⤬	Bridge
———	River/coast	♠	Buddhist temple
━━━	Wall	冂	Shrine
•---•	Cable car & station	▬	Building
Ⓢ	Subway	▢	Market
▲	Peak	⬭	Stadium
✈	Airport	⊞	Cemetery
◉	Accommodation	▦	Park

Kaesong

NORTH KOREA

Panmunjeom

DMZ AREA

Dongducheon

Bear's Town (ski resort)

Gyodongdo

Goindol

Heyri Art Valley

Odusan

Starhill (ski resort)

Uijeongbu

Seongmodo

Oepo

Paju Book City

Bomunsa

Ganghwado

Yangsu-ri

Gimpo International Airport

Yeongjongdo

Bucheon

SEOUL

Gwangju

Incheon International Airport

37

Muuido

Ansan

Icheon

Everland

Deokjeokdo

Incheon

50

Suwon

Korean Folk Village

Jisan Forest (ski resort)

15

GYEONGGI

Baengnyeongdo (Island) & China

WEST SEA

Pyeongtaek

Unjong

1

Cheongju

Cheonan

CHUNGBUK

Independence Hall of Korea

Taean

Seosan

30

Anmyeondo

25

CHUNGNAM

30

Gongju

151

25

Daejeon

N

0   20 km

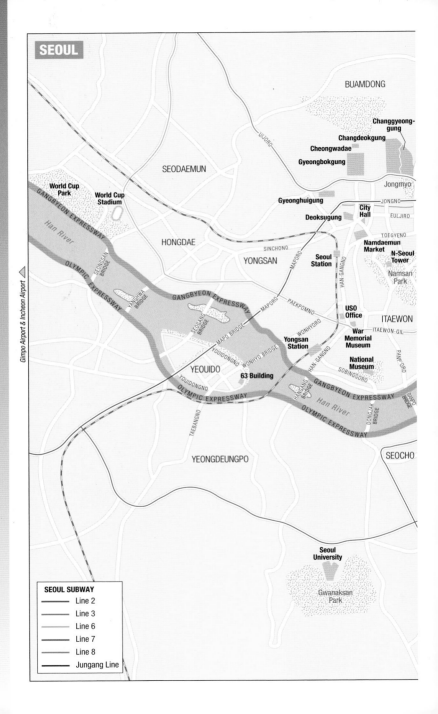

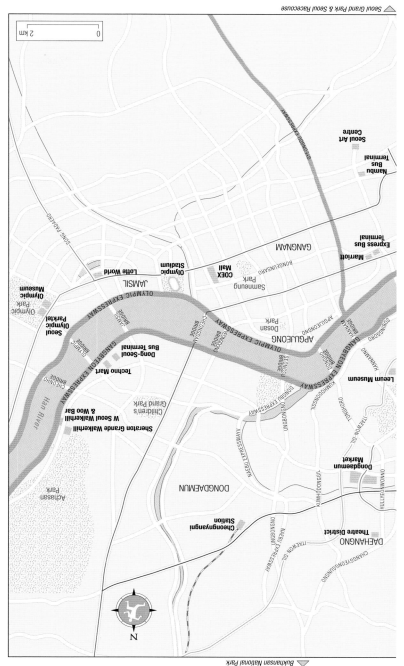

Achasan Park

Han River

Olympic Park
Olympic Museum
Seoul Olympic Parktel
Lotte World
Olympic Stadium
Olympic Expressway
Jamsi Bridge
Gangbyeon Bus Terminal
Olympic Bridge
Dong-Seoul Bus Terminal
Cheongdam Bridge
Techno Mart
Cheonho Bridge
Children's Grand Park
Sheraton Grande Walkerhill
W Seoul Walkerhill & Woo Bar

GANGNAM
COEX Mall
Samseung Park
Bongeunsaro
Marriott
Express Bus Terminal

APGUJEONG
Dosan Park
Apgujeongro
Olympic Expressway
Gangbyeon Expressway
Hannam Bridge
Seongsu Bridge
Yeongdong Bridge
Cheongdam Bridge
Dongho Expressway

Gyeongbu Expressway
Seoul Art Centre
Nambu Bus Terminal

Seong Padaro

Leeum Museum
Kumiho Bridge
Dongdaemun Market
Kumho-dongil
Hannamro
Itaewon-gil
Tongiro

DAEHANGNO
Theatre District
Changgyeonggungno
Naebu Expressway
Itaewon-gil

DONGDAEMUN
Cheongnyangni Station
Naebu Expressway

N

0   2 km

SEOUL SUBWAY